Being Open, Being Faithful

Being Open, Being Faithful

The Journey of Interreligious Dialogue

Douglas Pratt

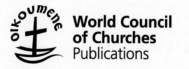

**World Council
of Churches**
Publications

BEING OPEN, BEING FAITHFUL
The Journey of Interreligious Dialogue

WCC Publications is the book publishing programme of the World Council of Churches. Founded in 1948, the WCC promotes Christian unity in faith, witness and service for a just and peaceful world. A global fellowship, the WCC brings together 345 Protestant, Orthodox, Anglican and other churches representing more than 550 million Christians in 110 countries and works cooperatively with the Roman Catholic Church.

Opinions expressed in WCC Publications are those of the authors.

Scripture quotations are from the New Revised Standard Version Bible, © copyright 1989 by the Division of Christian Education of the National Council of the Churches of Christ in the USA. Used by permission.

Book design and typesetting: 4 Seasons Book Design/Michelle Cook

ISBN: 978-2-8254-1575-7

World Council of Churches
150 route de Ferney, P.O. Box 2100
1211 Geneva 2, Switzerland
http://publications.oikoumene.org

CONTENTS

PREFACE

Good news rarely makes media headlines. Bad news always does. And too often, it seems, the bad news is religious—or at least there is an overtly religious dimension to it. Such news is no real reflection of religious life and values. Nevertheless, a secular and sceptical world looks on and shakes its head: religion seems inevitably part of the problem and not part of the solution; religions are forever at war with one another and not at peace. It would appear that religion is the worst measure of good intercommunal relations and of a harmonious society. Has any week gone by in recent times when this has not been the predominant portrayal of religion?

But is this portrayal fair? Is it the way things really are? And if there is a measure of truth to the portrayal, is it the full story? I hardly think so, but it is not an easy task to get local media, let alone the global giants, to take interest in something good and positive happening in the field of religion. This was the case with the National Interfaith Forum held in New Zealand in February 2012, an event of which I was the plenary chair. Even though some politicians attended, together with our national human rights commissioner, who launched a document detailing the rights and responsibilities of allowing space for religious observance within the work-place, the media refused to come; this was a minority affair of marginal interest to the general public, not worthy of media attention.

We have a long way to go for the good news to overcome the bad press religion too often receives. And what is this good news? It is none other than the fact of interfaith engagement and interreligious dialogue,[1] which are twin aspects of a climate of mutual openness among peoples of different faiths, a shift in orientation from mutual hostility to mutually appreciated hospitality. Christians of all shades, from Orthodox to Pentecostal, from Catholic to Independent, from so-called liberal to evangelical, are finding a myriad of ways of expressing good will toward people of many different faiths and of discerning modes of interfaith cooperation. In a world sorely vexed by much intercommunal strife, geopolitical upheaval and globalized conflict—much of this religion-oriented if not derived—such interfaith engagement is welcome good news indeed. What was once the dynamic fresh news of a Christianity discovering its own ecumenism is now a relational dynamic extending into the interfaith arena. Faith-identities remain, of course, but barriers of hostile perception and regard are coming down, albeit hesitatingly in many places.

What the world knows little about (and sadly, this encompasses a large proportion of people of religious faith, including many Christians) is that in recent decades there has been intense and growing dialogue between religions and increasingly wide interest in interfaith affairs. Rather better known, unfortunately, are the many contemporary situations of interreligious tension and strife throughout the world, situations where dialogue seems either absent or making no appreciable difference. Yet, as was once remarked, there can be no peace in the world without peace between the religions, and no peace between religions without dialogue between them. Today, more than ever, there is great and urgent need for renewed interreligious dialogue and interfaith engagement, both in the promotion of mutual understanding and acceptance and in the resolution of critical social and political issues. In a context where extremism emanating from one religion can spark a reactionary extremism from another—as in Christian extremists perpetrating violent acts in response to violence emanating from Muslim extremism—it can seem as if the cause of dialogue is lost before it has even begun. However, dialogue between Christians and Muslims, as also between Christians and peoples of many other faiths, has been actively pursued in many parts of the world over recent decades. This dialogue has been occurring at a multitude of local and informal levels as well as at highly intentional institutional events. Much of positive value is achieved when people of different faiths work together for the common good. Much more can yet happen when people of different faiths sit down together to share, in depth, the riches of their spiritual resources, and when they learn both to listen to and respectfully critique one another.

When it comes to the matter of Christians engaging in interfaith activities, and interreligious dialogue in particular, two issues seem inevitably to arise. On the one hand there is the question of motivation and rationale. Why should Christians do this? What theological reason can be given—and is it valid? On the other hand there is the question of effect and consequence. What difference does dialogue make, if any? And is dialogue meant to bring about change within the partners to dialogue? If so, what does that mean for Christian self-understanding? For surely, if we are firm in our belief and identity as Christians, a dialogical encounter with another religion is either superfluous or potentially dangerous. And it is not just the Christian side that asks such questions.

Nevertheless, for the Christian side, the World Council of Churches (WCC), which has been active in interreligious dialogue for well over half a century, has been exploring this issue on a number of fronts in recent years. In February of 2012 the WCC held a consultation on Christian self-understanding in the context of indigenous religions. Similar consultations were held with respect to Hinduism (2011), Judaism (2010), Buddhism (2009) and Islam (2008). Subsequently, the Interreligious Dialogue and Cooperation programme of the WCC brought this series to a reflective focus in the preparation of a document on the subject of Christian self-understanding in a religiously plural world in readiness for the 2013 WCC sssembly in Busan, South Korea. After decades of active promotion of interreligious dialogue, relations and cooperation, the realization has grown that dialogue is necessarily a two-way street; it has, therefore, a reflexive impact in the sense of a challenge, for each participant, to rethink and reconsider positions and perspectives held prior to dialogue. I attempt here to contribute to this wider discussion by addressing dialogical issues and providing an overview account of the contemporary engagement of the Christian church in this field. My interest arises out of a combination of active interreligious engagement (in my own country as well as internationally) and considerable scholarly investigation and reflection. I hope that what I have written and shared will resonate with the experience of some and contribute to the developing inquiry of others.

ABBREVIATIONS

CWME   Commission on World Mission and Evangelism
(of the WCC)

IMC   International Missionary Council

IRDC   Programme for Interreligious Dialogue and Cooperation
(of the WCC)

IRRD   Office of Inter-Religious Relations and Dialogue
(of the WCC)

OIRR   Office for Inter-Religious Relations (of the WCC)

PCID   Pontifical Council for Interreligious Dialogue
(of the Vatican; see SNC)

SNC   Secretariat for Non-Christians of the Vatican
(renamed in 1988, see PCID)

WCC   World Council of Churches

WSCF   World Student Christian Federation

INTRODUCTION

Interreligious dialogue, as an intentional and institutionalized activity that came to prominence during the latter half of the 20th century, is one of the most notable advances to have occurred in the field of religion. Indeed, it is probably the most significant development ever in the history of religions, for it marks a fundamental paradigm shift in the way, formally and more broadly, religions—and certainly Christianity—may and do regard and understand each other. Religions are embracing a new way of relating to each other. As far as Christianity is concerned, this represents a dramatic departure from almost two millennia of default hostile regard for the validity of other faiths. Furthermore, it is arguably only in and through this very recent development that the negative consequences of religious diversity (as expressed, for example, in the many violent interactions that have occurred in the name of religion) might be overcome. Sadly, as we journey into the third millennium of the Common Era, wars and rumours of war continue to abound; religiously motivated terrorism has become a feature of our time. Although, to be sure, all major religions share broadly common values as expressed in the many variations of the Golden Rule (treat others as you would have them treat you), it is also the case that religions can be caught up in the active promotion of violence and war. This is certainly evident in recent history and current events.

So, as Andrew Wingate has pointedly asked, "How do we account for the great commonalities between religions in the ethical field?" whilst at the same time asking, "And why do religions nevertheless fight each other?"[1] Wingate goes on to note that "in practice, major clashes arise wherever religions act in an aggressively missionary way and wherever religion is combined with nationalism or fanaticism."[2] This is not the sole cause of violence, of course. Nevertheless, a sharply competitive praxis can lie at the heart of a combative encounter between religious communities. It has certainly been the case within the history of Christianity, and it has often the case been (and in places continues to be) with Islam and Christianity, for these are, Wingate observes, "the religions most sure that they are right. They are both universal religions, with a self-understanding that they are to evangelise the world."[3] Wingate notes, though, that all religions have engaged in violent acts to one degree or another, including in recent times Hinduism and Buddhism in Gujarat and Sri Lanka.

As we know only too well, it is not uncommon for religion to be used as a tool or a rallying point in otherwise politically motivated conflicts. Paradoxically, the fact that religion can be so used is indicative of its pervasive importance in the scheme of things. If universally significant values, such as peaceful living and compassionate concern for others, as espoused by virtually all religions, are compromised by the recurrent juxtaposition of religious jingoism with political hegemony, the advent of a dialogical age means that, as never before, religions and their peoples have an opportunity to make good on shared values for the benefit of all. Indeed, for the most part, religions today view one another, at least officially, not so much in terms of competition and threat but as potential partners and actual neighbours. As was succinctly expressed at a World Council of Churches assembly just a few years ago, "Faith can make things better, or it can make them a great deal worse."[4] Our hope is ever with the former, even as we recognize the disquieting reality of the latter. So it is that the quest for appropriate relationship with other religions or, more specifically, with people of other faiths, has become a vital, though also contentious, element within the wider life of the Christian church.

Significant and fundamental shifts in practical perspective and concomitant thinking have been necessarily involved in this quest of new interreligious relationships; yet they have not been without difficulty. They are by no means uniformly embraced. Though atavistic detractors persist in tilting at the windmills powering change, the winds of a new era of interfaith engagement blow nonetheless, even if seemingly erratically at times. The positive promotion of interreligious dialogue has involved initiatives by the World Council of Churches (WCC) together with similar developments undertaken by the Roman Catholic Church since the early 1960s; both have been of critical importance.[5] The respective offices of the WCC and the Catholic Church, through the Vatican, have been at the forefront of Christian engagement in interreligious dialogue.[6] With the exception of some residual antipathies—and some disturbing new ones—from a few quarters, the normative position of the Christian church that emerged and consolidated during the 20th century is that other religions are to be esteemed. Cordial relations and an attitude of respectful regard have become the new presumption, expressed, in particular, through the WCC and the Vatican by way of the principal organs and offices charged with responsibility for interreligious dialogue, cooperation and allied interfaith relations. In this still relatively new context the need for better intercommunal relations is a vitally urgent issue; improved interfaith engagement is the sought-for goal for which interreligious dialogue is a *sine qua non*.

In today's world, we have the possibility of transcending histories of combative clash in favour of a future marked increasingly by cooperative engagement. People of different religions can and do engage in dialogical relationship one with another. Faith, in this regard, can make things better. At least that is the hope, even if the reality of everyday existence is yet to match. Such hope is engendered by a profound change wrought by the dawn of an age of interfaith relations, cooperation and dialogical engagement. Today, Christians join with members of other religions as interlocutors at dialogue conferences, as partners in interfaith organizations and in many common quests and cooperative ventures. Leaders from other religions receive hospitable welcome at the Vatican; the religiously other is received and welcomed as an honoured guest at WCC assemblies. Whereas, in days past, friendly and accommodating relational détente on the basis of mutual respect and regard would have been the exception, it is now the effective rule. Previously, people of other faiths were prime targets for outreach and conversion. If not amenable to that, they were at times subject to expulsion and on occasion even to execution if they lived within the borders of a "Christian" country. Alternatively, a dismissive condemnation was the theological and spiritual rule: rejection of the gospel would reap its own punitive reward. The relationship of Christians to the Jewish people has been a case in point. Such attitudes and responses, however, are thankfully no longer the order of the day.

Nevertheless, there remains much for faith communities to improve. Dialogue is the indisputable key to this improvement. As long as there has been any sort of mutual social contact, peoples of the world's religions have interacted with each other. Mostly, this has taken place in the everyday mundane yet largely positive encounters of commerce and related elements of social intercourse; sometimes the interactions have taken the negative form of hostile political events and allied warfare. On the whole, anything which today would be recognized as dialogue has been an exception, indulged in by the occasional enlightened leader or embraced by a scholar keen to engage in enquiry and debate, or perhaps the tentative outreach of an inquisitive seeker for truth and knowledge. This has been so with respect to most, if not all, religions, and especially in the case of Christianity, whose *modus operandi* has been predominantly that of missionary engagement in the quest for converts. But, as I have noted, things have changed. Now, some two millennia after Christ, the Christian church—here represented by way of the institutional structures of the Vatican and the World Council of Churches—has, without any abandoning of its missionary mandate, reached a position where interreligious relations and dialogue and, indeed, interfaith engagement at a number of levels, are affirmed and embraced. There would seem to be no going back. But, equally, the way ahead—what to do and think now, as a consequence of interfaith engagement—is not at all clear. A danger exists, I suggest, of *de facto* retrenchment into a ghettoized mentality, of a fall-back to an exclusivist fundamentalism, if, indeed, advances made in the 20th century are not consolidated and developed well and quickly in the 21st. Understanding the place and role of the church in interreligious dialogue and the quest for relationship with other faiths is thus not only of academic interest; it may indeed contribute to a critical dimension of contemporary religious life and theological concern, the priority of interfaith engagement as such. How has the present juncture come about? What has occurred down to the present time? In short, what has happened, why, and to what effect? In what way has faith tried to make things better?

In recent years, with the growing implications of further changes in religious demographics and the effects of media reactions to interreligious issues, new and significant needs and opportunities for interreligious dialogue and the work of improving intercommunal relations have emerged. Andrew Wingate notes that dialogue "begins when people meet people" and that this may be "by chance, or by intention" and furthermore, that many dialogical engagements take place "in an entirely informal context, between neighbours, friends, work colleagues, fellow students, and so on."[7] There is nothing special or extraordinary about this dialogue: it is part of everyday human interaction. It can proceed in an entirely pragmatic fashion, without suggesting or requiring any theological reflection as such. Before long, though, questions do arise, questions which can and do impact upon Christian self-understanding. Among the many questions that Wingate articulates are a number pertinent to note in the light of the issues we will address in this book. Two touch on the perennial issue of Christian mission and self-understanding: "How can the needs of community work and dialogue be balanced with the call to witness and respond to conversion requests?" on the one hand; and on the other, "How can we respond to those dogmatically certain within our own Christian community that they have the truth, the whole truth, and nothing but the truth?"[8] Different modes of interfaith engagement are signalled by questions such as "Where are the places we can join in common service to the wider humanity of different faiths?"[9] and "How do we use the scriptures in interfaith dialogue?"[10] Then there is the question "What ceremonies and prayers of other faiths can we participate in, and how do we decide?"[11] This last points us to the discussion and work on the issue of interreligious prayer and related activities that I will address in one of the chapters of this book. Wingate also reminds us that Christian identity and engagement in the world, including the world of other faiths, presupposes that we know both how to identify ourselves and how to communicate that identity—in order not only that "the world might believe," but more particularly that the world might know who is talking and why. "How can we engage in an appropriate form of Christian apologetic in a multifaith situation?" he asks.[12] There is a myriad of questions to be addressed, and across the globe there is a pressing Christian imperative to engage with interfaith contexts and issues. Reflection and action in the arena of interfaith engagement are today key challenges to the life of the church. This is so in many places around the world, not least in the Old World European heartlands of Western Christianity, but also in the relatively New Worlds of the Americas and Australasia and in the very cradle of the diversity of human civilization, Africa.

The ecumenical theologian Stanley Samartha once stated that dialogue "is part of the living relationship between people of different faiths and ideologies as they share in the life of the community."[13] The Indian-Catalan scholar of religions Raimon Panikkar made the following challenging statement, which remains fresh in its contemporary applicability:

Dialogue, to begin with, has to be *duo-logue*. There have to be two *logoi*, two languages encountering each other, so as to overcome the danger of double monologue. One has to know the language of the other, even if one has to learn it precisely from the other, and often in the very exercise of dialogue. Dialogue engages the intellect, the *logos*.[14]

Over the course of the last 100 years or so, the world's dominant missionary religion, Christianity, has embraced a wider range of relational modalities when it comes to its dealings with other religions and their peoples. Beginning with questions thrown up by missionaries in the 19th century, emerging in the context of a burgeoning ecumenical consciousness during the early 20th century, the move of the Christian churches toward intentional interreligious engagement has come to the fore, especially since the 1960s, within a horizon of seeking for better coexistence and the ameliorating of past patterns of negative interactions. The previously virtually exclusive "us and them" mentality has largely given way to a recognition that we are all of us but diverse members of the one human community, and must needs cooperate and strive for better intercommunal relations if, as a human race, we are to have a future. Nowadays the mood toward interreligious dialogue and wider interfaith relations is embraced by the leadership and representatives of most, if not all, of the world's religions. That this happens is of significance and importance, but it is not without opposition and some difficulty. Not everyone is on board and there are quarters of considerable concern and outright opposition. Nevertheless, the cause of interfaith dialogue is widely endorsed and is well embedded in the life of the wider church, as we shall see below.

It has long been recognized that interreligious dialogue, as an interpersonal activity, first and foremost occurs when people of different faith traditions meet and interact. So the first question, the first point of reflection, is: Just what kind of meeting—what kind of interaction—takes place? What happens—and what ought to be happening? Certainly interfaith dialogue, if it is to be in any way meaningful, must both presuppose and evoke mutual understanding and trust. But to what extent are these actively fostered? What more needs to be done? All being well, good interfaith engagement enables healthy communal relations and cooperative responsibility with respect to shared service in and to wider society. But how much, and to what extent, is this being promoted within the life of the church? To the extent it is *not* happening, why not? What strategies need to be put in place? Furthermore, good dialogue, and all it can portend, is often affirmed as a modality of authentic Christian witness. Yet how is this so? And just what is meant by "witness" in this context? If witness is viewed as the end-point, or justifying rationale, of dialogue, to what extent can dialogical engagement be said to be authentic?

Throughout the 20th century many developments in interfaith dialogue have emanated from within the Christian church, ranging from a diversity of local events to international initiatives sponsored by the WCC or the Vatican.[15] It was only as recently as 1969 that a dialogue occasion involving Muslims and Christians, with the theme of "Christian-Muslim Conversations," was held as "an attempt to take up the developing interfaith conversation on an international level."[16] The necessity for dialogue, and the recognition that Islam and Christianity have in common the same God but with different historical theologies, were the notable conclusions reached at the time. Furthermore, the gathering affirmed that the purpose of dialogue "cannot consist in arriving at artificial agreement. The encounter must not succumb to either syncretism or relativism. Dialogue must open the way . . . to meet and ask each other the true questions."[17] The invitation to interreligious dialogue was an invitation to a mutual quest for knowledge and understanding and to an engagement in openness and trust. Involvement in interreligious dialogue presupposes a desire to seek common ground as well as to explore what is distinctive, all with a view to countering misunderstanding and fostering a climate of respectful and cooperative relationships.

Nevertheless, it is fair to say that a dominant dialectical tension that is found in both the Roman Catholic Church and many member churches of the World Council Churches is the tension between evangelism and dialogue—or between those who promote conversion and those who promote conversation as the primary mode of relating to people of other religions. It must be noted, in this regard, that many Protestant evangelical churches, both members and non-members of the WCC, have eschewed interreligious dialogue as such and Christian-Muslim dialogical overtures in particular. Such churches tend to be suspicious of, if not opposed outright to, dialogical engagement with any other religion. They have tended to view interreligious dialogue as a compromise that poses an ideological threat to Christian faith *per se* and they have been quick to criticize the WCC for involving itself in the cause of dialogue. Similar threads of opposition have been and are still encountered within the wider life of the Roman Catholic Church as well. Further, and despite the promotion of a discourse of mutuality on many sides, the prospect for engagement is too often overshadowed by the suspicion, on the part of the prospective dialogical partner of another faith, of the existence of a hidden evangelistic agenda underlying overtures from the Christian side. The path to interreligious engagement is by no means smooth. But it is becoming, at least in some quarters of the Christian church, a more urgent and widespread challenge. A raft of local, regional and national interfaith organizations now exist in many countries. Many clergy and other church leaders today find themselves joining with clerics and leaders of other faiths in various public arenas and in espousing a range of public good causes. This is not just a matter of indulging in politically correct public relations. Rather, there exist a range of laudable and important reasons for interreligious engagement: they include social and community needs, the development of interpersonal relations among community leaders and the recognition that in a largely apathetic and religiously secularized, even antagonistic, world, it is the values and sensitivities of the religious communities in society that can make a critical difference. More poignantly, it is arguably the extremist behaviours emanating from some of the world's religions which are cause today for gravest concern: addressing the religiously motivated extremist threat is as much a concern for interreligious engagement as it is a charge laid upon security services of nations and communities.

It is issues and topics such as these that this book seeks to explore. The book's genesis lies in a combination of personal engagement, study and reflection on interfaith issues and interreligious dialogue, and opportunities to share these in a variety of forums (lectures, seminars, public addresses), within the United Kingdom, Germany, Switzerland, the USA, Egypt, Iran, India, Malaysia, New Zealand, and Australia. Such occasions have offered opportunity for further thinking and for the refinement of ideas in response to questions and comments. Thus I have brought together here a range of issues around the field of interreligious engagement, which includes interreligious dialogue, with a primarily Christian readership in mind, or at least a readership that sits within the culturally Christian world. I have divided the book into three parts. The first, comprising chapters 1 and 2, sets the scene by way of exploring some of the issues pertaining to the very prospect of engaging in, and before this, understanding the phenomenon of, interreligious dialogue; it also examines the issue of religious diversity, that is, examining the manner of responding to or contending with that diversity as the very context for engaging in dialogue. In the second part, chapters 3 and 4 provide an overview of the development of Christian engagement in interreligious dialogue from the perspective of the ecumenical movement (represented by the World Council of Churches) and the Roman Catholic Church (through the relevant offices of the Vatican) since the early 20th century. These chapters provide a wider context for what is happening today and they give an indication of the range of issues that have arisen—and show that what appears to be a newly pressing issue today may, in fact, have long been present in interreligious relations. Chapter 5 explores and propounds some key dialogical models and issues while chapter 6 outlines an ecumenical theology of interreligious dialogue. In the third part, chapter 7 examines the issue of Christian discipleship in the context of interfaith relations and dialogical engagement, while chapter 8 discusses the often contentious matter of interreligious prayer. Chapter 9 concludes the book with a discussion around the question of what it means to hold and maintain a Christian identity whilst being open to other faiths and their peoples. How can one be authentically Christian and at the same time engage authentically in interreligious dialogue? Although very different in structure and content, the purpose of this little book nevertheless rather echoes, at least in part, the purpose with which Andrew Wingate wrote his book *Celebrating Difference, Staying Faithful.* It has been written

> primarily for Christians who seek guidance in how to live in our multi-religious world; who would like to talk with those of other faiths with whom they live and work, and seek the confidence to do so . . . who want to reflect on biblical and theological questions in this field; or who are concerned about what the mission of the Church should be in our multi-faith society.[18]

Our hope is ever that interfaith engagement and interreligious dialogue will produce positive outcomes. Where this is not the case, it is not so much a matter of the failure of such engagement as a stronger challenge to succeed. The road to such success must necessarily involve the consideration—and resolution, or at least amelioration—of a range of critical issues. I have identified and touched on some of them here, with the principal underlying issue being that of the Christian perception of, and response to, the fact of religious diversity. I trust that you will enjoy accompanying me into an exploration of the selection of interreligious topics, questions and issues contained in this book.

Part One
Setting the Scene

1. PRELIMINARY CONSIDERATIONS
PROSPECTS FOR DIALOGUE

LYING BEHIND THE IMPETUS TO DIALOGUE WITH PEOPLE OF OTHER FAITHS is, for many Christians, the pressing question of how to live as religiously committed people in a multi-religious society. Whilst, for some, the presence of other faiths evokes neither curiosity nor attraction, but rather either polite ignoring or an anxiety about the effectiveness of Christian mission, for other Christians the presence of different faiths provokes an outreach and an accompanying theological quest: these too are children of God, created in the image of God, for whom Christ died, yet who have an alternate spirituality or God-relationship. What might it all mean for Christian faith? How might Christians live their own faith and at the same time cultivate a positive disposition (not to imply full agreement, of course) towards people of other faiths and, indeed, to their faith as such? Furthermore, towards the latter part of the 20th century there was mounting evidence within many societies of a widespread quest for an appropriate spirituality. If there had been an expectation during that century that religion was effectively passé, most likely to fade out in the face of rampant apathy born of consumerist and materialist satiation, it became increasingly clear late in the century that religion was here to stay, but maybe not in traditional forms, and certainly ushering in new modes of being religious and interacting religiously. Indeed, it has been observed that in this context it is sometimes the case that "religious persons from different faiths have much more in common than do a Christian and a person of no faith, even if they share the same culture."[1] Previous patterns and expectations of alliance and familiarity have been challenged. All this has led to new appraisals and appropriations of religious diversity.

This very diversity emerged as a significant issue impinging directly upon dialogue, for the question of faith-identity in a context of religious diversity is critical for interfaith engagement: it is this very diversity which sets the scene for that engagement. Further, religious diversity raises issues of the relativities of religious identities and the presumptions of absolute truth. It is the context of this very diversity that calls us to engage in dialogue with our neighbours of other faiths and to be open to new understanding and insight that might arise from that. In this chapter I shall discuss elements and issues that seem to me important in approaching the matter of interreligious dialogue. Then I shall identify some perspectives on dialogue as a relationship issue; I shall confront some of the difficulties and review some identifiable ideological perspectives that impinge upon prospects for this engagement. Finally I shall turn to the issue of dialogue methodology more directly. What kind of critical and cognitive tools are appropriate and applicable for dialogue to take place? Here I will be drawing upon my interests and expertise as both a theologian and a phenomenologist of religion.

Diversity and Dialogue: Question for Christians

Overcoming the competitive clash that has so often coloured religious interactions is one of the aims of interreligious dialogue. Religions that otherwise promote peace yet bless the battle-tanks of military might fuel the secularist's cry that religion must go if true peace is to be found. As has also been said in recent times, there can be no world peace without peace between religions, and no peace between religions unless there is dialogue between and among them. For Christians, however, the fact of religious diversity, and the question of relating to peoples of other faiths, raises acute theological questions: "Other religions exist and appear to thrive. Is this against God's will? Is it a temporary phase, until all are gathered in? Or is this part of God's provision?"[2] The answer to these questions determines the likelihood of Christian interfaith engagement. Even if that set of questions is set aside in the context of an everyday lived reality in a religiously plural world, Christians may well ask: "How do we account for the evident goodness, love and sense of spirituality found in people of other faiths? Is this the activity of the Spirit within them?"[3] Theodore Ludwig has usefully cautioned that expectations in respect to "the results of religious dialogue depend on how one views the relationship between the common human religious experiences, on the one hand, and the concrete, specific forms taken in the different religions, on the other."[4] How indeed, we may ask, are we to conceive and articulate "the common human religious experiences" in such a way as not to do an injustice to the specificity of a particular religion? In what way are we to take account of "concrete, specific forms" such that we may legitimately utilize generic concepts and terms? What methodological tools are required to allow us to bridge the gulf between uniqueness and specificity on the one hand, and valid talk of commonalities on the other, such that dialogical engagement may take place at the conceptual and ideological level? How can this engagement take place in a manner which does not presuppose that, indeed, different religions are but variations of the same thing?

Further, in order for dialogue to proceed, some basic attitudes or predispositions are important, even necessary. Ludwig identifies these as a firm standing in one's own religion; preparedness for growth in understanding, both with respect to one's own religious tradition and in relation to the other tradition; mutual respect; the willingness to learn; and the readiness to share. The context of religious plurality and the question of the meaning of religion are also directly addressed as the issue of religious dialogue is taken up. For many Christians, however, it is still the case that dialogue is perceived as either a non-issue or as a threat. But, as Ludwig has remarked,

> it is not necessary to give up critical thinking in order to dialogue with people of different religions. Dialogue involves a give-and-take that includes questions and challenges as well as respect and acceptance; comparing religious ideas and practices calls for accurate information and good critical thinking.[5]

So, the first task of dialogue is mutual correct knowledge, the educative task of getting to know each other; then the deeper issues may be addressed.

Framing the Dialogue

For interreligious dialogue to proceed in the hope, if not expectation, of a productive outcome, the misapprehensions of the past, together with the prejudices of the present, must be addressed in a climate of mutual and reciprocal acceptance as well as correction. This requires that we consider the very paradigms and perspectives whereby dialogue is framed and constituted, for the ideology of a dialogical encounter will set the context for the extent and nature of interreligious relationship. In this regard David Lochhead has identified five ideological dimensions that varyingly apply to the dialogical relationship.[6]

The ideology of *isolation* is the context for mutual standoff, for a climate of reciprocal indifference. It forms the context wherein the "isolated community defines reality for itself."[7] Furthermore, the "isolated community is not able to take seriously the existence of other views of reality."[8] Lochhead notes that the ideology of isolation supports the religious stance of exclusivism, as does the second type of ideology, *hostility*: maintenance of the purity of faith in isolation results in a faithfulness that requires the religiously other to be seen as "fundamentally ignorant and superstitious."[9] Indeed, for the exclusivist, openness towards other religions "would seem to be openness to idolatry. Faithfulness would seem to require a relationship of hostility to communities of other religious traditions."[10] The ideology of hostility means that the community is no longer isolated, but that "the impact of another construction of reality is experienced as a threat. The closeness of the other and the difference of the worldview of the other calls into question the community's own understanding. The challenge of the other community is experienced as a challenge to God."[11] Thus the ideology of hostility embraces three features: the other is perceived as threat; the error of the other is not naive but culpable (for example, "The other is a liar or a deceiver"); and the other is engaging in a deliberate undermining stratagem. This ideology of hostility yields up a rhetoric of hostility, including powerful images such as, for example in the case of Christianity, that of the Antichrist.

The ideology of *competition* is second only to isolation in typifying the predominant mode of interfaith relationship. It is marked by two features, namely that "competing communities implicitly acknowledge that they have some similarities" and that "competing communities place considerable stress on their differences."[12] Competition may or may not be hostile, but it certainly asserts the superiority of "our" community and religion over "yours." Competition allows the other a measure of validity whilst maintaining the claim of ultimate superiority—the undergirding motif of religious inclusivism. For most Christians, their very identity is given form and substance by the beliefs and dogmas expressed in creed and confessional statement demanding loyalty and assent. This fact has carried with it a considerable burden of responsibility, as Lochhead notes: "To fail to defend these definitions, to fail to insist on their non-negotiable character, as required in a competitive relationship with other traditions, implies a failure to be faithful."[13]

The fourth ideology, *partnership*, with its inherent values of cooperation and mutual respect, arose initially within the orbit of Christianity, but in practical terms, it may also apply between religions. As an ideology "it is based on the axiomatic affirmation that any real God must be a universal God."[14] A partnership ideology, somewhat akin to the *pluralist* perspective— the view that affirms the mutual relativity of religious worldviews—is vulnerable to the very charges the others seek to combat. Nevertheless, partnership ideology raises some profound theological challenges of its own. For instance, "to fail to see that God is revealed in all creation, and therefore in each and every religious tradition, makes one seem less than faithful to the universality and transcendence of God."[15]

As a mode of negotiation, dialogue aims at agreement that requires a measure of compromise, the dangerous side of which is, for some, syncretism. However, the first or primary goal of dialogue is understanding—not agreement as such, let alone the pursuit of some religious or spiritual amalgam. Lochhead suggests that dialogue may instead be viewed as *integrative*, for "dialogue with another tradition leads us to a deeper understanding of and loyalty to our own faith traditions."[16] This is so by virtue of the new light and perspective that knowing the other throws on the knowing of self. The dialogical process and attitude may be self-reflectively transformative without leading necessarily to either syncretism on the one hand or conversion on the other. This can be given explication through an analogy with bilingualism:

> When one becomes bilingual, one learns to operate within the categories that are appropriate to each particular language. Each language is considered to have its own integrity . . . one comes to understand one's own language in a more profound way by experiencing it in contrast to a second language.[17]

Thus dialogue has the prospect of integration, that is, of attaining a new level of self-reflexive understanding and awareness, as well as a concomitant understanding and sympathetic awareness of the other.

Phenomenology: Description in Dialogue

Broadly speaking, interreligious dialogue requires the parties involved both to carefully articulate their respective positions and to carefully hear and attend to the position of their dialogical partner. But, as I have indicated, the stance taken toward dialogue needs first to be clarified: too often it is assumed, at least from the perspective of the Christian partner, that the appropriate and indeed primary stance is theological. I contend that this need not and perhaps should not be so. I am not saying that dialogue has nothing to do with theology: far from it. Rather, prior to the introduction of theology and theological issues into the dialogical arena, another dimension needs to be attended to. Each partner to dialogue needs to know that he (or she) understands correctly, and can faithfully represent, the position of the other. To this end a primary discipline in the study of religion, namely the phenomenology of religion, may be usefully applied. The theological dimension of dialogue requires the careful analytic and non-judgmental descriptive acumen of the phenomenologist of religion; phenomenology requires the articulation of theological questions and issues in order to go beyond a mere polite posturing of mutually heard positions. So, for example, when Christian and Muslim, or Buddhist and Jew, meet in dialogical encounter, each first needs to know that she (or he) can faithfully represent and thereby empathically understands the position of the other.

The phenomenological method as utilised in the study of religion involves analytic description of a non-evaluative sort. "Phenomenological method" is, in effect, the technical term for the process referred to as *describing with critical empathy*. This method is interested in religious phenomena at two levels:

- What they are like, how they appear and where they are found, from an observer's point of view.

- What they mean, what their significance is and how they make sense, from a participant's point of view.

The first task of a phenomenology of religion is to make the observer's descriptions of the phenomena as accurate as possible. Then we can begin the second task, which is the attempt to appreciate what each phenomenon means for the participants. We do this by discovering how these phenomena fit into the wider belief system, tradition and social relationships within which the participants are situated. The attempt to explain religion and religious phenomena proceeds through the following steps:

- The suspension of presuppositions or assumptions about the truth, falsity or value of a religious set of concepts and actions (i.e., we set aside where *we* have come from).

- The attempt to articulate and elucidate, as fully as possible, what the concepts, actions, social associations—in other words all the dimensions and data that make up religion—mean for the persons involved with them (i.e., we try to portray accurately where *they* are coming from).

- The attempt to understand the various phenomena so articulated by engaging in analytic and comparative assessment (i.e., we try to comprehend *what is really going on*, how it all interconnects, what it represents and means).

It is also significant that the explanation arrived at by way of understanding and appreciation is not that of any dismissing or explaining away of the phenomena encountered. Religion explained— appropriate understanding—leads to a fuller appreciation of the diverse and complex reality of religion, whatever its manifestation. Thus, in essence, the phenomenological study of religion involves identifying the distinctive characteristics of religion through a systematic approach to the basic religious structures and functions across all faiths. The underlying goal is one of providing accurate meanings for the main terms used in the study of the religious field. Along with detailed information about particular faiths and their histories, the phenomenological method offers tools for understanding all faiths and the relationships among them; it places them within a common set of religious categories, together with their distinctive variations on basic themes.

In order for dialogue to be further advanced, once each side has established with the other the ability to hear and understand correctly, we need to examine the dynamics of the religious phenomena involved—

our own and the other's—with a view to sketching ways in which each may come to a deeper comprehension of the religious system of the other. We also engage in this learning process so that the possibility of a new mode of mutual understanding may emerge, something which belongs to the dialogue process itself rather than as the claim of one religion over against the other. Here we are touching on the realm of the "third partner in dialogue" that Norman Solomon identified with respect to Jewish-Christian dialogue,[18] namely, the realm of common conceptual language that allows for dialogue—in the sense of a genuine interaction of ideas and insight—to proceed.

Understanding Religion: Areas of Dialogical Encounter

We may note at this juncture some areas that are very often perceived as primary arenas for dialogical encounter between religions. Therein may be borne some fruit of common understanding, if not agreement. The dimension of *morality*, for example, reflects a fundamental dynamic of the way of being human: to be human is to be part of a process in which the individual relates both to the wider community and to the whole of the existing universe. There is an authentic way, or process, of human existence. The moral dimension of religion explicates this way, situating the way of being human within the context of a unique set of teachings and circumstances. That all religions have such a way, and that all such ways yield a set of common underlying values, is itself a commonplace of interreligious understanding. By contrast, the dimension of *mysticism* points to the possibility for, and modes of, transcendental understanding. What is presented to the senses and through experience is related to a wider worldview. Indeed, the worldviews that make up different religions generally have specific foci, what we might call belief-identifiers. These are the "catch-cry" slogan beliefs ("Jesus is Lord!" "Allah-hu-akbar!") whereby the followers or practitioners of a particular religion express their unique identity and allegiance. Another dimension of religion, *eschatology*, points up the dynamic of the salvific or transformative goal: religions have an aim, an end or *telos* (purpose, goal) in mind in their promulgation of a way to salvation or ultimate transformation. Salvation is both from something (the inadequacy or degeneracy of human existence) and to something (a realm or supra-state beyond anything the present existence can conceive or contain).

But we must return to our immediate task. I suggest that authentic interreligious dialogue requires a certain tool, a particular methodology, to enable genuine interaction to take place, and that this methodology, which necessarily involves the dimension of common conceptual language, may be found in the application of the phenomenological methodology as utilized in the field of religious studies. Indeed, the language in which I have couched my foregoing remarks concerning morality, mysticism and eschatology reflects this methodology. Furthermore, a word needs to be said concerning how we understand religion as such: how is religion to be defined?

We can begin by acknowledging two basic stances towards the issue of definition. The most common is to formulate an *essentialist* definition, to endeavour to encapsulate the essence of religion in a neat phrase or a succinct sentence or two. Usually, however, such definitions, whilst satisfying to their author, and generally reflecting the author's academic bias and emphasis, by no means satisfactorily encompass the many nuances of religion as experienced and expressed by religious practitioners. The essentialist definition may tinkle a bell of limited accuracy, but hardly peals a toll of encompassing sufficiency. Very often, too, essentialist definitions tend to be reductionist: the breadth and diversity of religion is narrowed down to one set of abstract terms. The sociologist Robert Bellah, for example, speaks of religion as "a set of symbolic forms and acts which relate man to the ultimate condition of his existence."[19] The philosopher Alfred North Whitehead says simply that religion is "what the individual does with his solitariness."[20] Essentialist definitions barely scratch the surface of, or do justice to, the manifest reality of religion.

Over against the tradition of essentialist types of definitions we can distinguish another set or type, the *phenomenological* or practical definitions of religion. These tend to be open-ended: they identify and categorize the range of phenomena that constitute religion by attending to the reality of religions as lived and experienced. Much contemporary scholarship approaches the matter of definition by taking account of, and accurately describing, the observable and recordable phenomena of religion: religion is defined in terms of the complex of phenomena of which it consists. The meaning of the term "religion" is thus found in objectively reportable religious activity or phenomena rather than in a construct of philosophical or theological speculation. Thus religion is defined—and our understanding of any religion is shaped—in terms of the functions, dimensions or structures which together comprise the milieu of any given religion. By the application of such an approach, commonalities may be discerned, although they have to be carefully teased out in order to be properly understood. Of course, the reality of the many distinctive characteristics that distinguish one religion from another must be clearly identified and not glossed over. The task of identifying and concentrating upon that which is held apparently in common is necessarily set alongside that which distinguishes and sets apart. To focus on one to the relative exclusion of the other is either to short-change the dialogical process or to render it an impotent exercise.

Addressing the matter of defining religion is an important prolegomenon for dialogue; so too is the issue of the way in which we go about the task of investigating, and so understanding, religion. The definition we hold to will either open the way to dialogue or place stumbling blocks before it. Christian definitions of religion, for example, have in the past often led to the presumption of irreligion so far as the faith of others has been concerned. The seeds of ignorance and bigotry can be easily sown, and in the process great stumbling blocks are put in the way of interfaith dialogical engagement and of peaceful and harmonious coexistence. Ignorance of many sorts is at the heart of many interfaith difficulties. Indeed, I suggest that ignorance may be manifest in at least three modalities, namely *innocent, blind* and *culpable*. On the one hand there is *innocent ignorance,* or ignorance *simpliciter,* namely the situation of a naïve not-knowing, which yields the direct and unequivocal "don't know" response when a question of knowledge or perception is posed. However, this form of ignorance may provide opportunity for correction through the provision of information and the processes of education. It implies no intentional prejudice on the part of the one who is innocently ignorant; it provides instead the possibility of an educative moment and openness to dialogical encounter for the sake of new understanding and relevant knowledge.

On the other hand, *blind ignorance* is something else again. It is ignorance born of an intellectual incapability, or cognitive barrier, that effectively prevents any seeing or knowing other than what has been dictated by the worldview or perspectives held. It yields a "can't know—it's beyond our ken" response. Knowledge of the other is so utterly proscribed by the worldview of the knower that no alternative perspective is admissible. Here the notion of applying a corrective simply through information is inadequate. Any educational process, if attempted, will require sustained and careful execution to effect any real change. Even if change is unwelcome or resisted, the premise of this mode of ignorance is basically cognitive inertia, which in principle can be overcome. Paradoxically it is this modality of ignorance that can yield to great changes in self-understanding, social ordering and cultural life as happened, for instance, in the momentous changes brought about in the USA by the civil rights movement, or the demolition of apartheid in South Africa, during the twentieth century.

There is, however, yet another kind of ignorance. It goes beyond even that occasioned by the blinding effect of a limited perspective and an intransigently closed mind. This third kind is *culpable ignorance*, that is, an active ignoring: the deliberate refusal to know, the avoidance of the challenge to cognitive change, the reinforcement of a prejudicial perspective by deliberately ignoring the issue at hand. This is ignorance born of an active dismissal of alternative possibilities, the out of hand rejection of options presented for alternate ways of thinking, understanding and interpreting. This modality goes hand in glove with the attitude and mindset that harbours most forms of fundamentalism. It produces an intentional "won't know" or "don't want to know" response. It is resistant to any information contrary to its own; it is inimical to educational process; it treats cognitive change as effectively, if not actually, treasonable. This is the mindset most resistant to dialogical engagement. Nevertheless, it does not vitiate attempts to dialogue; it rather sharpens the challenge. The critical contemporary task is to combat ignorance and overcome prejudice by getting our facts right: understanding what is really meant by "religion" and doing persons of other religions the honour and dignity of accurately portraying, and thereby appropriately comprehending, their actual religious perspective and framework. This is, in the first instance, a task of *intra*religious dialogue—dialogical engagement *within* a religion—which sets the scene for *inter*religious engagement. It is also and always a perennial underlying motif for, and a constant aim, of interfaith dialogical engagement.

Commonalities, Differences, and Dialogue

As a comparative scholastic exercise, the investigation of religion aims to attain deepened knowledge and understanding, not to assert one religion's being better or more true than another. Appropriate comparison can enable the discernment of meaning and the evaluation of what appears to be held in common and what is distinctive. This process must recognize and allow for difficulties with language and translation. Wherever possible it uses the key words of the religion itself rather than importing words from another religious tradition. This involves the discernment of dynamic parallels as much as, if not more than, the comparing of the details of concrete data. When dealing with the issue of salvation, for example, we may note that, generally speaking, nearly all religions express some form of transformative aim, by which I mean an underlying dynamic whereby the less-than-satisfactory now will yield eventually to a blissfully satisfactory (paradisiacal) future. But the details as to the how, why and wherefore of this transformation or salvation will vary greatly, and may even conflict. Even where there is reference to an apparent common heavenly end, descriptive details about it may vary—as is the case with Islamic and Christian notions of heaven, for example. The point is that from out of the comparative contrast of similarities and recurrent associations of commonalities on the one hand, and differences and variations that mark out what is distinctive on the other, we may deduce patterns and construct provisional perspectives to enhance our understanding and thereby enable fruitful dialogue to proceed. Genuine dialogue will only rise above an exercise in parallel prejudicial monologue to the extent there has been a proper effort at understanding.

But what of dialogue itself: how might we understand interreligious dialogue as such? A threefold aim of interreligious dialogue may be summarized as follows:[21] dialogue should lead its participants to greater mutual respect and better understanding of each other; it should raise questions which can lead each of the participating interlocutors to a deepening and a renewal of spirituality; and it should lead to the acceptance and fulfilment of common practical responsibilities. Each of the partners in dialogue should aim to achieve good understanding of the common and distinctive elements in each other's faith, history and civilization; respect for each other's religious and cultural integrity; common commitment to strive for social justice and for responsible development of the earth's resources; and a mutually challenging enrichment of spirituality which may also be a challenge to secular neighbours. As well, each partner should aim to avoid unfair comparison or caricature; any attempt to impose a syncretistic solution; complacency about static coexistence; and defensive and hostile attitudes to secular neighbours. To what extent these principles designed to guide dialogical engagement have been conscientiously applied is a matter of conjecture and would require careful investigation to ascertain. Certainly, in some parts of the world, there have been notable advances made by the intentional application of principles such as these. They remain a valid reference for anyone contemplating engaging in interreligious dialogue.

The ecumenical leader and theologian Wesley Ariarajah once noted the upsurge in the quest for religious identity and meaning that was evident in many contexts throughout the world, a phenomenon that shows no sign of abating. He remarked that this resurgence shows evidence of both promise and problems. On the one hand there would seem to be a genuine search for deeper, more profound and liberating meaning for religion coupled with a quest for an appropriate spirituality. On the other hand, there is clear evidence of a resurgence of fundamentalism and fanaticism that tend to destroy the very spirit and goal of religious life. The challenge of religious diversity speaks of the need for Christianity to "give a theological account for the presence of other faiths" as well as to ask "how [we] should . . . teach and learn theology in the context of religious pluralism and the emphasis on dialogue."[22] At a special conference on the theology of religions in 1990 which involved theologians from Orthodox, Protestant and Roman Catholic traditions, the issue of religious plurality was understood in terms of "both the result of the manifold ways in which God has related to peoples and nations as well as a manifestation of the richness and diversity of humankind."[23] Indeed, this significant Christian gathering stated that the "conviction that God as creator of all is present and active in the plurality of religions makes it inconceivable to us that God's saving activity could be confined to any one continent, cultural type, or group of peoples."[24]

In effect, any denigration of diversity, even religious diversity, can be viewed as a denial of the activity of the Creator. Put positively, the Creator is honoured as the rich diversity of creation is affirmed, and that includes human cultural and religious diversity or plurality: indeed, "Christian faith in God [provides the challenge] to take seriously the whole realm of religious plurality."[25] At the same time, the fact of plurality does not mean equality of value, nor does the affirming of diversity lack discriminatory diversification: an intelligent critical stance is called for. The issue of religious plurality and with it the question of religious pluralism as an interpretive, even ideological, response has been a long-standing issue and remains very much a lively question within the Christian church today.[26] In this regard Paul Hedges has noted the work of a number of scholars suggestive of an impasse in "understanding Christianity's encounter with other religious traditions," which may be articulated in terms of a tension between similarity and difference. Thus pluralism, as a positive disposition toward other faiths, tends to "stress the commonality of all religions."[27] Other responses to religious diversity stress the utter differences between religions. We shall pursue this topic in the next chapter. For the moment, we simply note the matter of Christianity's response to religious plurality is brought into focus in respect to the practice and understanding of interfaith engagement.

Some of the chief issues and concerns pertaining to the context of religious plurality that surfaced early on in the life of the ecumenical movement, and which are still very much alive, include the missionary vocation of the church; anxieties over the prospect that dialogue results in the compromising of faith; the slide into a false irenicism, where relational friendliness detracts from spiritual fidelity; the incipient danger of syncretistic outcomes; the putative promotion of a shallow relativism implying the idea of equal value of religions; and the prospect that dialogue might lead to any substantive doctrinal innovation. The fears that interreligious dialogue amounts to a betrayal of mission and to the opening of the flood-gates of relativism and syncretism were certainly early on dismissed as groundless within both the World Council of Churches and the Roman Catholic Church, even though such fears have resurfaced from time to time. The need to go in to bat for dialogue is a continuing call.

Conclusion

In broad terms, the Christian perspective on dialogue is that it is understood to include both witness to and exploration of the respective religious convictions of dialogical interlocutors. The practice of dialogue amounts to discerning and confirming religious value in the other. At the same time the identification of incommensurable values and genuine contradictions distinguishes Christianity from any other religion with which it engages. The fundamental Christian proclamation of "good news" and the new modality of engagement in interreligious dialogue are deemed to be interrelated, but not interchangeable: each has its own proper sphere and application within the wider mission of the church. A related issue concerns the paradigm shift signalled by the juxtaposition of the evangelical assertion of Jesus Christ as the normative way of salvation with an affirmation that no limit can be set to the saving power of God. Some years ago, a Lambeth Conference of the Anglican Communion stated that

> within the Church's trust of the Gospel, we recognize and welcome the obligation to open exchange of thought and experience with people of other faiths. Sensitivity to the work of the Holy Spirit among them means a positive response to their meaning as inwardly lived and understood. It means also a quality of life on our part which expresses the truth and love of God as we have known them in Christ, Lord and Saviour. [28]

The Lambeth report went on to say that there are "many opportunities today for Christians to stand alongside those of other faiths in the many tasks of nation-building, of seeking justice and peace, of working for the realization of the Kingdom of God."[29] Furthermore, the conference viewed dialogue as requiring the Christian to ask three questions: (1) What is there in the faith of the other that signifies the presence of God? (2) How is my faith received, understood and viewed by the other? (3) What is God saying to us within the dialogical context? Finally the conference concluded that (4) dialogue does not involve "a denial of the uniqueness of Christ" but rather leads to seeing that uniqueness "in inclusive, rather than in exclusive, terms."[30]

Advocacy of interreligious dialogue and interfaith engagement more widely implies a radical revision of the stance of Christianity towards people of other faiths, and this has been made obvious throughout the development of dialogical sensibilities such as undertaken by both the WCC and the Vatican. And arguably at the core of the gospel is the "good news" of reconciliation, for it presents the divine desire that creatures and Creator be reconciled into a right relationship. And in being reconciled to God, this very reconciliation flows outward, one to another. The teachings and example of Christ are pointers to what this means for daily life: love of God; love of neighbour; love one for another. Love that transcends the borders of racial, religious, socio-political, familial, and gender identities—as Paul so eloquently put it: In Christ "there is no longer Jew or Greek, there is no longer slave or free, there is no longer male and female'"—for all are one in Christ. Differences and identities are not lost or eliminated; rather, they are set in balanced and proper relationship one with another. In being reconciled to God we are challenged to be reconciled to our neighbour, including our neighbour of another faith.[31] This does not imply being in full agreement, nor does it require the disappearance of difference; far from it. Reconciliation, rather, means a deep level of acceptance, valuation, and appreciative interconnectedness *because* of difference. It means I see in the other something of value, something which contributes to my being and life, something that aids me in being authentically myself, even as there may be aspects to the other that I find irksome or not to my taste. So a first step for us is simply to recognize that the religious "other" does not necessarily represent something false or evil or in automatic opposition. God may yet be speaking to us through them. They may yet illuminate for us something new and different of the ways of God. We may indeed gain new insight and understanding of ourselves and our own faith out of our encounter with other people of faiths. And to discover this, we need to engage in dialogue.

Different models of dialogue apply according to circumstance and need. But wherever there is any substantive worldview or ideological content involved, whether in terms of articulating spiritual perceptions, religious values, or metaphysical theologies, then clearly what is being engaged is not just interpersonal relations. Dialogue involves a meeting of minds as much as an intercourse of friendship and a collaboration of concerns. For example, dialogue aims at understanding the other and reconfiguring an attitudinal stance toward the other as no longer a competitor, but a partner. It requires neither the rejection nor the acceptance of the religion of the other in any cognitive sense; rather it requires accepting the other as authentically a religious person, acknowledging the place and importance of religion as such, and honouring that with sincere critical engagement: affirming and endorsing where appropriate, challenging and critiquing where called for. This means being capable of both giving and receiving in authentic dialogical engagement. Jonathan Sacks has trenchantly observed that "great responsibility now lies with the world's religious communities. Against all expectations, they have emerged in the twenty-first century as key forces in a global age."[32] Sacks goes on to assert:

> Religion can be a source of discord. It can also be a form of conflict resolution. We are familiar with the former; the second is far too little tried. Yet it is here, if anywhere, that hope must lie if we are to create a human solidarity strong enough to bear the strains that lie ahead. The great faiths must now become an active force for peace and for the justice and compassion on which peace ultimately depends. That will require great courage, and perhaps something more than courage: a candid admission that, more than at any time in the past, we need to search—each faith in its own way—for a way of living with, and acknowledging the integrity of, those who are not of our faith. [33]

That is the challenge of change that faces all of us today. It is the challenge of diversity that has faced, and continues to face, the Christian community both globally and locally. The response to this challenge sets the parameters for engagement with those who are not of our faith.

2. CONTENDING WITH DIVERSITY
THE CONTEXT OF DIALOGUE

As we have already seen, a key issue confronting Christians and the church today is the unavoidable presence of many different faiths in our society. Religious diversity is a fact of life and is here to stay. It demands the considered response of religious thinkers. How is the fact of plurality to be comprehended from within the viewpoint of any one religion? Answers vary and often reflect the inner inclination of a particular religious worldview: some are more naturally accommodating of diversity and variety than are others. In many (particularly Western) contexts, this was, for a long time, an internal religious phenomenon: it was diversity *within* Christian religion that was at issue. The advent of secularization was one way of dealing with such diversity, religious as well as political. Nowadays it is the diversity of religions *per se* within many societies—Western as well as Eastern, South as well as North—that is the hallmark of our time. Australian sociologist Gary Bouma speaks of our "twenty-first-century postmodern and secular world where spiritualities are rife and religious diversity is an accepted feature" as the contemporary temporal locus of "a seriously multicultural society."[1] It is this diversity, and our response to it, that we must address. What is the meaning of diversity for faith and for dialogue?

Plurality and Pluralism

Plurality rules, in virtually all things. Religious diversity is our lived reality. But what does Christian faith make of it? First, it needs to be said, *plurality* is not the same as *pluralism*. The former denotes the fact of diversity; the latter names a response to the fact. Often the two terms are used synonymously to refer to the generic idea of "many-ness" and this can be confusing. As we shall see below, there are a variety of ways in which a religion such as Christianity can and does respond to—and so contends with—religious diversity, both within and without. Kenneth Cracknell puts the theological issue of pluralism—or rather, of religious plurality, the sheer fact of there being a diversity of religions—somewhat succinctly.[2] If there is but one God, Cracknell asks, how is it that there are so many religions? How are Christians to relate to peoples of other faiths—and, indeed, to their faiths or belief-systems as such? Are we caught up in a context of perpetual rivalry? Is the only peaceful option that of mute coexistence at the level of mere tolerance? Are we called to a life of cooperation with people of other religions? Are we not all fellow travellers in some sense? Today many people live in distinctly mixed religious contexts. This demands increased engagement in dialogue, at both the intercommunal and the interreligious level—and very often these two are so closely entwined that to engage one necessarily requires engaging the other. Religious diversity, which can be valued on the one hand whilst yet either ignored or regarded with suspicion on the other, is certainly an arena of concern for the church with respect to the discharge of its mission. If cultural and religious diversity is to be theologically valued, what then is the consequence for ministry and mission? Plurality poses intense questions and raises challenging issues. Contemporary ministry and mission within a religiously diverse context can certainly evoke an energized, positive response for dialogical relationship. But for others it results in an increase in assertively evangelical responses.[3] There is also an increased conservatism, if not fundamentalism, evident within many churches. Very often this is seen in the context of localized negative interactions with Islam, for example. The result is that there appears to be a growing resistance to, and dismissal of, interreligious engagement as a valid component of Christian life and church activity. In either case, plurality—or the sheer fact of difference and diversity—is undeniable.

If *plurality* is the fact of the matter, *pluralism* indicates one way of responding to, apprehending and interpreting the fact. Applied to religion, pluralism opens the way to situating particular religious identity within a larger framework of understanding and knowledge. As Peter Byrne remarks, "Pluralism is one important intellectual response to the fact of religious diversity."[4] The pressing question is: How may we think about religious plurality—or what may we do about it? In other words, how may we live with difference and diversity in the religious sphere? Religious *pluralism* is the idea and ideology that affirms something quite distinct about religious plurality. On the one hand, it contrasts with the idea and ideology of *exclusivism*, which amounts to a paradigm of plurality rejection. On the other hand, it may be compared to *inclusivism*, which is a paradigm of the incorporation of plurality. In this chapter we shall explore these three primary ways of responding to—or contending with—the plurality of religious diversity.[5]

Exclusivism: Paradigms of Plurality Rejection

In the context of discourse on interreligious dialogue, *exclusivism* has been posited as the default position inimical to dialogue and against which, through the application of either *inclusivism* or *pluralism*, positions of openness to dialogical engagement have been contrasted and advocated. Close analyses show, however, that inclusivism and pluralism do not denote discrete paradigms but that each refers, in fact, to a range of sub-paradigms that may be better thought of as expressing relative positions upon a continuum. Furthermore, it can be argued that, in the end, the pluralist must necessarily be an exclusivist of some sort and that the paradigm of inclusivism, when pressed, also tends to collapse into some form of exclusivism. The critical issue for interreligious engagement today is not so much the vexed issue of pluralism, nor even problems raised by inclusivism, but questions posed by the persistence—even growth—of religious exclusivism. Indeed, the phenomenon of contemporary religiously driven extremism and terrorism shows the presence of a distinctive and rigid form of exclusivity inherent to the paradigm of religious fundamentalism. Such exclusivity can certainly be understood as a variant of the paradigm of exclusivism, and exclusivism is itself an element of fundamentalist ideologies, whether religious or otherwise.

A fundamentalist perspective, for example, is inherently absolutist: all other relevant phenomena are simply explained on its terms, or viewed with reference to this perspective in a relativizing, even negating, way. Fundamentalism, as a mind-set, is a mentality that expresses the modern quest for universality and coherence writ large: only one truth, one authority, one authentic narrative that accounts for all, one right way to be. It is not just religion that can manifest this mind-set, but this mind-set is certainly something that exists within most religions today. As a response to plurality, the paradigm of exclusivism may be formally defined as *the material identity of particular and universal*. That is to say, religious exclusivism involves the identification of a particular religion (or of a form of that religion) as being, in fact, the essence and substance of true universal religion, thereby excluding all other possibilities. From this viewpoint the exclusivist's religion is "The Only Right Religion" because there can be only one religion that is right or true. Given the assertion, for example, that from a religious viewpoint, truth and salvation are universal values, the exclusivist position holds that this universality is materially identified with but one religion, that of the exclusivist. The Harvard scholar of religion Diana Eck once commented:

> The exclusivist affirms identity in a complex world of plurality by a return to the firm foundations of his or her own tradition and an emphasis on the distinctive identity provided by that tradition. . . . Exclusivism is more than simply a conviction about the transformative power of the particular vision one has; it is a conviction about its finality and its absolute priority over competing views.[6]

For the exclusivist the mutually tolerant coexistence of religions is simply not possible. In general terms, Christianity has long held an exclusivist line with respect to salvation and eternal destiny; this can be denoted as *salvific-eschatological exclusivism*. It is both a militant and a triumphant expression of religion and it is adamant that there is but one way to God, one way to access this salvation and eternal destiny. Specifically, it is based on the claim that Jesus is the only way to God or heaven, the only name whereby salvation may be attained, and further that this salvific means was vouchsafed to, and is only obtainable through, the church. Thus since the epoch of the early Church Fathers and up to the Council of Florence (1442 CE), the view that no one outside the church could possibly be saved was developed and refined.[7]

In general terms religions can be thought of as manifesting a way of life and a path of salvation. With respect to this, the position of Christian exclusivism regards all but its own way and path as invalid or void. From the Catholic dogma of *extra ecclesiam nulla salus* (outside the church there is no salvation) to various conservative Protestant declarations of condemnation of any but their own viewpoint, the "controlling assumption," said the late John Hick, "is that outside the church, or outside Christianity, there is no salvation."[8] According to Hick, exclusivism today is adhered to within Christianity by only a relatively few Catholic ultra-conservatives and Protestant fundamentalists. I think it is a little more widespread, at least at the level of many of the popular and conservative forms and expressions of Christianity. Although perhaps discounted in formal church stances and statements, exclusivism remains a problematic impinging more on the practical and pastoral dimensions of interreligious relations than on the realm of theoretical reflection. Yet exclusivism also has an impact on theoretical reflection, and attending to this is a necessary task to which I now turn.

I suggest that the paradigm of *exclusivism* is present today in at least three variants: *open, closed,* and *extreme* (or hard-line) *rejectionist.* By its very nature exclusivism is hostile to any form of interreligious dialogue or rapport; nevertheless, it impinges on interfaith engagement, most often contributing to outright resistance, or at least to the undermining of efforts toward interfaith engagement. Exclusivism is varyingly undermining of interfaith engagement; this is where nuanced variations of the application of the exclusivist paradigm may be more clearly identified.

An *open exclusivism,* while maintaining cognitive and salvific superiority, may at least be amenably disposed toward the other, if only to allow for—even encourage—the capitulation of the other, for instance by way of conversion. Some early twentieth century open exclusivists include Willem Visser t' Hooft, a leading ecumenical figure, who argued against what he viewed as "incipient pluralism," wherein syncretism and the notion of a single world faith were viewed as inexorable outcomes of taking a non-exclusivist line. Nonetheless Visser t' Hooft affirmed the value of cultural plurality.[9] Similarly, Hendrikus (Hendrik) Kraemer, for many years a missionary in Islamic Indonesia, popularized and promoted the view that, at the level of human institution, Christianity was no different from other religions in being yet another religion.[10] However, following the Swiss neo-orthodox theologian Karl Barth, Kraemer argued that with respect to its basis in revelation and the uniqueness of its truth claims, Christianity is essentially other than the religions. For Barth and Kraemer, religion names the human seeking for the divine; Christianity, by contrast, is the sole authentic arena of the divine encountering the human. Christianity stands apart, holding a position of exclusive privilege: "Christianity understands itself not as one of several religions, but as the adequate and definitive revelation of God in history."[11] Kraemer upheld the validity of cultural plurality, as did Visser t' Hooft. Nevertheless, the open exclusivism espoused by these ecumenical Christian leaders of the 20th century asserted a triumphant christocentric salvific proclamation of essential Christian identity. Openness for them had limits, at least in so far as what openness might mean for the self-identity of the person or group taking a stance of openness. Their stance of *open exclusivism* implied—and for those who share their views, continues to imply—openness to some form of relationship with another without any expectation or possibility of consequential or reciprocal change of self-identity with respect to that relationship. The other is acknowledged, but only as an antithetical other whose presence calls forth either patronizing or polemical engagement—or both.

In contrast to the open variety, *closed exclusivism* simply dismisses the other out of hand. Relationship to the other, especially the religious other, is effectively ruled out. The other may be acknowledged as having his or her rightful place, but that place is inherently inferior to that of the closed exclusivist, who prefers to remain wholly apart from the other. An open exclusivism may yet entertain a dialogue of sorts—perhaps a conversational interaction—if only with a view to understanding the perspective of the other in order, then, better to refute it and so proclaim the Only One Right Religion. By comparison, a closed exclusivism will spurn interaction with another religious viewpoint altogether: imperialist assertion is the only mode of communication admissible. The contrast between the open and closed forms of exclusivism is exemplified by two closely related denominations of Protestant Christianity, the Open Brethren and the Exclusive Brethren, found particularly in Australia and New Zealand, but also elsewhere in the Western world.[12] The former function as an ultra-conservative Christian community; the latter live a sectarian existence, effectively withdrawn from the wider world. The Exclusive Brethren, as their very name suggests, see themselves not just as superior to other forms of Christianity but indeed, as the only true form which must be thus protected from contamination with lesser and corrupt forms of the faith.

However, as I have indicated, the open and closed variants are not the only forms of exclusivism. The third variant is that of *extreme exclusivism*, which marks a shift from the closed exclusivism form, understood more simply as the exercise of a right to withdraw into itself. *Extreme exclusivism* gives expression to hard-line rejectionist exclusivity, the viewpoint that asserts an exclusive identity to the extent that the fact and presence of an other are actively resisted, even to the point of taking steps to eliminate the other. While examples of such extreme forms of exclusivism are present within the history of Christianity, it is also the case that today the more obvious instances are to be found at the extremities of most major religions, with Islam currently to the fore. The distinguishing feature denoting extreme exclusivism is the negative valorizing of the other—howsoever defined—with concomitant harsh sanctions and limitations imposed upon that other. We see this today across many religions: Islamists of various ilk, Hindu extremists in the Punjab and elsewhere and ultra-orthodox Jews in Israel, to name but some of the more prominent. It is this level of exclusive religion which, in its hostility to variety or "otherness," inherently invalidates any "other" incompatible with its worldview. It is this level of religious exclusivism which lies at the heart of so much religious strife, not to mention terrorism and insurgency, and thus poses an acute challenge to those who would advocate religious freedoms, toleration and peaceful co-existence. It is this exclusivism that inheres to the extreme wings of religious fundamentalism. But let us now turn to the second way of contending with plurality.

Inclusivism: Paradigms of Plurality Incorporation

In general terms I define religious *inclusivism* as *the effective identification of a particular religion with the universal*, with some allowance made for other religions. This paradigm suggests that the other is included surreptitiously, by being understood as already "anonymously" and indirectly within the fold of true religion, identified, of course, as being the religion of the proponent, the Only *Fully* Right One. Within Western Christianity the paradigm of religious inclusivism has been embraced formally by the Roman Catholic Church since Vatican II, and it reflects most official contemporary Protestant church positions. However, there are, arguably, two classic examples of Christian inclusivism. The first may be denoted as *cosmic-rational inclusivism*. It is derived from the doctrine of the *Logos*. The author of the fourth gospel made use of this term, *logos* (eventually capitalized as *Logos*), meaning the Word which was with God and which was God-like or divine. This led to the idea of Christ as the *Logos*. In concert with some classical Greek philosophical views, the *Logos* came to be viewed by early Christian thinkers as the creative and organizing agency of the cosmos. Justin Martyr, a second century Christian theologian and one of the earliest Christian apologists, focused on the idea of Christ as the *Logos*. He proposed that, as the energetic (*dunamis*) Word, the divine *Logos* was the creator and organizer of the cosmos, and that as the seminal (*spermatikos*) reason or Word, the *Logos* in fact inspired the Greek philosophers and is present in all humans, indeed all creation. Knowledge of God within creation is a response to the revelation brought about by the *Logos*, for creation itself is a divine manifestation. Another early Christian theologian, Irenaeus, also in the second century CE, explained that all divine manifestations take place through the *Logos*. Knowledge of God within creation is itself a response to the revelation brought about by the *Logos*, for creation (as it is for Justin) is a divine manifestation. Thus, by virtue of the universal principle of creation, all that is created is brought into being by the *Logos* of God. All is included within its cosmic sweep.

The second classic example of religious inclusivism is that of *implicit christocentric fulfilment*. While the majority of early Protestant missionaries operated on the mandate of carrying the light of the gospel to a "heathenish darkness," some showed remarkable openness. Bartholomäus Ziegenbalg (1682–1719), the first Protestant missionary to India, perceived the sense of a Supreme Being and "broken lights" of a higher truth among the Hindus. G. U. Pope (1820–1907) was fascinated by the devotional fervour of the Shaiva community in southern India and saw in it a spirituality "awaiting fulfilment." J. N. Farquhar (1861–1929) wrote the famous *The Crown of Hinduism*, in which he argued that Christ and Christianity fulfils all the aspirations of Hindus and bring to the highest point all the noble values of Hinduism. He highlighted Jesus' words that he came "not to destroy but to fulfil." This approach has been taken and expounded by several Christian theologians of religious inclusivism since then. F. D. Maurice (1805–1872) affirmed that the reign of God is a present reality and Christ is redeemer of humanity in all ages. He observed deep truths in Hinduism and regarded Muhammad as a witness for God. This observation, for him, provided a basis for further dialogue with Hindus and Muslims. In short, this form of inclusivism is based on the idea that Jesus is the absolute fulfilment of human destiny. Christianity claims to be the absolute religion, but not so as to exclude all others absolutely. Rather, Christians may consider non-Christians as "anonymous Christians"[13] because of the ever present divine grace touching each individual. At different stages many are on the way to salvation, yet preaching makes them realize the victory of grace and join the church, the social form of salvation.

In its modern form, inclusivism, I suggest, comes in at least five variant forms, or at least it displays these variant perspectives of expression and self-understanding, which I call *gatekeeper, incognito ubiquity, imperialist, mutual co-inherence* and *participatory* forms of inclusivism.

Gatekeeper inclusivism allows for limited connections with respect to other religions, but the validity of such connection is found only through one religion—"mine"—as being the point of entrance into the realm of the One Fully Right Religion. A measure of generosity of heart can be extended inasmuch as the religiously other is perceived as not completely beyond the pale: other religions may be said to enjoy a measure of veracity, or limited representation, of the Universal Truth. However, even these religions must, in some sense, go through the gate of the inclusive religion to obtain full religious or salvific validity. The governing context is clear and unequivocal. The religion of the gatekeeper inclusivist is the only *fully* right way to salvation, the only and ultimately valid bearer of religious truth. It constitutes the gate wherein, at best, others may be admitted to the fold.

By way of contrast, what may be termed *incognito ubiquity inclusivism* allows for the partial validity (truth value) as well as partial efficacy (salvific value) of other religions. This is more than a matter of gate-keeping with a generous heart. There is a hint of pluralism inasmuch as some theological value is accorded to other religions, but there is no doubt as to how that is contextualized: others are viewed as variant and limited expressions of the universal or religious truth that is yet best expressed by *our* Right One. The "our," of course, is important: any religion could theoretically, if not actually, take this view. Each religion can view itself as possessing in full that which others lack or have but partially. An illustration of this paradigm may be found in Islam, with its view of Judaism and Christianity as "religions of the book": within this paradigm Islam has, knows and lives fully that which has been given to these others, but which they now express in only a limited, if not corrupted, fashion.

The third variant, *imperialist inclusivism*, also allows for the partial truth validity and salvific efficacy of others (but, again, only those deemed "authentic" religions) in that such others are viewed as legitimate variant outworkings of the only *comprehensive* Right One. That is to say, as a sort of advance over the notion that other religions, in some incognito fashion, express in part what the inclusive religion has in full, there is in this variant of inclusivism an allowance that certain other religions may, indeed, be living out, in their own authentic though partial way, that which is nevertheless to be found fully in the one comprehensively true or right religion. Other religions, at least under certain conditions, are already and "anonymously" included within the worldview framework of the dominant religion in this schema. These other religions enjoy a partial measure of being right relative to that religion which is, of course, fully right. From the Christian perspective, Diogenes Allen expresses this paradigm when he asserts that "a Christian theology of other faiths reaches out toward other faiths, retaining the conviction that Christ is the Savior of the world, and bringing another faith or aspects of it into a vital relation to Christ."[14] In the end the generic inclusivism stance is modified by an imperialist assertion of non-negotiable or superior perspective. Imperialist inclusivism highlights the basic assumption inherited from the exclusivist stance: the total identification of a universal value, such as religious truth or salvation, with the particulars of one religion.

A fourth variation on the paradigm of inclusivism is that of *mutual co-inherence*. It derives from the work of Raimon (Raimundo) Panikkar,[15] who claimed that Christianity and Hinduism meet only in Christ, for although the man Jesus is certainly the Christ, Christ is not only Jesus. Panikkar regarded the Hindu reality of the personal Lord (*Isvara*) as identified with Christ, the personal Lord. This form of inclusivism is less a matter of a one-way including of the worldview of one religion within that of another; it holds rather that at certain critical points there is a measure of mutual including, especially where there is a careful deepening of doctrinal understanding, as with the issue of delineating what is meant by "Christ" from the understanding of the person "Jesus," for example.

Participatory inclusivism, the final variant I have identified, derives from the work of Indian theologians P. D. Devanandan (1901–1962), the founder-director of the Christian Institute for the Study of Religion and Society, Bangalore, and his successor M. M. Thomas (1916–1996).

Devanandan and Thomas bridged the perspectives of the early Indian Christian theologians, who suggested points of contact and interpretive tools in certain Hindu religious categories such as *avatar*, and the more radical stand concerning the universal presence and action of God, where the inclusivism motif is more readily discerned in a notion of the different religions equally yet differently participating in the greater outworking of God's active presence in the world. Devanandan and Thomas saw the work of the Spirit as effective within the modern religious and secular movements of India, particularly the reform and renaissance movements of their time. They viewed history as God's platform of interaction. They regarded Christ as the beginning of a new creation for which the church is called to witness through word and service. In particular, Thomas, interpreting salvation as humanization, was open to the inspiring thoughts and alternative models of community coming from other religions and even secular ideologies. He centred them on Christ, but had no fear of syncretism if it was Christ-centred.

Pluralism: Paradigms of Plurality Affirmation

The essential idea of *pluralism*, as the third way of responding to the fact of plurality, is to posit *a multiplicity of particular expressions of that which is deemed to be universal*, as opposed to the idea that there can only be one valid or fully valid expression of the universal. In essence, pluralism embraces the fact of plurality and gives it a positive interpretation. Religious pluralism, as a conceptual construct, may be viewed as an assertion of a "measure of equal standing between the major religious traditions" at the very least. It entails a denial of any type "of uniqueness and absoluteness claimed for one tradition or another."[16] It may appear that this means a relativistic reductionism where everything is equal because nothing stands out as different. But this is to misunderstand pluralism. In essence the affirmation of plurality sets aside the a priori presupposition taken by many that their religion is absolute in all respects, with the implication that, as there cannot be competing absolutes, any religion other than theirs is necessarily false. This is, of course, the position of exclusivism. Pluralism simply asserts all religions as being both different and valid.

This means that different religions are equally valid expressions of some universal religious reality. Specific religions are co-equally valid expressions of some universal notion of true religion. Thus both difference and equality are affirmed. Religions are not all the same: their differences are important; yet religions are no better or worse than each other as equally valid expressions of the universal. On this basis, no one religion can lay claim to an objective superiority, or to superlative congruence with the universal religious reality, with respect to other religions. Of course, the moment we engage in exploring the possibility of a pluralist response to religious plurality we run into a number of critical issues. To what extent, and in what way, can the notion of value equivalence be applied? Is not an affirmation of plurality the beginning of a slippery slide into relativism and reductionism? Does this not reduce religion to a matter of indifferent alternatives? Is commitment then vitiated? These are fair questions, but should not be taken as rhetorical criticisms of pluralism, for rightly understood pluralism affirms commitment, counters indifference, and neither reduces nor relativizes. As Byrne has noted,

> some versions of the pluralist response focus on truth, affirming that all religions are equally true. Other versions focus on salvation, affirming that all religions are equally valid paths to salvation. Yet others focus on the notions of religious experience and encounter, affirming all religions to be equally good means of encountering a divine transcendent reality.[17]

I take this recognition of the diversity of pluralist perspectives a little further, however. Indeed, I suggest there are a number of discrete subsets and sub-paradigms within the paradigm of pluralism. Some are more obvious and well known; others are somewhat novel.

Standard Pluralism

The first subset, which may be termed *standard pluralism*, comprises the standard definitional paradigms of pluralism, namely *common ground pluralism* and *common goal pluralism*. These two tend to predominate in any discussion of religious pluralism. The subset they constitute is the default position on pluralism that is most often discussed and the basis upon which religious pluralism, as an ideological response to plurality, is most often criticized. *Common ground pluralism* views religious differences, or the variety of religions, as contextualized variable expressions of or from a universal source. The fundamental idea is clear: there is a common ground of religious reality from which the different religions of the world derive. John Hick, a leading representative of this view, argues that the since the middle of the 20th century a new consciousness of human existence set in one world with many world religions has arisen. New conditions and contexts demand new thinking. If our neighbour is someone with whom one can engage in conversation and dialogue and, in so engaging, make discoveries about the relativity of values in respect of religious identities, then, Hick asks, are members of one religion, Christianity for example, demonstrably any better (morally or behaviourally) than members of other religions? He draws the conclusion that "it is not possible to establish the unique moral superiority of any one of the great world faiths."[18] All religions contain examples of great good and of great evil. Says Hick: "We need to compare apples with apples" (not apples with lemons).

Hick views his own work as a kind of Copernican revolution which "involves a shift from the dogma that Christianity is at the centre to the realisation that it is *God* who is at the centre."[19] Indeed, he argues that "the different encounters with the transcendent within the different religious traditions may all be encounters with the one infinite reality, though with partially different and overlapping aspects of that reality."[20] Hick reminds us that the great world religions, seen in historical context as movements of faith, "are not essentially rivals. They begin at different times and in different places, and each expanded outwards into the surrounding world of primitive natural religion until most of the world was drawn up into one or other of the great revealed faiths."[21] Hick's approach is essentially one of reconciling the aspectival relativism that embraces complementary diversity. The variant expressions of divine reality contained within the different religions are not necessarily or automatically mutually exclusive, but rather necessarily limited, yet complementary, images or manifestations of the divine Reality, "each expressing some aspect or range of aspects and yet none by itself fully and exhaustively corresponding to the infinite nature of the ultimate reality."[22]

The second variant or sub-paradigm within standard pluralism, closely allied to the first, is *common goal pluralism*, which holds that religious differences reflect the variety of salvific paths leading, or drawn to, the universal goal. In this view, the key idea is that there is a transformative goal that is the end-point of all religions, even though it may be differently expressed (in concert with the narrative tradition within which each religion dwells uniquely) and differently attained (again in keeping with the unique transformative or salvific narrative of each religion). As Hick remarks, "different religions have their different names for God acting savingly towards mankind."[23] Hick further suggests that the variant salvific paths of religion indicate that religions themselves may be regarded as

> [D]ifferent manifestations to humanity of a yet more ultimate ground of all salvific transformation. . . . the possibility that an infinite transcendent reality is being differently conceived, and therefore differently experienced, and therefore differently responded to from within our several religio-cultural ways of being human.[24]

Ground and *goal*, though complementarily linked, are nevertheless two variant paradigms of the pluralist hypothesis forming the standard paradigmatic subset. The fundamental ideas are clear—there is either a common ground of religious reality from which the different religions of the world derive, or a transformative goal that is the end-point of all religions. These constitute the substance of what religions have in common, and so provide a basis for dialogical encounter or a basis of interfaith engagement more generally.

Radical Pluralism

The second paradigm subset, *radical pluralism*, consists of two variants or sub-paradigms. First, *differentiated pluralism* holds that religious differences signal irreconcilable differentiation of religious identities. That is to say, there is no reasonable ground to assume a link across religions: their individual, or particular, identities militate against any such linkage as inferred by the predominant standard paradigm-set of pluralism. What are conveniently called religions cannot be said to be variant examples of any single category in the first place. The difference between them is of such a nature that, strictly speaking, it is illicit even to consider that there is any point of meaningful conceptual contact among the religions. A leading exponent of this variant is the US theologian and philosopher John

Cobb.[25] He may be identified as a "pure pluralist" for whom religions are not mere variant expressions of the one divine reality, but are genuinely plural in respect of the realities they represent. Thus, for example, the outcome of dialogical encounter may well be mutual transformation as opposed to mutual reinforcement.[26] Cobb demonstrates an open-ended, non-common-ground pluralist position which is suspicious of any organizing or categorical terms that might prejudge or limit dialogical conversation. He raises objections to the notion of "universal theology of religion" and sketches difficulties that he sees with the term "religion" as a denominating label. Cobb asserts the need for all traditions, including the Christian, to affirm their unique centres of meaning. He protests "that the pretense to stand beyond all traditions and build neutrally out of all of them is a delusion" and clearly asserts the uniqueness of his own religious tradition—Christianity—but eschews any suggestion that this implies any necessary superiority: he argues for "the rejection of all arrogance, exclusivism, and dogmatism in relation to other ways."[27] The attractiveness of this paradigm lies in its clear assertion of the individual identity and integrity of the religions: none can be adequately interpreted in the terms of another; none can be viewed as in any sense subsumed within another. To that extent there is no confusion of dialogical motive. But this still leaves the question that there are some religions—Judaism, Christianity and Islam, for instance—where historical, if not theological or ideological, linkages militate against this paradigm as the most apposite context for the conduct of dialogue. Cobb's perspective finds echo in the category that some refer to as "particularities," associated in particular with George Lindbeck, Gavin D'Costa, John Milbank and others.[28] In my view the idea of particularities is a variant of radical pluralism, not another separate category.

The second sub-paradigm in this radical set is *eschatological pluralism*, suggested by Mark Heim, who proposes a hypothesis of "multiple religious ends."[29] For Heim, distinctive testimonies of different religious traditions, undergirded by a concrete texture of myths, rituals and experiences as well as conditioned by different cultural-linguistic components, reveal the distinctive ends which are most desirable and ultimate for communities concerned. One should not devalue the other and impose one's vision of ultimate goal but recognize the overlapping nature of religious life including interior experiences and exterior behaviour. Heim's view can be summarized as proposing a relative value equivalence of otherwise distinctive, and thus uniquely different, religious ends or goals.

Interdependent Pluralism

Another paradigmatic sub-set, *interdependent pluralism*, also has two variants, *complementarity holistic pluralism* and *dynamic parallel pluralism*. The former holds that religious differences may be discerned as complementary particular expressions which together comprise the Universal Whole. Paul Knitter exemplifies this category in that he proposes an idea of unitive pluralism.[30] He argues that "in the contemporary pluralistic world there cannot be just one religion, but neither can there be many that exist in 'indifferent tolerance.'"[31] Knitter holds a relational view of truth wherein the differences and particularities of religions are reconciled, but not materially equivalent. The plurality of religions is not so much a matter of non-competing variant out-workings of a common ground or goal, but rather the mutual complementarity of different parts together comprising a complex whole. The world's religions together comprise the whole of what religion is as such. The divine reality encountered and expressed in variegated ways in and through different religions is not the One Reality behind religions, as it were, but the One Reality that is comprised by them all.

In similar fashion, *dynamic parallel pluralism* holds that religious differences reflect a parallelism of religious phenomena. This paradigmatic perspective may be gleaned from the phenomenological study of religion espoused by Ninian Smart and others.[32] The affirmation of pluralism asserts authenticity of phenomena without commenting on matters of validity or veracity. What is observed as a result of analysis of presented data—the phenomena that together comprise any given religion—is the presence of dynamic parallels rather than substantive sameness. Religious plurality may then be interpreted in terms of dynamic parallels of religious intuition and response, for example. This yields a point of commonality that preserves the integrity of difference. Religions are not variants of the same thing, but they may variably express parallel processes. The inference is that the reality of religion lies in the dynamic processes rather than the veracity or otherwise of supposedly commensurable substantives. The question of commonness of goal or ground, let alone the notion of religions as parts that collectively comprise a whole, is not the focus. Rather, from observation and concomitant analysis of religions can be discerned a number of parallels that are dynamically operative in and through the various narrative traditions of the religions of the world. For example, all major religions contain a narrative account of an inherent less-than-satisfactory state of affairs for human existence, howsoever arrived at in terms of specific narratives. In all cases, however, this state of affairs requires some transformative action to overcome and so enable the attainment of an ultimate outcome or destiny. The stories expressing this vary, as do the doctrines and teachings relating thereto. But the dynamic contained within the differing narratives redounds with parallel similarities. Religious plurality may be interpreted in terms of dynamic parallels of religious intuition and response. This is the point of commonality that yet preserves the integrity of difference. Religions are not variants of the same thing, but they are variant expressions of parallel processes.

Ethical Pluralism

A further subset of the pluralism paradigm is that of *ethical pluralism*. Mutual understanding, peaceful coexistence and cooperation for common welfare among people of different faiths are not new ideas. However, they have been reinforced with new slogans and novel frameworks. The Global Ethic of Hans Küng represents a serious theological exploration in dialogue with partners from other religious traditions; he has chosen to promote an idea which is appealing and widely respected on the world scene today.[33] When Küng launched his new project on global responsibility and a world ethic in 1990, his concern was very clear: no world peace without peace between the religions; no peace between the religions without dialogue between the religions. Paul Knitter has gravitated to this ethical perspective and likewise is an advocate of the addressing of, and responding to, religious plurality through the lens of an ethical pluralism.[34] Only on the basis of a pragmatic, values-oriented engagement can religions truly cooperatively work together for the future of humankind and the planetary ecosystem, for example.

Comprehensive Integrated Pluralism

Ethics and common-cause values are not necessarily the only or even the most convincing basis for an appreciation of plurality—or for a response to plurality that endeavours to discern a connection without running the risk of reductionist commonality, and to affirm uniqueness without vitiating the prospect of an appropriate harmonious interplay.

This last paradigmatic response of plurality affirmation, that of *comprehensive integrated pluralism*, is suggested by the work of Stanley Samartha (1920–2001), a pioneer of interfaith dialogue at the ecumenical level through the World Council of Churches.[35] Samartha warned against a kind of relativism which can make persons non-committal, passive and indifferent but argued that there can be a positive act of relativizing if the starting point is a deep commitment to a particular faith and community, however imperfect it may be. According to Israel Selvanayagam, Samartha was fond of the images of travel and pilgrimage, but not without commitment and openness: "We are always *on the way*," he wrote. "Every arrival is a point of departure, and every journey looks for a new destination."[36] It is in the light of the lead given by Samartha that, indeed, a way forward may be found in terms of a comprehensive integrated pluralism which affirms religious plurality in a context of concrete religious commitment and firm religious identity; which is marked by a stance of critical openness to the other and to the greater truth and understanding that lies beyond our inevitably partial and particular expressions of them; which rediscovers and carefully articulates a transcendental meta-narrative inclusive of the otherness of the other; and which therefore is able to pursue and develop a new theology or ideology of the religious other.

Conclusion

The paradigms of exclusivism and inclusivism remain quite problematic as an adequate context for the promotion of interreligious dialogue. Does this mean pluralism as such offers a way forward? Perhaps, but the multiple paradigms of pluralism are no less problematic. The notion of dialogical engagement being based on a context of a preconceived common ground "Reality" or a common salvific goal, seems now to be somewhat presumptuous as well as cognitively constraining. It requires the dialogical interlocutors to commence from a supposed third position and reconcile the two they represent to that third position. In the end, these two sub-paradigms of pluralism seem increasingly to be variants of the inclusivism paradigm, which tends more to curtail genuine dialogue than facilitate it. By contrast, the radical and ethical paradigms tend to be variations on the theme of highlighting the need for a positive approach to plurality as such. Perhaps the paradigms of complementary holistic pluralism or dynamic parallel pluralism, undergirded by a development of the idea of a comprehensive integrated pluralism, may offer a more realistic basis for contemporary interfaith engagement.

Living with difference is not a matter of reconciling perspectives and worldviews across any two or more religions, but of seeking to grow in mutual understanding as well as deeper self-understanding. Genuine difference and distinctiveness can be affirmed, but there is scope for real advance in mutually beneficial and challenging dialogue as well as scope to pursue actively other modes of interfaith engagement. Because actual religions are very different in many respects, neither has an inherent upper hand, so to speak, and therefore there is no *a priori* limit to the dialogical conversation.

Part Two

The Church Engages

3. FROM CONVERSION
TO CONVERSATION
THE EMERGENCE OF DIALOGUE

AT THE PORTO ALEGRE ASSEMBLY OF THE WORLD COUNCIL OF CHURCHES in February 2006, interreligious dialogue was acknowledged "as one of the most pressing needs of our time."[1] In fact, this pressing need has been the subject of intense activity and reflection by the Christian church for some sixty years and more. It was further remarked that in "addition to the theological issues arising from the shrinking of the world and the ever more porous boundaries between communities, religion has become an increasingly significant component in inter-communal relations."[2] So it is that, as the 21st century of the Common Era gets underway, the Christian quest for appropriate relationship with other religions and their peoples has become a vital element in contemporary church life. However, the modern impetus for Christian involvement and interest in interreligious dialogue derives initially from nineteenth century missionary activities and concerns. Very early in that century the English Baptist missionary, William Carey (1761–1834), called for a major gathering of missionaries to address common concerns. The first such conference was not held until 1846, and from this London event was born the Evangelical Alliance as an interdenominational missionary-oriented umbrella organization. At this stage, of course, missionary interests did not extend to dialogical explorations with people of other religions. Rather, Christian paternalism towards people of other faiths was very evident. For example, Muslims were viewed, at best, as religious cousins to Christians. The concerns of evangelical proclamation and salvific conversion were uppermost in Christians' minds.

Then, toward the end of the 19th century, a momentous event in the history of religions occurred—the 1893 Parliament of World Religions held in Chicago, USA. It was a gathering of those "who believed in the cooperation of religions and who hoped that their respective insights were convergent."[3] It marked a watershed in religious development of the 19th century that was to become a defining feature of the 20th century, with the fostering of mutually appreciative interactive relations between religions. Subsequently, from the time of the World Missionary Conference at Edinburgh in 1910, a multiplicity of events, occasions, organizations and movements of people aimed at fostering beneficial interfaith relations has blossomed. The Melbourne Parliament of World Religions in December 2009 was one of the recent major events in this trajectory of development.[4] Although this rapprochement has become, for some Christians, a source of major challenge to all forms of missionary praxis and thinking, nevertheless since around the middle of the twentieth century Christian involvement in interreligious dialogue has become, in effect, a permanent and formally endorsed activity.

It was not always so. Indeed, the standard Christian position in relation to any "other"—particularly any other religion—had been, for centuries, one of antagonism, whether muted or openly expressed: other religions were regarded as necessarily false, simply by virtue of being other. The principal way whereby Christians related to people of other religions down through the centuries had been, on the whole, that of seeking conversion rather than meaningful and mutually engaging dialogical conversation. Evangelical imperative and missionary activities had been powerfully predominant. And the evangelical imperative continues, of course. The issue, to which we shall return elsewhere in this book, is how that ancient imperative sits with the relatively new imperative to relational and dialogical détente. For the moment our focus is on the story of interreligious dialogue from a Christian perspective. How has it come about? How and why has interreligious dialogue developed in the life of the church? Despite the rise of religious fundamentalism and related extremisms, and without abandoning its missionary mandate, the Christian church has clearly reached a position where interreligious relations and dialogue has been affirmed and embraced. There would seem to be no going back. Indeed, the promotion of dialogical engagement through the work of the WCC together with the development of similar engagements promoted by the Vatican since the early 1960s, have been in the vanguard of this development throughout much of the 20th century.

In this chapter we will attempt to come to some understanding, in broad terms, as to what has occurred and why. The first task will be to understand something of the background and historical development within Western Protestant Christianity that led to the embracing of dialogical engagement as a legitimate activity. The turning point is the second world war, both in the hiatus it occasioned with regard to some early ecumenical developments amenable to dialogical interaction with other religions and, in the aftermath, which precipitated great migratory shifts and concomitant demographic changes that made of dialogical interaction an imperative concern. So, the post-war developments are critical and we shall briefly review some key elements pertaining to the work of the WCC and the Vatican up to the mid-seventies. The next chapter will effectively take up the story from that point.

Early 20th-Century Ecumenical Developments

The most significant event, so far as identifying the track of key developmental factors is concerned, was the first World Missionary Conference held in Edinburgh in June of 1910.[5] This event marks the effective beginning of the Christian ecumenical journey into interreligious dialogue. The work of the conference was divided into a number of commissions of which the two relevant to the eventual emergence of dialogical activities were Commission I, "Carrying the Gospel to All in the Non-Christian World," and Commission IV, "Missionary Message in Relation to Non-Christian Religions." The 1910 gathering resulted in the formation of the International Missionary Council (IMC) which played a key role in debates about, and the development of, interreligious dialogue. Other trends and developments during the 1920s were to spur this on, most notably the emergence, particularly in North America, of the Social Gospel movement as a new development of liberal theological thought, together with a growing sense of ecumenical openness more generally. A dialectical counterpoint was, of course, found in the neo-orthodoxy of Karl Barth. Two specific and important developments, the Life and Work Movement, and the Faith and Order Movement, also emerged during the 1920s. Each sought to interlink Christians and churches around significant arenas of life and concern. Later, these two movements would merge to form the structural basis of the World Council of Churches.

The second World Missionary Conference, now the province of the IMC, was held in Jerusalem, on the Mount of Olives, at Easter in 1928. At both of these critical conferences "the issue of religious plurality, and the proper Christian response to it, received a great amount of attention."[6] The Jerusalem Conference attempted to span a range of concerns by utilizing the language of "sharing," which "had a dialogical connotation."[7] Christian and non-Christian alike were seen to be in need of redemption or salvation; other religions were called upon to join with Christianity in the struggle against secularism. Although this latter was a controversial initiative, to be severely criticized some ten years later, it nevertheless prefigured one of the platforms of dialogical engagement that was to emerge later: working together in a common cause. As a consequence of the Jerusalem meeting, the "stage was being set for the need for a clear, concise, and considered Christian position in relation to people of other faiths."[8] But the way ahead was by no means clear. There soon emerged a wave of conservative reactions against liberal overtures to the nascent pluralist perspective and the call for dialogical engagement that the debates at Jerusalem had signalled. Indeed, it has been said that the 1928 Jerusalem conference "was the last occasion in the ecumenical history where one spoke of Christianity as one among other religions, and where one saw religious values as possible bridges of contact."[9] Certainly this has been the case until relatively recent times, and it was effectively underscored by another IMC event, the third World Missionary Conference, which met in the city of Tambaram, India, in 1938.

The Tambaram meeting was to become famous within the ecumenical movement as the platform wherein the conservative bulwark against dialogical openness and religious pluralism was forged, largely as the result of the impact of the missionary theologian Hendrik Kraemer. Kraemer propounded a viewpoint of "biblical realism" which focused on the "sovereign God encountering the sinful human person for decision."[10] For Kraemer, only Christian revelation is true or authentic revelation: all other religions pursue knowledge or insight cognitively, but this is not the same as that which obtains to Christian faith. Jesus is the revelation *sui generis* of the revealed yet hidden God.[11] The outcome of Kraemer's work, which was to remain highly influential until quite late into the 20th century, was to popularize and extend the distinction between revelation (divinely given through Christ alone) and religion *per se* (all forms of human seeking for the Divine). This distinction had been persuasively articulated by theologian Karl Barth. Christian faith was raised above all other faiths, even if some value in other faiths was acknowledged or allowed for. However, critics of Kraemer contended that his position was too narrow and quite unable to affirm the religious life of any other than Christianity as genuine. Nevertheless, the report of Tambaram was a triumph for Kraemer and his supporters. Indeed, Ariarajah notes, "Kraemer succeeded in convincing the majority of the participants that the gospel was in discontinuity with world religions. At Tambaram the church-centred mission theology that sought to replace the world religions regained its place in mission history."[12] However, although Kraemer had made a significant impact, "the Tambaram debate itself was inconclusive. Even those who had welcomed Kraemer's clear and forcefully argued rationale for mission had lingering questions on some of the strong positions he had taken vis-à-vis other faiths."[13] Tambaram affirmed both continuity and discontinuity: Christianity, as religion, is one of many religions; yet revelation in and through Christ sets Christianity apart from all religion.

Mid-20th-Century Developments

With the cessation of hostilities the post-war Western world engaged in reconstruction and recovery; this included picking up the pieces of stalled ecumenical initiatives. So it was that in 1947 the International Missionary Council convened in Whitby, Canada to resume its particular interdenominational efforts. Then, in 1948, the first assembly of the newly formed World Council of Churches (WCC) was held in Amsterdam. The WCC was initially formed by the amalgamation of the two pre-war ecumenical movements, Faith and Order (focused on theological reflection) and Life and Work (focused on social action). In these two areas of Christian life the constituting churches of the new umbrella organization believed it was right to do as much as possible together rather than to continue apart. In 1952 the IMC met again, this time in Germany. Here the church-centred view of mission was affirmed, although not without critical opposition. The meeting also affirmed a necessary relationship between mission and ecclesial unity: each presupposes the other. Ecumenical unity was set in the context of universal mission: the church is "One" in its proclamation of Christian salvation for all. The implications were significant. Wesley Ariarajah observed the importance of the event at which the "attitude of countering the liberal ideas on relationships with people of other faiths emphasized at Tambaram" was reaffirmed "and became one of the main streams within the Protestant churches both inside and outside the World Council of Churches."[14] Relationship to persons of other religions was to be primarily, if not solely, evangelistic and *not* dialogical. "The overall note was one of caution against possible syncretism and the loss of the sense of mission."[15] The uniqueness of Christ's lordship was affirmed over against relativism and syncretism, both of which were deemed to be "rampant."

The second assembly of the WCC was held in Evanston, Illinois (USA) in 1954. It saw some shift in ground towards a more inclusivist stance, and thereby a new openness to, and respect for, other religions, with the concomitant possibility of genuine dialogue being mooted. A new mood in respect to other faiths was evident. There was an affirmation of the ecumenical heritage coupled with a new note of humility. The pre-war language of "sharing" re-emerged. There seemed to have been something of a thaw, a warming openness to the religiously other, expressed, for example, in the acceptance and high valuation of Asian Christian leadership which promoted positive relating to other religions. In this regard, following the second assembly, Asian theologians such as D. T. Niles, in speaking from their lived experience of daily dialogical encounter with people of other faiths, argued for "a more open and perceptive approach to the religious situation in the world."[16] In 1955 the WCC central committee discussed the theme "Christianity and Non-Christian Religions." The directions taken by the Tambaram conference in the late 1930s were re-examined and the conference's debates and dialogical issues were again addressed. The basic question that had been left unresolved then was now re-defined: there was still a priority given to the missionary imperative, but now the issue of an interactive relationship with other religions was gathering momentum. The drive to engage in serious interreligious dialogue was underway. As a consequence, by 1956 the WCC had initiated a study programme entitled "The Word of God and the Living Faiths of Men," which ran until 1971. It involved a number of study centres around the world, together with regional ecumenical consultations held in Israel (Jerusalem), Burma, Hong Kong and India. Arguably, it was this programme which enabled interreligious dialogue to be taken up by ecumenical Christianity in a way never before possible. Furthermore, carried out in cooperation with the International Missionary Council, the programme helped pave the way for developments during the 1960s which, together with radical changes within the Roman Catholic Church, made this decade a turning point in the relationship between Christianity and other faiths. But at the commencement of this decade a new development occurred which was to be of considerable importance to the growing interest and work in interreligious dialogue from within the ecumenical movement.

At the third assembly of the WCC, held in New Delhi, India, in 1961, the International Missionary Council formally merged with the WCC. This led to the formation of the Commission on World Mission and Evangelism (CWME) as a sub-section of the WCC. The effect, it would seem, was to reinforce a more conservative ideology and theology suspicious of, if not hostile towards, interreligious dialogue, or indeed any form of rapprochement with other religions. Indeed, this antagonistic current has resurfaced from time to time and impacted negatively upon ecumenical dialogical endeavours. However, it is worth noting that the then contemporary context for dialogical discussion within the ambit of the WCC was not religious plurality but rather secularization. It was this contextual factor that had the most significant impact upon the still dominant Western bloc within the WCC. The theological significance and impact of the process of secularization held the WCC's attention, not the presence within the world of other religions. Nevertheless, the stimulus to local reflection and development of an interfaith outlook afforded by the programme "The Word of God and the Living Faith of Men" in the end managed to bring the issue of interreligious dialogue back into the spotlight and to place it firmly on the agenda of the WCC. At this juncture the cause of interreligious dialogue within the ecumenical movement had run into heavy waters. By contrast, in the Church of Rome things were about to get going in a radical and epoch-making fashion. What happened?

Vatican II: Catholic Initiatives for Interreligious Dialogue

For centuries the Roman Catholic Church had lived, to all intents and purposes, wholly within its own worldview framework: acknowledgment of the religiously other, even other Christian churches, was muted. Certainly no salvific value was accorded to any other religion, and the notion of establishing any kind of dialogical relationship with any other religion was a fringe idea in the extreme. Religious exclusivism held sway. The doors and windows of the institutional edifice were firmly fixed. But with the advent of a courageous and far-sighted pontiff, John XXIII, things were about to change. The doors and windows were thrown open to allow a new breeze of perception to blow through and a new light of sensitivity to illuminate the doctrines and practices of this ancient institution. The pope called a special council of all the bishops of the Roman Catholic Church, which met in four sessions during the years 1962 to 1965. Only one other such council had been called in modern times, during the nineteenth century. Now known as the First Vatican Council ("Vatican I"), it was interrupted by the Franco-Prussian war, hence the reference to the 1960s meetings as the Second Vatican Council ("Vatican II"). With the untimely death of John XXIII in 1963, after only one session of Vatican II, it was the new Pope, Paul VI, who took up the reins of change.

In many respects the Catholic interest in interreligious dialogue that emerged from Vatican II can be set in the context of the papal encyclical *Ecclesiam Suam* issued by Pope Paul VI in 1964. This statement presents a model of the relationship of the church and the world "in a series of concentric circles, the outermost representing the Church's dialogue with humanity in general."[17] The next circle represents dialogue with non-Christian religions; the following circle represents the ecumenical dialogue with "separated" sister churches; the innermost circle represents the dialogical life within the Catholic Church. A dialogical pattern, inherent to the very life of the church, was thus asserted, and it is in this context that the specifics of interreligious dialogue can be placed. But Paul VI was not just a promulgator of theory: he took concrete action with respect to the Vatican's relationship with other faiths. The overriding concern of the Vatican was, and has continued to be, pastoral. Innovation in both policy and practice was aimed at enhancing the life of the Catholic Church and its people. Accordingly, Pope Paul VI established the Secretariat for Non-

Christians (SNC) in 1964 to oversee relationships between the Catholic Church and non-Christian religions. The office has since (in 1988, at the initiative of Pope John Paul II) been renamed the Pontifical Council for Interreligious Dialogue (PCID). Significantly, this office, or dicastery, to use the technical term for it within the operations of the Curia (Vatican governmental bureaucracy), was inaugurated directly during the course of Vatican II by papal decree, not by the council itself. In many respects it could be said that the pope was prefiguring where Vatican II was yet to arrive. And arrive it certainly did. The early work of the SNC was focused on preparing church members for dialogue with other faiths through training and the production of a range of publications. The SNC produced its first formal guidelines in 1969. In relations with Islam, for instance, the first higher level delegation of Muslims from Cairo was received in Rome in 1970. The Vatican had moved "from a position of condemnation to the acknowledgment that Muslim beliefs are a set of beliefs in their own right."[18]

Of the many documentary outcomes of Vatican II, all signalling quite remarkable changes in a wide variety of areas of church practice and teaching, there were some which both directly and indirectly paved the way for the engagement of the Catholic Church in interreligious dialogue including, in particular, dialogue with Jews and Muslims.[19] One of the most important documents promulgated at Vatican II, *Nostra Aetate*,[20] is a declaration on the relationship of the Church to non-Christian religions which "advocated openness to other religions along with an uncompromising stand on the uniqueness of Christ."[21] A critical passage states:

> The Catholic Church rejects nothing of what is true and holy in these religions. She has a high regard for the manner of life and conduct, the precepts and doctrines which, although differing in many ways from her own teaching, nevertheless often reflect a ray of that truth which enlightens all men. Yet she proclaims and is duty bound to proclaim without fail, Christ who is "the way, the truth, and the life" (John 14:6). In him, in whom God reconciled all things to himself (cf. 2 Co. 5:18-19), men find the fullness of their religious life.[22]

Nostra Aetate also speaks of the Church's "high regard for the Muslims" and goes on to acknowledge the "many quarrels and dissensions" that have obtained in the past between Christians and Muslims, seeking to go beyond that past and urging "that a sincere effort be made to achieve mutual understanding."

The first step by the Church of Rome toward genuine and mutual dialogue with other religions was thus taken. An open attitude to other faiths was encouraged and, in a preceding Council document, *Lumen Gentium*, the salvific validity of other faiths, especially that of Islam, was given recognition: "the plan of salvation also includes those who acknowledge the Creator, in the first place among whom are the Muslims: these profess to hold the faith of Abraham, and together with us they adore the one, merciful God."[23] Other documents further reinforced the Vatican's changed stance toward other religions. The overall picture to emerge from a study of the relevant documents of Vatican II may be summarized as follows: on the one hand dialogue is promoted as expressing openness toward persons of other religions; on the other hand the finality and supremacy of Christ, and the mission of the Church in that regard, are also necessarily affirmed. As with the ecumenical movement's explorations into dialogue through the WCC, Catholic efforts through the Vatican have been dominated from the outset by the ideological tension between mission and dialogue and the effective subsuming of the latter under the former. For the most part it would seem that missionary motifs tend to triumph over dialogical détente. Nevertheless, it is clear that it was in the decade of the 1960s that Catholic sensibilities toward other religions and dialogue with them changed dramatically. This was also true of the historic Protestant churches on the whole, together with the Eastern Orthodox who were also part of the ecumenical movement. It is to developments within the wider ecumenical context that we now return.

Ecumenical Developments through the 1960s

The first meeting of the CWME, held in December 1963, signalled a rather cautious stance with respect to relations with other faiths. The report of this meeting "attempted to hold together the need to continue the missions to the non-Christian world and the desire to emphasise partnership with non-Christians in the post-colonial situation where there was little or no choice but to engage with others in nation-building."[24] The primacy of evangelical witness was asserted as the chief ecumenical concern. To the extent this was acknowledged, dialogical engagement was subsumed under evangelical witness: dialogue could be understood and accepted only in the context of mission. However, as mentioned above, much good work was being engendered by the study programme "The Word of God and the Living Faiths of Men." Toward the late 1960s, as this programme was entering its second phase, the stage was set for something of a breakthrough. On the one hand there was the burgeoning interest in interreligious dialogue that had been stimulated thus far; on the other, there was the impact of a special consultation on Christian-Muslim encounters that took place in 1966. The breakthrough itself occurred with an ecumenical conference on interreligious dialogue held in Kandy, Sri Lanka, in 1967.

The Kandy consultation, on the theme "Christians in Dialogue with Men of Other Faiths," was notable in that for the first time such an ecumenical consultation involved representatives from the Vatican together with Protestant and Orthodox theologians. This conference and the joint statement it produced[25] were seminal for the WCC and the ecumenical cause of interreligious dialogue. Whereas previously, and in contrast to evangelical proclamation, dialogue had had no ecclesiological relevance within the WCC, now both proclamation and dialogue were affirmed as "essential for the church and the communication of the Gospel."[26] Dialogue was given high value:

> Dialogue means a positive effort to attain a deeper understanding of the truth through mutual awareness of one another's convictions and witness. It involves an expectation of something new happening. . . . Dialogue implies a readiness to be changed as well as to influence the other. Good dialogue develops when one partner speaks in such a way that the other feels drawn to listen, and likewise when one listens so that the other is drawn to speak.[27]

The Kandy statement also affirmed that

> Christian theological response to other religions should be formulated *in dialogue* with adherents of . . . other religions. Instead of approaching

other religions from predisposed doctrinal formulations and ideas, the discussion partners agreed to reflect theologically on religious plurality while actually being in dialogue with those of other faiths.[28]

There were yet two other significant outcomes of the Kandy consultation, the first of which tended to detract from interreligious dialogue as such and the second, on the other hand, providing a substantial theological rationale for it. The Kandy meeting distinguished between *secularization* (*qua* historical process) and *secularism* (a God-denying or transcendent-disavowing ideology). It affirmed the former and called for dialogical engagement with the latter. Thus, at this juncture, inter-ideological dialogue was given pride of place over dialogue with other religions. There was recognition of common humanity as the basis for common human responsibility concerning social problems.

The ecumenical debate about interreligious dialogue, in general terms, was now determined by three elements. First, the idea of dialogue as a two-way communication was viewed as a principal and proper form of relationship to people of other faiths in distinction from a narrowly one-way missionizing proclamation. Second, effort was put into determining a framework of thinking that attempted to make theological sense of dialogical interaction from a Christian perspective. Third, such communication and theological reflection was to take place within the horizon of actual interreligious encounters: "dialogue was seen as a justified correction of the kind of evangelism that disregards what others have to offer to Christians."[29] The Kandy consultation had successfully countered the dominant ideology that had prevailed for three decades since the Tambaram conference. It was an undoubted turning point in the ecumenical journey into interreligious dialogue.

Although at the time it appeared dialogue had the green light, in fact the way ahead was not to be entirely smooth or without resistance. The debates of, and subsequent to, the Kandy consultation highlighted "a deep division within the ecumenical movement over the theological approach to people of other faiths and its implicit significance for the Christian understanding of mission" and, furthermore, in

the tension between those who had an exclusivistic understanding of the Christian faith and therefore viewed other faiths primarily as "mission fields," and those who wanted to understand the phenomenon of other religions as somehow within the salvific purposes of God, the more mission-oriented group had almost always prevailed.[30]

The outcome might be best summarized as being a dialectical tension between a closed or exclusivist theology of mission that sees no virtue in genuinely mutual interreligious dialogue, and an open, albeit inclusivist, theological perspective that seeks serious intercourse with other religions on the assumption that all should be able to be fitted into some greater conceptual whole.

The year following the Kandy meeting, 1968, saw the fourth assembly of the WCC, in Uppsala, Sweden, move away from dialogue as a valid ecclesial activity in its own right. Instead, it placed renewed emphasis on "God's saving work in all of human history," thus taking a strong missiological line.[31] Interreligious dialogue and the outcomes of Kandy were subsumed under the section "Renewal in Mission." The assembly declared that "God's mission . . . aims at creating one truly whole humanity that is no longer divided by conflicts and separations of race, class or gender" in which "the divisions caused by religious traditions were explicitly included."[32] However, the assembly endorsed the Kandy initiatives to the extent of casting dialogue firmly within an inclusivist theology: "Christ can be met in, and understood more deeply through, dialogue."[33] But dialogue could in no way be substituted for "witnessing and proclamation."[34] At best, interreligious dialogue was acknowledged to be a legitimate part of the process of evangelical proclamation. Nevertheless, following Uppsala there was a positive development of interest in genuine interreligious dialogue and related issues. The threefold aim of dialogue as (1) engendering mutual respect and better understanding, (2) leading to mutual deepening and renewal of spirituality and (3) promoting the accepting and fulfilling of common practical responsibilities, emerged out of ensuing consultations. Dialogue was certainly deemed an urgent task, implying a radical rethinking of ecumenical theology and strategy. Traditional forms of mission, antithetical to dialogue, came in for substantial criticism.[35] Even so, the purposes of dialogue were still subsumed to the aims and objectives of missionary theology and enterprise. So, at the close of the decade of the 1960s, the prospects for ecumenical development in interreligious dialogue seem to be quite positive. But before turning to an exploration of how things turned out, we need to catch up with what was happening in the Catholic camp.

Catholic Developments Immediately Post-Vatican II

On many occasions during his pontificate, Paul VI did one or the other or both of two things: he affirmed interreligious dialogue as part and parcel of the church's new directions in its life and mission post-Vatican II, and he reasserted the priority of evangelistic mission and, in the process, delimited the scope and expectations of interreligious dialogue.[36] As indicated above, the early work of the Secretariat for Non-Christians was focused on preparing church members for dialogue with other faiths through training and the production of a range of publications. The objectives of the SNC have been summarized as the opening of "friendly relations, communication and dialogue" with followers of other religions; the promotion within the Church of knowledge of other faiths with a view to stimulating this dialogue and communication; and the supporting of the process of local church enculturation "which is a true form of continuing dialogue in the local Churches . . . between the Christian message and the religious cultures of the particular place."[37] The first goal of the Secretariat had been "to establish contact with the local Catholic communities in those areas where Catholics are in contact with believers of other religions" by way of visits, attending various events, organizing meetings, publications, and other means, "to continue to spread the spirit of the Second Vatican Council as expressed in its document *Nostra Aetate*."[38] To this internal ecclesial activity a great variety of dialogical engagements and reciprocal visits with other faiths had been added. Within but a few years of Vatican II the change of stance was well embedded with regard to concrete actions: the Church of Rome was now active in engaging dialogically with other religions.

Early 1970s: Ecumenical Advances

In March 1970 a change from conversations about dialogue to direct engagement in dialogue occurred at a conference held at Ajaltoun, Lebanon, which brought together adherents of a number of religious traditions.[39] This conference was the first in a continuing series of WCC-sponsored or co-sponsored dialogical events wherein the focus was purely interreligious, as opposed to involving dialogical engagement with secular ideologies such as Marxism. A follow-up ecumenical meeting in Zürich was called to reflect upon the outcomes of the Ajaltoun consultation. It resulted in a communiqué, now known as the Zürich Aide-Memoire,[40] which set out some basic principles for engaging in dialogical relationships with peoples of other faiths.[41] This document affirmed dialogue and "saw in God's incarnation in Christ a gesture toward all of humanity that should have consequences for . . . dialogue."[42] It also asserted that "only in dialogue could Christians gain deeper insight into God's purposes with religious plurality." Further, the aide-memoire noted, dialogue is not just with the great traditions but also with local contexts and traditions. The recurrent threat of syncretism was dismissed as a red herring: indigenisation was equated with contextualisation. Jan Hendrik Pranger remarks that "the participants in the Zürich consultation tried to make a new start with the issue of interreligious dialogue . . . the Zürich Aide-Memoire sees in dialogue . . . the only suitable form of communication between Christians and adherents of other faiths."[43] It would seem, at this point, that prospects for ecumenical development in interreligious dialogue were quite positive.

In 1971 the Central Committee of the WCC met with interfaith dialogue as its principal agenda item. In consequence, it issued a landmark document, *An Interim Policy Statement and Guidelines* ("*Guidelines*")[44] and undertook a restructuring exercise that paved the way for new developments in dialogical activity. A new Sub-unit on Dialogue was created within the bureaucratic structure of the WCC. A key element in this development was the formation of the special programme "Dialogue with People of Living Faiths and Ideologies," which ran until 1979. Addressing dialogical concerns was now to be set within the context of the programme and sub-unit, instead of being addressed from within the Department of Mission and Evangelism. The positive effect was to allow the question of interreligious dialogue to come of age within the orbit of ecumenical affairs. The promulgation of the *Guidelines* both validated the enterprise of dialogue as a *bona fide* ecumenical activity and provided some theological underpinning for it. A major issue which had arisen was "whether witness and proclamation presupposed dialogue and could only take the form of dialogue, or whether dialogue itself was already a threat to mission and evangelism."[45] In the light of this issue, the *Guidelines* steered the activity of dialogue away from confrontational encounter—as in theological debate, for example—and preferred to encourage the dialogue of life in terms of stimulating common action, mutual understanding and the legitimate processes of indigenization.[46] Dialogical consultations thus explored issues of practical cooperation, mutual concerns and modes of common life. But there were no conferences addressing specifically religious or theological issues as such; arguably this dimension of dialogical engagement was too sensitive and difficult to tackle. Indeed, "discussion about the meaning and relevance of interreligious dialogue for the ecumenical movement . . . did not primarily take place at these conferences, but in the reflection on these meetings in the subunit on dialogue, and in the broader discussions in the WCC."[47] At a pragmatic level, the 1971 initiatives had resolved the issue of dialogical content so far as the WCC and the ecumenical movement, more widely speaking, were concerned. However,

> it had proved impossible to find acceptance, in the WCC, for the characterization of interreligious dialogue as a collective religious quest, or a discourse on religious themes. The fear of syncretism, and the claim of the uniqueness of the Christian Gospel amidst other religions, did prove insurmountable obstacles for this interpretation of the meaning and significance of dialogue for the ecumenical movement.[48]

On the other hand, dialogue was grounded, in the view of leading ecumenists, in the conviction that it was "the precondition for all forms of relationship and communication in situations of religious plurality."[49] Dialogue was promoted as not just an adjunct to, but actually a precondition of, mission and evangelization, as well as having valid reference and scope in its own right.

Since the Uppsala assembly in 1968, dialogue had been made more acceptable to the Christian church by placing it in an instrumental context: it was the tool *par excellence* in the quest for human unity and an inclusive human community. But interreligious dialogue was also advanced in the context of reflection on religious plurality, even though this provoked conflict in a number of ecumenical discussions.

One problem that emerged, particularly pertinent to Christian-Muslim engagement, was that produced by having on the one side a formal and representative body—the WCC—whilst on the other side there was usually no equivalent entity. Dialogue therefore became more and more the province of a select group of interested individuals who may or may not have had any substantive and authoritative representative status. Alongside this problem of equality of dialogical partners lay the issue of initiative for dialogue. One Muslim researcher has noted that in contrast with such global Christian institutions as the WCC and the Vatican, Muslim institutions do not "express the same enthusiasm that the Churches and their units and councils show on the question of dialogue. In a sense, Muslim institutions respond as institutions as far as dialogue is concerned, but are not initiators of dialogue with other religions and beliefs."[50] Historical and political context are important in explaining this. Many Muslim countries have had their energies and agendas directed by their various struggles to come out from under Western colonial domination. Questions addressed by Muslims in these countries were more likely to be about "how to counter the Western political forces who were occupying their lands and were in control of all their important institutions" than about addressing finer theological points of interreligious debate.[51]

Another significant problem had to do with the fact that the WCC dialogue programme was not charged with advancing interreligious dialogue alone, but also inter-ideological dialogue. However, dialogue with ideologies was never really engaged in by the programme unit and this element of its agenda was eventually moved elsewhere. The original inclusion of ideologies reflected the then lack of proper awareness and understanding of other religions and the unique relationship between them and the Christian faith, which is different from ideologies that generally reflect secular, or even anti-religious, sentiments. That this juxtaposition happened in the first place was because of the dominance of a particular theological anthropology:

> To avoid the suggestion of a common ground with other religions, and to open the dialogue to secular world views, the WCC refused to make a theological distinction between religions and secular ideologies. Christians engaged in dialogue with others on the basis

of "our common humanity". The theological anthropology that decided the understanding of this humanity was, however, a *secular* perspective on the meaning of being human. The refusal to distinguish between dialogue with other religions on the one hand, and dialogue with ideologies on the other, had the aim of keeping interreligious relationships and dialogue away from the "religious" realm, and to relate it to secular history . . . the other religious traditions (by being bound to the secular presumption) were not taken seriously as full partners.[52]

In 1974 a significant multireligious conference on the theme "Towards World Community" was held in Sri Lanka as a preparatory exercise for the forthcoming WCC assembly in Nairobi (1975). As it happened, it was also "the first interreligious meeting where the significance of dialogue as a prerequisite for, and an expression of, greater community between religious groups was explored."[53] The issue, in this multi-religious context,

> was how the different religious perspectives on unity and community could be related to one another, especially since each of the religious communities saw itself as the centre of human community . . . The Christian ecumenical movement saw itself confronted with other religious ideas of unity and community, and had to relate itself to them in the search for community in the global society.[54]

The result was that the phrase "World Community" was replaced in ensuing documents with the phrase "community of communities" with a view to the simultaneous expression of "the need to preserve the identity of each community, and a positive perception of plurality, increasing openness, cooperation and communication."[55] The fact of religious plurality predominated: there was little by way of an agreed outcome from this consultation. And so it was that at the 1975 Nairobi assembly the cause of interreligious dialogue in the ecumenical context reached its nadir, and it is to this development that we shall turn in the next chapter.

4. ECUMENICAL INTERRELIGIOUS ENGAGEMENT
THE PROGRESS OF DIALOGUE

STANLEY SAMARTHA, DURING HIS TIME AS DIRECTOR OF THE WORLD Council of Churches' programme "Dialogue with Men of Living Faiths and Ideologies," published an article which originated in a paper presented to the Consultation on Inter-religious Dialogue held in Kyoto, Japan, in October 1970.[1] In considering "the hard conflicts between religions in various parts of the world," Samartha was cautious in offering any measure of value to dialogue and noted "the necessity for clarifying fundamental concepts and attitudes in order for inter-faith relationships to have a deep and lasting basis."[2] He warned:

> While recognizing the progress made in inter-religious understanding one should be careful not to claim too much for what has been done so far or what may be possible in the coming years. The suspicion and distrust between religions and the memories of fanaticism, intolerance and persecution built up during centuries cannot be so quickly removed by a few conversations between individuals of different religions most of whom are academicians.[3]

It would seem little has changed since Samartha's time. Certainly, Samartha identified the fear expressed by Christians that interreligious dialogue amounts to a betrayal of mission and the opening of the flood-gates of relativism and syncretism as a key element detracting from, impeding, even opposing dialogue. In this regard he referred to syncretism as "a kind of 'fruit-salad' type of religion with little nutritional value" and argued that syncretism "is an uncritical mixture of different religions. It leads to spiritual impoverishment, theological confusion and ethical impotence. To eliminate fundamental differences between religions in the interests of a shallow friendliness would be foolish."[4] At the same time, evincing a feeling of superiority with regard to one's dialogical partner, or entering a supposedly dialogical relation carrying a burden of concern about losing one's religious identity, are also inimical to genuine dialogue.[5] With respect to the former, people of other faiths are likely to be concerned that Christians might use dialogue for missionary purposes, thus vitiating one of the principle tenets of interreligious dialogue, namely a mutuality of respect in regard to each other's religious integrity.

Samartha also usefully noted a variety of factors that contribute to the promotion of interreligious dialogue. "Dialogue can help bring people together in the face of cultural plurality," he said. It also allows for a "focus on co-operation in the task of nation-building" which, in Samartha's day, was a leitmotif in the discourse about the need for dialogue. Finally, dialogue "is important with a view to the conflict between the sacred and the secular and highlights the growth in personal relationships between religious people regardless of labels."[6] Samartha also enumerated six "positive guidelines" for the conduct of dialogue. These include an attitude that combines commitment to one's own faith together with openness to the faith of others; the avoidance of any superficial consensus; an attempt to move beyond the level and limitations of academic discussion to a point of mutual trust; paying attention to the devotional and worship aspects of the religions engaged in the dialogue; active cooperative engagement in "common human concerns," in particular the cause of peace; and finally, that dialogue should include a study of the "fundamental questions in the religious dimension of life."[7] Samartha was a critical voice in the early promotion of interreligious dialogue within ecumenical circles and a key contributor to the development of ecumenical thinking about this dialogue. Much of what he observed, the perspectives he held and the advice he gave remain as pertinent as ever. In the previous chapter we traversed the emergence of interreligious dialogue as a church concern and focus of activity. In this chapter we take the story further to see something of how this dialogue developed during the last decades of the 20th century. We will see something of how things changed, and how they did not: there is yet much to be done, much to be developed.

Ecumenical Progress

The fifth WCC assembly (Nairobi, Kenya, 1975) was significant in that it marked the first time the subject of interreligious dialogue was dominant at a WCC assembly. But it was in that context that considerable opposition arose, based on both genuine concern and much misunderstanding. For the first time, members of other world faith groups were welcomed as guests at a WCC assembly.[8] Against the then predominant tradition of an exclusivist-inclined ecumenical ideology, an attempt was made at Nairobi to propose a response to the manifest religious plurality of the human community based on an inclusivist understanding of the universality of the presence of Christ. Thus the theological motif of *Christocentrism* was harnessed in the attempt to render interreligious dialogue more widely acceptable. This move, however, was less than successful. In many ways the Nairobi assembly was primed to entertain a radical rethinking of ecumenical identity and of the relevance of the Christian church and mission within the world. The ecumenical ideal of overcoming tension and division within the body of Christ was now extended to the full *oikoumene* (the whole inhabited earth) itself. The ecumenical movement was being recast "within a common human universalism."[9] But the assembly resisted: delegates raised the spectre of syncretism and gave voice to the fear that dialogue threatened the distinctiveness of the gospel. Many, especially European, delegates betrayed a firm exclusivist approach: Christ is only within his church, not outside it. Nevertheless, points promoting dialogue were clearly enunciated: dialogue enriches, rather than diminishes, the faith of those involved; it is actually a safeguard against syncretism; it promotes a wider and deeper spiritual vision.[10]

Perhaps the wrong questions were being asked. Or rather, the questions that were articulated gave the game away. M. M. Thomas's query "Should we not make greater efforts to discern how Christ is at work in other faiths?" rather belies an inclusivist Procrustean bed into which the reality of the plural context must be made to fit. It does justice neither to pluralism nor to christology. From the evangelical perspective, the purpose of dialogue can only be as a propaedeutic to evangelism: anything beyond that will lead to the quagmire of syncretism. Whilst the Nairobi assembly affirmed the issues of pluralism and dialogue as important and endorsed the search for "wider community," it rejected any notion of a "wider ecumenism" as apparently implied by the advocacy of interreligious dialogue.[11] Clearly,

> the issue of interreligious dialogue evoked a serious confrontation in the WCC. It centred on the questions whether dialogue led to the corruption of the mandate for mission, and whether it would lead to syncretism. Dialogue as a relationship and a form of communication remained subjugated to mission and witness. . . . [T]he Nairobi assembly reaffirmed the traditional ecclesiological identity of the ecumenical movement, which was based on an exclusive Christology.[12]

For Samartha, as the director of the WCC's Dialogue Sub-unit,[13] Nairobi was "an inevitable clash of attitudes between those for whom dialogue had become a matter of daily experience and others who did not live with religious plurality in any significant way."[14] Dialogue, in the ecumenical context, was down; but it was not out.

After Nairobi the next major WCC development occurred in 1977, when a follow-up dialogue consultation took place in Chiang Mai, Thailand. Once more the key issue was that of the meaning and relevance of interreligious dialogue as such. In the event, the product of this meeting, *Dialogue in Community*, was accepted, with some additions, by the WCC central committee in 1979 to replace the 1971 *Interim Policy Statement and Guidelines*. It was promulgated under the title *Guidelines on Dialogue with People of Living Faiths and Ideologies*, a document that remained in place until quite recently.[15] The 1979 *Guidelines* were developed in order to promote interreligious dialogue at the local level "because of common social, political and ecological problems that different communities face together" and at the global level "as a means of cooperation."[16] The *Guidelines* specifically view dialogue as an intentional activity of the church. The church is enjoined to seek opportunities for dialogue and to work with prospective dialogue partners on the planning of dialogue events. Importantly, dialogue partners must be free to define themselves. Dialogue involves an educational dimension and requires taking stock of local contexts. Communal co-existence is the key: the *Guidelines on Dialogue* champion the dialogue of daily life, where "participants actually share their lives together," and the dialogue of action, wherein there is cooperation for the sake of a common enterprise. The *Guidelines*, which were recommended to the churches for study and action, made the following theological affirmation:

> It is Christian faith in the Triune God—Creator of all humankind, Redeemer in Jesus Christ, revealing and renewing Spirit—which calls us Christians to human relationship with our many neighbours. Such relationship includes dialogue: witnessing to our deepest convictions and listening to those of our neighbours. It is Christian faith which sets us free to be open to the faiths of others, to risk, to trust and to be vulnerable. In dialogue, conviction and openness are held in balance.[17]

The *Guidelines* end with an exhortation:

> To enter into dialogue requires an opening of the mind and heart to others. It is an undertaking which requires risk as well as a deep sense of vocation. It is impossible without sensitivity to the richly varied life of humankind. This opening, this risk, this vocation, this sensitivity are at the heart of the ecumenical movement and in the deepest currents of the life of the Churches.[18]

The promulgation of the *Guidelines on Dialogue* both validated the enterprise of dialogue as a bona fide ecumenical activity and provided some theological underpinning for it. An emphasis on bilateral dialogue tended to be the dominant stress in these provisional guidelines for interreligious dialogue.[19] Meanwhile, a key theological issue had arisen: "whether witness and proclamation presupposed dialogue and could only take the form of dialogue, or whether dialogue itself was already a threat to mission and evangelism."[20] In the light of this, the *Guidelines* steered the activity of dialogue away from confrontational encounter—as in, for example, theological debate—preferring rather to encourage the dialogue of life to stimulate common action, promote mutual understanding and pursue legitimate processes of indigenization.[21]

The closing two decades of the 20th century saw both a process of consolidation and a continuing controversy in terms of interfaith relations and dialogue; they also witnessed the undertaking of new initiatives. In particular, there emerged a close working relationship between the WCC's Office for Inter-Religious Relations (OIRR), which succeeded the Dialogue Sub-unit, and the Vatican's Pontifical Council for Interreligious Dialogue (PCID), which by the end of the 1980s had succeeded the Vatican's Secretariat for Non-Christians (SNC). The sixth assembly of the WCC, held in Vancouver, Canada, in 1983, again gave specific attention to the matter of interreligious dialogue. Guests from other religions were present once more. However, as one commentator has remarked, interreligious dialogue

> had not become less controversial. The question of the relations between dialogue, mission and evangelization proved, again, an impediment to a deeper and more fundamental discussion. The proposed formulation "we recognize God's creative work in the religious experience of people of other faiths" was, because of resistance in the assembly, later changed to "we recognize God's creative work in the seeking for religious truth among people of other faiths."[22]

Interreligious dialogue within the orbit of the WCC continued to be both advocated and resisted. The key aim of the Dialogue Sub-unit was to promote dialogue with people of living faiths and secular ideologies (although, as noted above, this later dialogical aim never really bore fruit); to encourage theological reflection on issues that arise; and to help the churches to discern the implications of dialogue for their life and for the understanding and communication of the Gospel in different situations. With respect to the task of theological reflection, the sub-unit embarked upon a study programme and produced a study booklet entitled *My Neighbour's Faith—and Mine: Theological Discoveries through Interfaith Dialogue.*[23] The programme received wide promotion and did much to raise the profile of interreligious dialogue within the member churches of the WCC.

Meanwhile, the 1989 World Mission Conference of the CWME, held in San Antonio, Texas, gave attention to the dialogue of life, in which dialogue has its own place and integrity and is neither opposed to nor incompatible with witness or proclamation. In this context dialogue was portrayed as an invitation "to listen in openness to the possibility that the God we know in Jesus Christ may encounter us also in the lives of our neighbours of other faiths."[24] But if this signalled a thaw in the evangelical perspective on dialogue, it would appear that the cooling breezes of resistance had already done their work so far as the ecumenical movement was concerned. Indeed, in the early 1990s the WCC Dialogue Sub-unit was closed and its operations subsumed within the General Secretariat of the WCC. This administrative development reflected a response to financial constraints but also a renewed religio-ideological pressure. It has been argued that the WCC "could not decide how relations should be established between 'mission to' non-Christians as well as 'dialogue with' them" and, at the same time, that there was very considerable pressure brought to bear by the evangelical churches which were members of the WCC. The overall outcome was "a lack of clarity" with respect to the relationship between "mission to" and "dialogue with."[25] This did not help the cause of either mission or dialogue.

Controversy within the ecumenical movement continued at the seventh WCC assembly at Canberra in 1991. Invited guests from other faiths were subject to protestors bearing placards with messages of opposition and disapproval. A vocal minority of assembly participants made their exclusivist point loudly, although theirs was not the only voice of objection to or dissent from interfaith overtures. At one point a group of Orthodox delegates took exception to a presentation which, to them, bordered on blasphemous syncretism. The debates of Canberra can be said to have illustrated two points, namely "the fundamental ecumenical importance of the intra-Christian conversation about the response to religious pluralism" and the interweaving of dialogue "with other ecumenical concerns."[26] The cause of interreligious dialogue seemed to be on the back foot once more, although in reality much happened quietly, steadily and without fuss or fanfare, throughout the nineties. Something of a positive turning point, however, occurred at the next WCC assembly, in 1998. Since the Canberra assembly, the OIRR had focused less on ongoing organization of interfaith dialogues than had been the case with the sub-unit it replaced. A subsequent report stated that the OIRR "encourages and enables churches in their own relations with neighbours of other faiths, monitors developments in interreligious relations, and responds to specific interfaith issues and situations of conflict in which religion plays a role."[27] Increasing evidence of religion fuelling conflicts and violence meant that "renewed seriousness about religious convictions worldwide has provided surprising and often troublesome challenges in what many had considered a secular age."[28]

In its report to the 1998 Jubilee Assembly of the WCC, the OIRR highlighted its work under a number of headings including Christian-Muslim relations; Jewish-Christian dialogue; Hindu-Christian relations; interreligious prayer and worship; new religious movements; and religious plurality and religious education. The report also noted in particular a cooperative venture, a joint project on interreligious prayer, undertaken in partnership with the Vatican's Pontifical Council for Interreligious Dialogue.[29] The moderator of the Interreligious Advisory Group, Bishop Fjärstedt, remarked that in the move from engaging directly in dialogue to that of more generally "fostering relations," there was a certain lack of definition and specificity which had both positive and negative sequelae. He criticized the divorce between the interfaith concerns of the OIRR and the addressing of theological and mission questions, undertaken elsewhere. It was clear that dialogue had gone from something of a "hot issue" in the 1970s to something of a "lukewarm" activity at the end of the century. Yet the matter of relations between Christianity and other faiths—especially Islam—was a major pressing issue. A key question, Fjärstedt asserted, was "What does it mean to be Christian in a pluralist world?" Both the WCC moderator and the general secretary indicated in their respective reports that the Christian church "cannot go it alone, blithely ignoring other faiths." In noting that sentiment, Fjärstedt alluded to the self-reflective dimension of dialogue: religious plurality and relations to other religions require a new mode of theology, the seeking of a theological rationale for religious plurality and a new method for dialogical engagement.

The work of the OIRR was endorsed and supported by the Jubilee Assembly on the grounds of the need to address universal and international issues and the requirement for support and encouragement of local initiatives with resources, guidelines, and reflection. Significantly, however, the daily newspaper produced at the 1998 assembly reported from the second session of a hearing on the General Secretariat the assertion that the

world of religious plurality requires of World Council of Churches (WCC) to adopt a "global view of things" [and also that] assembly participants [expressed] regret that despite the reality of a multicultural and multi-religious world, [the] WCC maintained an understaffed department dealing with inter-religious relations. . . . Some participants contended that Indian religions were neglected by the department due to its understaffing, which also prevented it from giving Christian–Muslim relations their deserved attention.[30]

Clearly, at the close of the 20th century, there was much that needed yet to be attended to. Indeed, the WCC general secretary, Konrad Raiser, noted in his report a number of uncertainties facing the WCC and the ecumenical movement: "We seem to be at a crossroads . . . Understandings of Christian mission in a world of religious and cultural plurality differ widely."[31] Religious pluralism was also seen as a pressing issue with respect to Christian education.[32] Together with globalization and contextualization, pluralism was identified also a key area for study and reflection with regard to mission and evangelism.[33] The multi-religious and multi-cultural context within which the mission of the church is situated was becoming ever more the lived reality to address as well as an urgent theological issue in it's own right.[34] Following the assembly, "dialogue," in its wider sense of both activity and reflective theological concern, was incorporated once more into the appellation and mandate of the newly renamed Office of Inter-Religious Relations and Dialogue (IRRD). For the next several years, until further WCC organizational restructuring following the 2006 assembly, the IRRD contributed a necessary mechanism to promote a global view of interreligious work, and its cooperative work with the PCID bore witness to the truly ecumenical context in which Christian engagement with other faiths often takes place.

In June 2005 one of the largest-ever interreligious consultations took place in Geneva, Switzerland, with the theme of "Critical Moment in Interreligious Dialogue." Over 130 participants representing 10 different religions gathered to reflect on the state of interreligious dialogue and prospects for its future development. The conference was cast as a landmark event, reflecting the fact that, in the words of the WCC general secretary Samuel Kobia, "Dialogue with other faiths has become a core issue for the WCC."[35] Ecumenical theologian Hans Ucko remarked that the conference was unique "because it sought to assess dialogue, and looked at ways of fostering relations which are more realistic and less idealistic."[36] This event clearly acted as both confirmation and spur to the continued commitment of the WCC to the path of interreligious dialogue. In his speech to the conference, the moderator of the WCC, Aram I, Catholicos of Silicia, spoke of interreligious dialogue as "an ecumenical priority" and that "there is a great awareness of the need for a credible and relevant interreligious dialogue" which, hopefully, might "help religions to reach a coherent and holistic approach to crucial issues stirring the life of societies and lead humanity to healing and reconciliation."[37] More recently the WCC nomenclature was further changed, and today there is no longer an "Office" as such but, rather, the Programme for Interreligious Dialogue and Cooperation (IRDC).

Having now surveyed landmarks pertaining to the development of interreligious dialogue engagement by the WCC, what can we say of the Vatican, the Christian organizational partner to the World Council of Churches in the field of interreligious dialogue?

Catholic Developments

Five months into his pontificate, Pope John Paul II issued his "manifesto" encyclical, *Redemptor Hominis*,[38] which echoed and developed the earlier *Ecclesiam Suam* encyclical of Pope Paul VI. *Redemptor Hominis* is arguably "one of the most important statements of the Catholic Church's teaching office on the question of how Christians are to relate to the followers of other religions."[39] *Redemptor Hominis* views both Muslims and Jews "as worthy of esteem on the part of Christians" and the Pope urged that "dialogue, contacts, prayer in common, investigation of the treasures of human spirituality" be the order of the day in matters of interfaith relations.[40] Furthermore, the encyclical views dialogue as an activity that ranks alongside that of mission and, that, as well, lends itself to ecumenical cooperation. Advocacy of the value of understanding the other "does not at all mean losing certitude about one's faith."[41] The church is open toward the religious other, for the seeds of God's word may be found in other religions. At the same time, the centre of the life of Christian discipleship and mission remains—and must ever remain—the person and work of Christ. *Redemptor Hominis* is but the first of at least eleven documents comprising the Solemn Magisterium of John Paul II in the matter of teaching on interreligious dialogue.[42]

Although the initial members of the Secretariat for Non-Christians (SNC) were appointed in 1969, the first plenary of the SNC was not convened until a decade later. Together with secretariat members and other Vatican officials, there were also three representatives of the WCC present. Of the work of the SNC, its then secretary-general stated: "We are conscious of the limits of our mandate and capacities, but we are entrusted with the ministry to the non-Christians, we represent the external sign of the interest of the Church for the immense multitude of the followers of religious traditions in the world."[43] The SNC had three principal aims: (1) "establishing relations, communication and dialogue with non-Christian religions"; (2) "arousing interest in, and promoting knowledge of non-Christian religions within the Church, yet respecting local contexts and encouraging ecumenical co-operation"; and (3) "assisting the Church in its rightful process of enculturation."[44]

As with ecumenical efforts, dialogue with other religious traditions raised questions of ultimate purpose. Marcus Braybrooke argues that, from the beginning, the missionary motivation and intention of the church was reflected in the brief given the Secretariat.[45] Indeed, "the Secretariat's understanding of dialogue . . . is seen as complementary to the Church's overall mission of proclaiming the gospel. The view that other religions have 'saving significance' is expressly rejected and the salvation of non-Christians is seen as a secret dialogue between God and the individual soul."[46] To the suggestion that dialogue marked the end of missionary endeavours and implied some grand design for religious unification via the amelioration of difference, if not by outright organic amalgamation, there came the retort that such had never been the case. Indeed, "It was made clear from the beginning that the creation of the Secretariat did not mean that Mission had been replaced by Dialogue."[47] Dialogue is not meant to supplant mission; rather it is there to help. Dialogue is a new tool in the outreach of the church to the "other." Hence the purpose of dialogue was early seen by its Catholic proponents as being a matter of promoting understanding in order "to acquire an objective knowledge of different spiritualities and of the different ways the human mind expresses its approach to God."[48] The dialogical methodology of the SNC, which in turn reflects its understanding of dialogue, was given clear expression in 1974 as follows:

The first characteristic of our method is that we meet our non-Christian brethren in the capacity of religious persons endowed with religious values, and we join them in a dialogue because we believe alike in a Reality which transcends this world and our senses. . . . The second characteristic of our method is to work within the local Churches and in collaboration with them and to stimulate and help them to dialogue.[49]

The author of this comment, Pietro Rossano, secretary of the SNC, went on to indicate that, in respect to the content of dialogical engagements, "our point of contact with the others is the religious experience; that is, the quest of an Absolute, which transcends the empirical experience and throws a special light on human life and activity."[50] The reason for this distinctive focus is given in terms of the understanding of human being as religious being, based on "a definite theological evaluation of religiosity and a positive estimation of the fundamental religious experience" which rests in the prior theological conviction of humankind created as *imago Dei* (in the image of God).[51]

The year 1984 was something of a milestone, as it marked the 20th anniversary of the Vatican's Secretariat for Non-Christians. A major document, entitled *The Attitude of the Church toward Followers of Other Religions*, was issued by the secretariat, and a new presidency commenced, that of Cardinal Francis Arinze, which would last another twenty years. The plenary session of the SNC held that year affirmed dialogue as "intrinsic to mission, included within mission in the broad sense, as is the whole of the Church's activity."[52] The modality of dialogue does not just apply to the context of relations with other religions, of course. It was in fact seen by the SNC as "a mode of relating both inside and outside the Church" and was advocated as but "one of the many ecclesial activities" which the church ought to be undertaking with respect to the "followers of other religions."[53]

An important multi-religious event, and indeed a watershed for the involvement of Pope John Paul II in the cause of interreligious dialogue, occurred in Assisi, Italy, in October of 1986. Here can be seen, perhaps, the pinnacle rationale for dialogue enacted: the coming together of religious leaders in order together to pray in the cause of the promotion of world peace and, *inter alia*, harmonious interfaith relations. The great diversity of religious leaders in attendance, representing all the major traditions of the world, came at the invitation of the pope.[54] The Assisi gathering was a momentous event and of sublime significance in the development of Christian interfaith engagement.[55] Significantly, the gathered religious leaders were not invited to pray together: interfaith common prayer is at best a problematic exercise and not one the pope could reasonably entertain. Rather, "to avoid any semblance of syncretism, the Pope proposed that . . . each religious group should have its own place to pray. In this way, each group could feel free to worship in strict accord with its own tradition."[56] The point of the exercise was not to propose and enact some lowest common denominator of interfaith togetherness, even in a noble cause, but to demonstrate the possibility—and the reality—of peaceful cohabitation of religions in the authentic exercise of the religious life. After each religious tradition had undertaken its own prayer-act in the allotted location, religious leaders gathered together in the piazza in front of the Basilica of St Francis for a closing ceremony at which representatives read aloud a prayer from their own tradition. The others who were gathered there listened respectfully, in silence. The event itself provided an opportunity to highlight the promotion of dialogue as such and to reflect on the meaning and significance of dialogue as a now established and high-profile dimension of the church's ministry and mission.

Following the 1988 papal promulgation of the Apostolic Constitution *Pastor Bonus*,[57] the Secretariat for Non-Christians was renamed the Pontifical Council for Interreligious Dialogue (PCID). This move came as part of a set of wider reforms of the Roman Curia. The significance of this particular change was in its confirmation of the importance of the ongoing work of interreligious dialogue and of interfaith relations more generally. The secretariat, in being reformulated as a council, was to be seen as no "temporary or experimental" office. It was observed that a "positive title is better than a negative one and is more respectful towards other believers."[58] The aim of the council was expressed in terms of promoting and regulating relations with other religions. Dialogue with followers of other religions was couched in terms of producing "various forms of relationships" and promoting "human dignity and common spiritual and moral values."[59] The PCID itself, in its role "as the arm of the Pope in his dealings with the followers of other religions," identified as its primary task "encouraging Christians and other believers in each country to 'enter into dialogue': to examine the roots of tension and conflict, to seek out areas of cooperation, and to take a stand on those matters which touch their lives as people for whom God is a real and meaningful presence in the world."[60] Interfaith dialogue of all sorts takes place in many local, national, and regional contexts: the PCID "works in close collaboration with these, and encourages their formation where they do not yet exist."[61]

A most significant encyclical, *Redemptoris Missio*, was issued by Pope John Paul II on December 7, 1990.[62] It advocated a two-dimensional respect: for the human quest seeking answers to deep questions on the one hand, and for the universal empowering and motivating action of the Spirit within human existence on the other. Indeed, this perspective is found throughout much of the pope's comments on dialogue.[63] *Redemptoris Missio* declares that "the universal activity of the Spirit is not to be separated from his particular activity within the Body of Christ, which is the Church." The work of dialogue is at the same time the work of the mission of the church. The encyclical places interreligious dialogue firmly within the sphere of the "dialogue of life" wherein "believers of different religions bear witness before each other in daily life to their own human and spiritual values and [help] each other to live according to those values, in order to build a more just and fraternal society."[64] For *Redemptoris Missio*, dialogue is an element of, not an alternate activity alongside, the church's mission of bringing redemption to the world.

Redemptoris Missio was followed in May 1991 by a ground-breaking document issued by the PCID jointly with the Congregation for the Evangelization of Peoples, *Dialogue and Proclamation*. Subtitled *Reflection and Orientations on Interreligious Dialogue and the Proclamation of the Gospel of Jesus Christ*,[65] the document views dialogue as integral to mission: the linking of the dialogical task with evangelism is of profound importance. This new development both reflected the emerging understanding of the role and place of interreligious dialogue thus far and served to establish a normative perspective. Thus a new component of the church's tradition was being forged. The document is an important indicator of the official Catholic theological perspective on interreligious dialogue, both at the time of its promulgation and since then.

Although *Dialogue and Proclamation* was a document emanating from the Holy See, addressing the Catholic Church primarily, it nonetheless spoke to a universal Christian issue—the relation between interfaith engagement and evangelical mission—and it received positive endorsement from a number of non-Catholic quarters.[66] Evangelical proclamation and engagement in interreligious dialogue are deemed by *Dialogue and Proclamation* to be interrelated, but not interchangeable: each has its own proper sphere and application within the wider mission of the church in which "the members of the Church and the followers of other religions find themselves to be companions on the common path which humanity is called to tread."[67] Dialogue with and among other religions is a modality wherein the church fulfils its inherent sacramental role of being "a sign and instrument of communion with God and unity among all people" so making interreligious dialogue "truly part of the dialogue of salvation initiated by God."[68]

Conclusion

Christian perspectives on dialogue and other religions are notoriously diverse. The sheet-anchor to progress has ever been a concern with "syncretism, loss of mission, and compromise of the uniqueness and finality of Jesus Christ."[69] As we have seen in the previous chapter, the early positive attitude toward religious plurality that had emerged in the first couple of decades following the 1910 Edinburgh missionary conference, and that prefigured the prospect of an ecumenical theology of religious pluralism, gave way to conservative ecumenical neo-orthodoxy. Missionary agenda and evangelical concerns predominated. But religious plurality remains a fact, a rock of certainty against which the tides of conversion activity have not been able to prevail. The work to reconcile theologically the fact of religious plurality with the gospel-derived missionary imperative that drives Christian outreach has yet to be satisfactorily completed. It is also clear that the issue of secularism predominated during the third quarter of the 20th century and effectively distracted attention from the interreligious arena. Some of the key secularist ideologies and programmes have now collapsed, but rampant materialism and secularism (amongst other issues) remain a part of the predominating free-market ideology which has the globe in its grip; the prospect of the religions of the world finding common cause to address them is now a real and urgent issue. Alternative authentic Christian responses are possible; there are emerging theologies of pluralism and religion which have yet to be harnessed in any sustained way within the orbit of ecumenical thought and action.

Is dialogue a modality of polite and friendly conversation and a means of fostering neighbourly relations and promoting peace and goodwill, or a mode of theological engagement with people of other faiths? It is clear that the thrust of the WCC has been largely with the former, though it does not discount totally the latter. This question is a perennial and key issue. Dialogue is, of course, primarily a mode of interpersonal relationship: it is people, together, who, face-to-face, engage in a dialogical encounter. But there comes a time when intellectual perspectives on the metaphysics and ideologies which permeate and undergird any given religious worldview need to be addressed and critiqued. It is at this juncture that concerns about the distracting and deleterious effect of postures of religious superiority, or claims (whether declared or undeclared) to hold the only valid or central position, come into focus. The internal problem facing anyone who is party to dialogical engagement is how to maintain the sureness of religious identity without succumbing to a presumption of religious superiority, let alone to a supersessionist perspective. Here the necessary corollary task of careful rethinking of one's own faith from a dialogical perspective—and the need to cast even one's own self-understanding against a wider horizon of truth and meaning—must be engaged. It can be done, and it must be done. Indeed, during the first decade of the 21st century the WCC has undertaken a number of bi-lateral dialogues with other religions as part of a project exploring Christian self-understanding in a religiously plural world. The future of interreligious dialogue requires that urgent attention be paid to the intrafaith issue of conceptual theological reconstruction in response to two contemporary realities: religious pluralism and the concomitant contemporary dialogical imperative.

5. DIALOGUE PRAXIS
MODELS AND ISSUES

TODAY, IN MUCH OF THE WESTERN WORLD, THERE IS A CONTEMPORARY upsurge of interest—even governmental and other institutional interest— in matters of interfaith concern and allied intercommunal relations. Very often this is in response to local political pressures and to the wider quest for harmonious multicultural coexistence and, of course, the current war on religiously based terrorism.[1] Nevertheless, interreligious dialogue remains somewhat "fragile" and is still rather "elusively defined," as Mark Hensman notes.[2] Raimon Panikkar, a venerable Christian voice championing interreligious dialogue, regards such engagement as "unavoidable; it is a religious imperative and a historical duty for which we must suitably prepare."[3] Chester Gillis notes that, in contrast to much of its heritage, in the present age "Christianity must understand itself not in contrast but in relation to other religious possibilities and traditions."[4] Dialogue is first and foremost a mode of interpersonal relationship: it is people, face to face, who engage in a dialogical encounter. Dialogue is a modality of relational engagement, a way of loving one's neighbour. Furthermore, the experience of dialogue can precipitate change: "Things look different when one meets at the boundaries, or when one is invited into the spiritual realm of the other."[5]

Models of Dialogue

There have, indeed, been many attempts at articulating models of dialogue.[6] In the development of interreligious dialogue a standard four-fold pattern or typology has clearly emerged. First, the everyday, typically informal *dialogue of life* occurs when interactions between people of different faiths take place within the ordinariness of daily existence. This form of dialogue may involve awareness of religious differentiation, but generally takes place without any intentional interreligious engagement as such. Second is the often community-focused and practical *dialogue of action* that will, in varying degrees, acknowledge the differentiation of religious identities involved and will likely draw on references to common values and perspectives across religions in the context of cooperative efforts to address a concern or cause held in common. The third model, the *dialogue of experience*, involves an intentional coming together of religious practitioners and adherents to participate in some aspect of each other's life (as in the interchange of Buddhist and Catholic monks in visits to each others' monasteries, for example), or else the coming together of peoples from different faith traditions to join in some sort of responsive experiential act (for example, interreligious prayers to mark or be part of a wider community response to a traumatic event, or the occasional "days of prayer for world peace" when the pope has convened a gathering of faith leaders at Assisi).

The fourth model, the *dialogue of discourse*, is often viewed as the default meaning of dialogue and is where, in effect, the dialogical phenomenon began: the gathering of representatives of diverse religions to discuss, debate and explore at an intentional intellectual level the tenets, perspectives and beliefs that pertain to the agenda which has been the prompt for the purpose of the gathering. But it is widely agreed that this is the hardest form of dialogue and best occurs in a context where dialogical participants have had experience of the other three types. A multi-faith conference that took place in May 2006, jointly sponsored by the WCC and the Vatican and involving participants from a variety of religions, provides an example of the dialogue of discourse. The focus of the conference was the controversial issue of cross-religious conversion. Participants aired differences and reported that their "deliberations" helped in the development of "a convergent understanding of the several aspects of the issue," in the process "making [them] more sensitive to each other's concerns, and thus strengthening [their] understanding that such concerns need to be addressed through appropriate action locally, nationally and internationally."[7] The conference further stated that meaningful interreligious dialogue "should not exclude any topic, however controversial or sensitive, if that topic is a matter of concern."[8] The conference concluded by articulating the need for an agreed code of practice with respect to activities leading to conversion and it also stated that during our dialogue, we recognized the need to be sensitive to the religious language and theological concepts in different faiths. Members of each faith should listen to how people of other faiths perceive them. This is necessary to remove and avoid misunderstandings, and to promote better appreciation of each other's faiths.[9]

The standard models as outlined above have informed the practice and understanding of interreligious dialogue as undertaken by the Christian church, or by various church agencies and other relevant groups, during recent decades. However, these are not the only models that have or can be applied, especially in the context of the interreligious work engaged in by the WCC and the Vatican. An exploration of the relatively distinct models of dialogical engagement which can be identified with the work of the WCC on the one hand and the work of the Vatican on the other extends our understanding of dialogical praxis. Furthermore, a measure of ecumenical compatibility may be discerned, for at the official level of policy pronouncements, practical guidelines and *modus operandi*, the WCC and the Vatican, if not speaking with one voice exactly, may certainly be regarded as singing from the same hymn-sheet.

World Council of Churches: Models of Dialogue

I suggest that three models of dialogue have applied to the interreligious activities of the WCC. I identify these as *systemic*, *communitarian* and *relational*. The first, *systemic dialogue*, refers to the notion of dialogue as a discursive interaction between faith-systems, mediated through the meeting of minds. This is the arena of discussion, enquiry and debate undertaken by representative experts. It is more or less the classic understanding of what dialogue is about: an intellectual exercise and quest. However, the focus of the systemic model of dialogue is on the interaction of faith-systems as such. This contrasts with an intellectual interreligious discourse around any given agenda that brings to bear on the subject matter the perspectives of the different religions engaged in the discourse. That form of interreligious discourse is more like the mode of discourse necessarily accompanying the dialogue of action. Although systemic dialogue was one of the earlier models employed, it was also, relatively early on, eschewed by the WCC in favour of the communitarian and relational models. This was on the basis that dialogue is primarily an interpersonal engagement and not an intellectual exercise. Intersystemic dialogue was thus dismissed as an abstract and arid exercise, effectively the antithesis of "genuine" dialogue, for dialogue was understood to be primarily, if not solely, a relational and interactively engaged experience, a meeting of persons of different faiths set within a context of community engagement for the purpose of achieving common goals and aims.

The second WCC model, *communitarian dialogue*, emerged very much in the context of the community-seeking rationale for interreligious dialogue: dialogical engagement as a modality of community-building, an interpersonal exercise where the agenda was of a socially enhancing nature—the quest for peace, the promotion of harmony, the agitation for justice, the combating of social ills. Correlatively the third model, *relational dialogue*, is enacted where dialogue is promoted on broadly educational bases: the facilitating of mutual enrichment, deepened understanding and the task of combating ignorance and prejudice, together with the aim of building interpersonal relations of goodwill, especially among leadership personnel. It is clear that these two models have been dominant within the WCC orbit for the past 40 or more years, with perhaps the communitarian as the predominant one. Arguably it is the dismissal of the systemic model which has contributed to problems in addressing theological issues and in particular to the severing of theological reflection and engagement from the promotion of relationships that governed much of what occurred during the 1990s. However, interreligious dialogue is today a stated priority within the life and work of the WCC, and it would seem that pressing theological questions are again able to be taken up. Perhaps there is a new opportunity to recover the systemic model and interweave it quite intentionally with the other two. If this occurs, dialogical discourse would play a proper role supportive of, and so extending, the wider field of interfaith engagement.

Vatican Models of Dialogue

It was primarily through Roman Catholic developments that the standard fourfold model for dialogical engagement discussed above (*life, action, experience* and *discourse*) was articulated. I suggest that other distinctive models are also operative in the Roman Catholic Church, for this Church, through the Vatican state (the Holy See), engages in formal diplomatic relations. As an official Vatican organization, the Pontifical Council for Interreligious Dialogue (PCID) tends to have contacts with the wider world of interfaith communities at a high governmental or other institutional level. The dialogue in which it is engaged is often a dialogue between leaders. At the same time, the task of interreligious dialogue is a work of the church at large, supported and nurtured by the Vatican, in particular through its interreligious dicastery to which has been given "the apostolate of promoting dialogue with the followers of other religions . . . and contributing to the formation of people who engage in interreligious dialogue."[10] Wherever there is dialogue there is also proclamation: for the Catholic Church, the mission of salvific announcement forms the default horizon within which, for the most part, dialogical engagements take place. Therefore, three distinct and mutually interactive models of interreligious dialogical engagement may be identified: *ambassadorial, propaedeutic,* and *humanitarian.* These may be seen as marking emphases or stages, as well as denoting discrete types, of dialogical engagement.

In the first place, *ambassadorial* dialogue reflects the fact that the Vatican is a sovereign state with all the diplomatic responsibilities and relationships that pertain thereto. This is not to be underestimated. It influences the means of engagement and relating to any "other" as such. Ambassadorial dialogue is the implicit precondition for any dialogue of action. Cooperative ventures require, in the first place, a context of mutual respect and functional communication. Many countries have ambassadors accredited to the Holy See, and in turn the Vatican has ambassadorial representation and relationships around the globe. Thus it should not be surprising that this modality of relationship is found to the fore with respect to interreligious relations. In many situations, of course, state and religious relations coincide.

A mark of the ambassadorial mode is that steps are taken to maintain long-term relationships: specific dialogical events may be themselves *ad hoc,* infrequent and irregular, but the relationship between dialogical parties can be nurtured over time nonetheless. The annual goodwill message to Muslims throughout the world during the fasting month of Ramadan may serve as an example. Over the years there has been a steady increase in these reciprocal greetings "and expressions of gratitude" by way of response.[11] Since 1995 similar annual messages have been sent to Hindus on the occasions of *Diwali* and to Buddhists on the occasion of *Vesakh*, significant festivals of these religions. Furthermore, in the ambassadorial mode of dialogical relationship there is—or at least there is a presumption of—an encounter of equals; the establishment and maintenance of cordial and functional working relations are the order of the day. In this context the undergirding task is the patient and mutual self-presentation of one side to the other in the interest of fostering mutual authentic knowledge and respect. Within the context of interreligious relations, the ambassadorial mode is a way of relating that requires clear assertion of identity. Vatican representatives know what it is, and who it is, that they represent. Catholic interlocutors in dialogue are unmistakably clear in their Christian identity and concomitant assertions concerning the nature of ultimate reality.

The second, *propaedeutic*, model refers to the style or dimension of interreligious engagement that goes beyond the presenting of credentials to the careful explanation of the self to the other as a means of preparing the ground for further development and deepening of relationship. This allows for mutual invitation and responsive engagement. As is the case with the *ambassadorial* model, the *propaedeutic* model is premised on the reciprocities and protocols of the host-guest relationship paradigm. Inherent in this model is the fact that much careful attention is paid to identity explanation. This involves articulating an apologia and bearing clear witness, rather than simply engaging in informative self-presentation. Pains are taken to assert and explain what it means to be Christian— indeed, to be Catholic—in the context of this dimension of engagement. References to this type of interreligious engagement abound with the language of proclamation, mission and outreach. Dialogue is spoken in terms of clearing of the way for appropriate evangelical "invitation and witness." Dialogue is also itself a kind of conversion or call to conversion for its participants. Cardinal Francis Arinze, a former president of the PCID, has also spoken of a conversion that is concomitant to, if not inherent within, interreligious dialogue. There is, he wrote,

> a sense in which we can rightly speak of conversion as a needed mental state and as a result of dialogue. It is the sense of greater conversion to God. Every believer who meets other believers in interreligious contact

should strive to be more and more open to the action of God. God can speak to us through our encounter with other believers. Such can become occasions in which we are challenged to become more faithful to the deeper calls of our faith.[12]

Arinze would hold, however, that religion "should be proposed, not imposed."[13] The propaedeutic dialogue model is undoubtedly a valid form of interreligious engagement, one that is premised on both respecting the integrity of the other and upholding one's own assertions and truth references. However, it is difficult to see how a genuine mutual dialogue of discourse might proceed in this context; rather it would seem effectively excluded, or at least severely delimited.

The third Vatican model may be called *humanitarian* dialogue. This is found, in particular, in the dialogue of action, where engagement is not so much in attending to issues of identity, relationship and understanding—such as would be expected in the context of dialogues of discourse and religious experience, and implied within the dialogue of life—but rather in the coming together of two or more parties in the quest for a common goal or the commitment to joint action for the greater good of the human community, whether in a local or wider context. Such dialogue, more particularly, is an expression of the local or regional church in action. But a number of PCID-sponsored dialogues, such as various conferences and consultations on Jerusalem or the Middle East more broadly, have focused on socio-political issues and allied humanitarian concerns with respect to questions of justice, human rights and religious freedom. The humanitarian model stands alongside, and may even intertwine with, the propaedeutic and ambassadorial models.

I suggest that the distinctive Vatican dialogical models sit alongside and complement those of the approach of the WCC. Together and complementarily these models paint a fuller ecumenical picture of interreligious dialogue. Arguably, however, there is another model that arises out of these, one which might yet enable an advance in interreligious dialogue. Can dialogue go yet further in the cause of interfaith engagement? I wish to argue that, arising out of the dialogical trajectory thus far, a specific dimension or model of dialogue is logically suggested as the next step in the extending and deepening of interfaith engagement. It arises out of the dialogical praxis described above; it represents a dimension of theology after—or arising from—dialogue that then provides impetus and mandate for renewed engagement. It is to this model that I now turn.

Transcendental Dialogue: Toward Deeper Engagement

The substantive focus of interreligious dialogue is not simply the fomenting of good interpersonal relations across religious traditions, vital though that may be. There is a further dialogical perspective, I suggest, that complements and extends all those discussed so far. This is what I call *transcendental dialogue*, or the dialogue of *intentional cognitive* (that is, theological/ideological) *engagement*. Paradoxically, this form of dialogue would appear to echo something of the original intention for dialogue which was undertaken within the ambit of the WCC, but which was, in effect, set aside in favour of the promotion of practical relationships. In this model the dialogue of discourse might come into its own more properly, not to supplant the more practical, relationally affirmative modalities of interfaith engagement, but rather to undergird and support them on the one hand, and to address issues which often underlie practical interfaith engagement on the other. To some extent, perhaps, this is already the case with aspects of the dialogue of religious experience. But this perspective can also be seen in the burgeoning examples of highly intentional interreligious dialogical engagements such as with the Christian-Muslim "Building Bridges" annual seminar series established a decade ago by the Archbishop of Canterbury.[14] Although an Anglican initiative, it is very much an ecumenical exercise. It represents the ideal of theological dialogue at its best: the open-ended quest for truth and understanding which, by way of insight gained in and through the dialogical encounter, takes interlocutors deeper into, as well as beyond, their own tradition. This is also much the case for the various dialogical engagements within and across the Abrahamic traditions known as "Scriptural Reasoning" and, within Germany (for the past decade), for the Stuttgart-based Christian-Muslim Theological Forum (*Theologisches Forum Christentum-Islam*).[15]

The key to such intentional cognitively oriented dialogue is careful and mutual exploration of critical issues and questions of ideological and theological differentiation, and sharing in the development of mutually authentic interpretation and cross-conceptualization. The aim is not to provide an intellectual panacea or to presume that cognitive engagement is the superior dialogical modality. Rather, I would contend that the proper function of such transcendental dialogue is to roll back the barriers that inhibit diaconal and cooperative modalities of engagement (with respect to the dialogues of life and action) and so to foster the dialogue of discourse as more than polite posturing and mutual sharing of information about ourselves. Transcendental dialogue extends and complements the WCC and Vatican models as adumbrated above. It requires that each partner in the dialogue be secure and comfortable in his or her grounding identity, but is not thereby closed to having that identity critiqued, extended, even challenged—and thereby also enriched. It presupposes addressing the deep and thorny matters of theology and religious ideologies and worldviews as a priority for interfaith engagement rather than, as has so often been the case thus far, leaving such issues aside in favour of a more homogenous, often praxis-focused, agenda. Instances of this mode of dialogue in action are not so obvious; indeed, it has been intentionally shunned at points, and certainly not actively pursued for the most part. The caveat that dialogue should not effect change to Christian identity, teaching and self-understanding, for example, recurs in varying ways throughout much Catholic material on dialogue. The dominant Vatican view might be said to be that dialogue as the discursive component to cordial relations is one thing, but that dialogue which suggests a challenging rethinking of one's own position and presuppositions is not to be entertained; indeed, that form of dialogue is effectively curtailed. Nevertheless, transcendental dialogue may well be approximated in situations such as the monastic exchanges between members of Zen Buddhist and Catholic Benedictine orders, for instance. However, whilst the Vatican understanding of dialogue admits recognition of the "risky search" for truth, at the same time it seeks to minimize any risk of fundamental change to its apperception of truth by way of the sheet-anchor activity of the Congregation for the Doctrine of the Faith.[16]

In principle, both the WCC and the Vatican should, or could, be open to advocating and engaging in what I call transcendental dialogue; but for both it would require strong leadership and clear sanction to proceed. The reality, I suspect, is that transcendental dialogue is more likely not to be the modality of the more formal institutionally oriented events. Nevertheless, I suggest, there is a clear need and challenge to develop and promote this modality of dialogue across the ecumenical spectrum. For if the pressing issues facing global humanity today are to be successfully addressed, and their impacts appropriately ameliorated, this will require a considerable deepening of interreligious dialogue in order to resolve impasses. The goal of mutual understanding is not the only legitimate aim of dialogue: mutual critique with respect to "judgement and criticism of religious beliefs or practices" and with a view to probing to the depths the challenging issues of the day is inherent to good and needful dialogical engagement.[17] Deeper dialogue cannot be shunned. In truth, as theologian Mark Heim writes,

> Christian resources for interfaith encounter must encompass a spectrum
> of elements, some more directly relevant to one kind of encounter than
> another. . . . If the whole Christian church is to meet the challenges of
> religious diversity faithfully, it will have to draw deeply upon both its
> catholicity and its ecumenicity.[18]

Dialogue is always a risky business, of course: it carries with it the possibility that, in consequence to genuine openness, the outcome may well be radical change.[19] Much more can be said about this, but, for the moment, from this consideration of the models and modalities of dialogue, we turn to a brief exploration of some issues pertaining to interreligious dialogue.

Theological Issues in Dialogue

Two issues that stand out in the context of Christian engagement in interreligious dialogue may be usefully considered at this juncture as an example of how a deeper transcendental dialogue might proceed, or rather of the kind of topics such a dialogue could engage. The first has to do with the fundamental understanding of *the nature of divinity* or God. The second is the issue of *our human destiny*—the relationship with and response to God, what this involves and means and how it relates back to interreligious dialogue. There are, of course, many other issues, but these two, *divinity* and *destiny*, seem to me to be critical self-reflective theological issues that are both thrown into sharp relief in the context of dialogical engagement and necessarily pre-dialogical: they form part of the important theological thinking, from a Christian perspective, that is required before any discursive dialogue can be properly entered into.

Deity: Understanding the Nature of Divinity

One of the key areas of theological self-reflection to arise out of the experience of interreligious dialogue is undoubtedly the understanding of Ultimate Reality, which can be spoken of in general terms as "divinity" or "deity," but which for Christian theology is God. The first step is for Christians to critically rethink what is meant by and understood as the sources of knowledge of God—scripture, tradition, reason and experience—and, importantly, the relationship between them. For example, theology that privileges scripture above all else may appeal as being overtly "religious," but it is open to the degradations of a narrow biblicism or to the pitfalls of bibliolatry, in which the Bible is treated as an oracle through which one directly accesses (or reads off) the supposed words of God. Theologically, the words of the Bible are then confused with the living Word (*Logos*) of God. On the other hand, a shallow approach (which can be either liberal or conservative) privileging contemporary experience all too easily results in the reductionism of what I would call an "affective theology" where rational belief, which seeks the balance of scripture, tradition, reason and experience, is replaced with subjective feeling alone: if it feels right, it must be so; if it feels objectionable or wrong, it is that.

The second step, which assists in maintaining the balance of the components of the first, has to do with the art and quest of hermeneutics, the challenging task of interpretation. For how the sources—scripture, tradition, reason and experience—are themselves interpreted and applied is critical to the matter of both self-understanding and contemporary identity in a multi-religious dialogical context. This task leads directly to the third step in any theological rethinking of the nature of divinity, the trinitarian definition of God which has been, and is still, a central tenet of Christian belief.[20] In the context of interreligious dialogue it is a critical issue. Loose Christian language can all too easily give the impression of tri-theism—where God *is* the Father, Jesus *is* God's *son*, and the Holy Spirit *is* some*thing* that the other two somehow produced (to echo the dynamic of the Western version of the Nicene Creed). In fact, the great creeds really attempt to assert the unity of God who is mysteriously named or experienced as a three-fold identity: God the Father, God the Son, God the Holy Spirit. God is not a triumvirate of three separate beings co-existing as a divine community but is rather a singular entity comprising three points of identity, or reference, in and of the One Being. With respect to interreligious encounter, especially that between Christianity and Islam, the Trinitarian construct needs to be revisited so as to underscore divine Unicity on the one hand and divine relatedness on the other.[21]

And so we come to the fourth step: the thinking through of a relational theology where the dynamics and connections of relationship—between God and humans, between human persons and communities—replaces the kind of theological outlook that premises Christian truth on the notion of static absolutes as the essence of reality, including the reality of God.[22] Indeed it is just such a theology which is called for in the Christian response to the recent Muslim invitation to a renewed dialogue on the basis of the common affirmation of love of God and love of neighbour.[23]

Destiny: The Human Response to Deity

Next to notions of deity (theology), it is perhaps concerns about destiny (eschatology) that take prominence. Relationship to neighbour, as embedded by way of a commandment within the Jewish, Christian and Muslim scriptural texts and traditions, for example, provides the first element in the understanding of destiny as a response to deity. Indeed, much of pragmatic interreligious dialogue—that is, the dialogues of life and action—has to do with precisely this theme expanded out into concerns of justice, community and peace, among others. A second element within the theme of destiny would be that of salvation. Of course, it is not Christian salvation which is in any way a common theme of interreligious dialogical engagement, nor even some generic notion of salvation, notwithstanding the theological distinction between "general" and "special" salvation somewhat in parallel to the distinction often made concerning revelation. Where Christianity is "special" to the "general" of other faiths, an inclusive theology is presupposed, which arguably does not do justice to the phenomenology of religion as such. For, on their own terms, other religions do not deal in salvation; they rather deal in other sorts of relationship and responses to the divine, whether conceptualized as "God" in a personal sense or by way of some other, usually non-personal concept such as "Ultimate Reality." Instead of salvation as the destiny-oriented religious focus, we find Torah-fidelity for Judaism, submission to the Divine Will for Muslims, attentiveness to Buddha-*dharma* for Buddhists and fulfilment of one's *varnashramadharma* for Hindus, for example. Other religions have other terms and concepts. Certainly, from one perspective, the paths of Christian salvation and Muslim submission, for instance, lead to the same goal: access to heaven and the avoidance of hell as the graciously bestowed gift or reward. Phenomenologically the transformative processes involved to attain the ultimate goals are different, but the theological imaginary of the goal is effectively the same. Out of dialogical encounter Christianity must necessarily rethink the meaning and understanding of the essential theological dynamic embedded in the ideas of salvation: Is salvation to do with some form of transformation, whether at personal or communal levels? Is it fundamentally a metaphysic of posthumous rescue of the soul? Or is it something else entirely?

A third element of the focus on destiny is that of eschatology. Narrowly conceived as having to do with a concept of post-death existence or resting place—so heaven and hell, again—the term more widely denotes not just an end-point, but also the "game-plan" that enables an end-point. This broad arena of ultimate values, purposes and intentions that govern both individual and corporate existence is ripe for both an intentional—transcendental—theological dialogue and, among other processes, critical Christian self-reflection and rethinking. Much the same can be said for ecology, which I would name as the fourth element within the concern for destiny. Here issues of stewardship of finite resources, the care of creation and the quest for sustainability across many fields of human existence and endeavours come to the fore. Ecological concern is rightly on the agendas of many dialogues of action. It requires some profound thinking as well as action. Some fundamental analysis, critique and conceptual reworking of religious perspectives may well need to occur—and for Christian theology, it is both pressingly needful and underway.

The Future of Interfaith Engagement

The immediate future of interfaith engagement—that is, of the Christian church actively engaging with other faiths and their peoples—is somewhat unclear. In some quarters the need to press ahead is obvious and unquestioned, and often attendees at interreligious conferences and allied occasions report that such events are a vital occurrence in today's world. But equally church leaders otherwise sympathetic, even enthusiastic so far as interreligious dialogue is concerned, are likely to find themselves under pressure to downplay, or desist engaging in, interreligious activities. At the same time, as previously noted, there is an increased societal as well as political interest in interreligious dialogue being expressed in many quarters. Often, of course, it has to do with the promotion of harmonious intercommunal relations within a wider horizon of contemporary security concerns. Even as part of wider society, the church also needs to be involved. To be sure, dialogue is primarily about relationship: it is people who engage in dialogue together. And whilst engagement in dialogue across religious divides is widely affirmed, if only for the sake of a common human good, often it is the substantive content of dialogue which is perceived as threatening. For in authentic dialogical interactions we may find our ideas about each other—and about ourselves in consequence—changing. Dialogue is continuously affirmed as important, yet it continues to be a controversial issue.

Interreligious dialogical engagement, and the theology arising from the practice of dialogue, have thrown up "deeper questions about the Christian understanding of other faiths (the area of the theology of religions), and about Christian beliefs and theological formulations which do not take serious account of the reality of other people's beliefs."[24] The key issue here has been to identify the subsidiary questions and find ways of addressing them. Along with the issue of plurality, the church in the 21st century must freshly rethink its approach to mission; these two issues are symbiotically related and are integral to the church's approach to interfaith engagement and dealing with allied issues.[25] Indeed, the context of religious plurality in which, today, more and more people live, primarily in consequence of demographic changes and the post-*fin-de-siècle* upsurge of socio-political activity involving religion, suggests more, not less, external impetus for interreligious dialogical engagement. At the same time there is a paradoxical response evident from within the wider Christian church. On the one hand the dominant missiological stance tends to favour non-confrontational partnering arrangements as expressive of mission in regard to people of other faiths. (Of course, a conversionary response would rarely, if ever, be parried; the wider context of religious freedom, advocated in particular by the Catholic Church, would allow for that in any case.) On the other hand there is increasing evidence of a resurgent assertive, if not aggressive, evangelical missionary stance that adheres to many Christian groups which lie outside, or exist at the fringes of, both the Catholic Church and the ecumenical movement.[26]

Arguably, advocacy of interreligious dialogue, or of interfaith engagement more widely, implies a radical revision of the stance of Christianity towards people of other faiths; this has been made obvious throughout the development of dialogical sensibilities with respect to both the WCC and the Vatican. Yet Wesley Ariarajah, for example, has asserted that "in the interfaith field, the WCC, despite all the contributions it has already made, has done much less than what can and must be done."[27] Nevertheless, Ariarajah is hopeful that "the contribution of the WCC to the interfaith reality in the future can be even greater than has been in the past."[28] The recurrent desire and perceived need for a theological lead, if not an authoritative position statement, to emanate from the WCC, has had a habit of being elided in favour of interactive study exercises which, at best, can do little more than collate and edit the divergent perspectives of member churches. As an organ of the member churches, the WCC functions rather more as a coordinating clearing house seeking a distillate of consensus from an ever-widening constituency of diversity and contention than as a locus of ecumenical theological leadership as such. As far as the Roman Catholic Church is concerned, a solid theological contribution and commitment to interfaith dialogue has marked the engagement of the Vatican thus far. The upholding of the magisterium since Vatican II, and affirmations given by Pope Benedict XVI, constitute grounds for confidence in the future of Catholic engagement in interreligious dialogue, even though there are concerns aplenty generated by shifting sands of curial politics and theological shifts away from the dialogical détente that marked Vatican II.

In some ways, perhaps, the term "dialogue" has become over-worn, even to the point of being unhelpful. In the course of the development of interreligious dialogue, the WCC emphasis shifted more towards "relations" as a signal that interreligious engagement was much more— even other than—discursive dialogue: actions are so much more important than words. But words are by no means unimportant, and "dialogue" has been rehabilitated in the WCC context, albeit alongside co-operative "relations." For the Vatican, it has ever been the case that dialogue is to be understood as a diverse phenomenon, inclusive of word and action. I would argue that the phrase "interreligious (or interfaith) engagement" might be a more useful term to employ. It is inclusive of both "relations" and "dialogue" and yet more open-ended than either. The term "interfaith" has come into greater prominence in the context of public discourse. The term "engagement" connotes, I suggest, a wider relational dynamic than does the term "dialogue" *simpliciter*, despite the teasing out of dialogue modalities. Nevertheless, the dialogical task and focus *per se* remain important and multifaceted. Thus we might say that interreligious dialogical engagement, as both modality and activity, remains of vital significance for the life of the churches and for relations between the Christian church and peoples of other faiths. Nevertheless, people of other faiths are sometimes concerned that Christians might use dialogue for evangelical missionary purposes, thus vitiating one of the principal tenets of interreligious dialogue, namely, a mutuality of respect in regard to each other's religious integrity. This, too, must be resisted. Chester Gillis rightly articulates the significance of interfaith dialogical engagement for theology:

> Dialogue is not an end in itself but it is an essential component of the contemporary theological enterprise. Contemporary theology simply cannot be done adequately from a single-source vision. The very nature of theological discourse itself is affected by the dialogical exchange between and among religions. Theology for the twenty-first century must be attentive to interreligious dialogue as a resource, and interreligious dialogue must seek reliable theological insight.[29]

Dialogue impacts upon theological thinking in a profoundly self-reflexive manner; if it does not, it is not really dialogue. The contemporary challenge of interfaith engagement is to address pressing critical concerns of peace, justice, human rights, the environment and intercommunal coexistence, to name but a few. To successfully do this, dialogue needs to be more than mere talk-fest: it needs to engage deeply, to employ the model of transcendental dialogue—or something rather like it.

6. TOWARD A THEOLOGY OF DIALOGUE
ECUMENICAL CONSIDERATIONS

MAURICE WILES, FORMERLY OF THE UNIVERSITY OF OXFORD, ONCE commented that "for Christians who want to embark on dialogue with people of other traditions in a way which is consistent with the integrity of their own Christian profession, there is need to reflect about the theological basis on which they are so doing."[1] I could not agree more. Wiles distinguished the theology *of* dialogue as that which emerges out of interreligious encounter from the theology *for* dialogue as that "which prepares for that encounter."[2] The way of doing dialogue has itself evolved, of course: "the concept of interreligious dialogue has ranged from communication for the purpose of pre-evangelism to communication for the purpose of a fruitful and mutual exchange of meaning."[3] But the time comes, in any sustained encounter, when deep and thorny issues must be openly and honestly confronted and addressed. It is at this point that the fine line between witness and openness to the other needs to be both defined and walked. Martin Conway, a former study secretary of the World Student Christian Federation (WSCF), once commented that the responsibility of mission belongs, in reality, with God in Christ, "and [is] ours only in a derived sense. But it gives us a freedom and flexibility to respond in appropriate ways to the actual circumstances."[4]

With respect to these two observations, I suggest that a theology of interreligious dialogue, or dialogical engagement, may be understood in terms of three dynamic moments or dimensions, namely, theology *for* dialogue, theology *in* dialogue, and theology *after* (or consequent upon) dialogue. Rather than suggesting a linear sequence, I regard these theological moments as encompassing both a logical progression and something of a hermeneutical circle: they mutually interact, inform and interpenetrate. They are symbiotic dimensions of dialogical theology *per se*. Once we have made the case for interreligious engagement, identifying the agenda of that engagement and asking what the engagement suggests by way of the need for consequential reflection are natural corollaries.

This extension of theology of dialogue can result in a further rethinking of the rationale for subsequent or continued engagement as well as a recasting of the engagement agenda so as to address relevant new issues. Thus will theological self-reflection be engaged anew; the reflective task is perennial. So, the question to be asked, and which we have explored above, is: What has taken the Christian faith, in and through its principal ecclesial structures, into dialogical engagement with other religions? In other words, what is the theological rationale for dialogue? The uncovering of what has been going on in terms of the development of policy and praxis allows for the discernment of the mandate for interreligious engagement—theology *for* dialogue. This refers to the justification that allowed Christianity, in its twentieth century, to take up this relational modality with respect to other faiths in a way that is wholly new vis-à-vis the preceding history and paradigms of interfaith engagements.

The fundamental heuristic task also allows for the discernment of key issues that have emerged within the context of dialogical engagement: What have been—and still are—the theological issues and concerns that comprise the dialogical agenda? What has been engaged and what has been set aside as "too hard"? In other words, what comprises the contour and substance of theology *in* dialogue? Again, we have explored something of this in previous chapters. We are now brought to the question of theology *after* or *consequent upon* dialogue. Given an assumption that dialogical engagement is taken seriously and viewed as an open-ended exercise—dialogue as genuinely "*duo*logue" (Raimon Panikkar's term) and not parallel monologue—what are the implications of dialogical engagement for Christian thought? That is to say, the obvious question that emerges in response to the experience of interfaith engagement— on the presumption that dialogue is, indeed, an interaction of mutual encounter, confrontation and learning—concerns the implications of dialogue for theological thinking and expression. In what follows I shall sketch out my ideas concerning theology *for*, *in* and *after* dialogue.

Theology *for* Dialogue:
Rationales for Interfaith Engagement

Throughout the process of the development of interreligious dialogue, some key rationales and endorsements have emerged and have been expressed as part of the overall formal theological apologia for dialogue. Lead theological rationales may be summarily grouped into five categories: *contextual, communal, theocentric, responsive* and *salvific*. I suggest that these provide elements for a putative ecumenical theology *for* dialogue. *Contextual reasons* to engage in interreligious dialogue during the latter part of the 20th century include a post–Second World War situation of openness toward, and positive regard for, other religions and cultures. There had been other earlier intimations, but the emerging globalization factors and post-war awakenings to religious and cultural "others" as emerging "neighbours" particularly contributed to this openness. This openness included articulating a new Christian affirmation of compatible values that may be found in other religions as well as affirming a more general value of other religions: those religions, too, have their place in the greater scheme of things.

The newly emerging positive regard of the fact, if not the substance, of other religions coincided, of course, with a growing affirmative response to, and concomitant regard for, the phenomenon of religious plurality as such. New appreciations and related new thinking were in the air. Indeed, it is quite clear that the context of religious plurality, and with it the emerging perspective of religious inclusivism and later that of religious pluralism as paradigms for comprehending and dealing with diversity, have been longstanding factors in the overall rationale for dialogue. Religious diversity, or the context of multi-faith plurality as the now virtually normative *Sitz im Leben*[5] of much of the contemporary Christian world, continues as a principal justification for the interreligious dialogical imperative. Arguably, another significant contextual factor is the impact of the process of secularization: the perception of the underlying ideology of secularism was viewed by many religions as a common threat, or at least a challenge, to religion, and so led to secularism being regarded as one of the first grand "common cause" issues providing good reason to engage in interreligious dialogue. Other issues can be added—particularly the quest for global peace and justice and, more recently, inter-communal tensions, the worldwide economic recession and related problems, global environmental issues and the HIV/AIDS pandemic.

The quest for community, in both localized and global senses, can also be seen as providing a lead rationale for dialogue. One argument in favour of dialogical engagement is, at least in part, that of the maintenance and promotion of practical cooperative communal relationships for the sake of social harmony and security. A necessary connection between the Christian community and other faith communities was clearly given in the widespread promotion of "dialogue in community." Indeed, motifs of human solidarity along with human community are long-standing elements of a rationale for interreligious dialogue held within both Catholic and wider ecumenical thinking. From the very outset the fundamental purpose of dialogue from the Catholic perspective was articulated in terms of the social good of humanity, as noted above. The corollary requirements were that of mutual learning—hence educational efforts within the churches—and an intentional engagement at many levels. Interreligious dialogue, at the very least, serves the cause of social justice and healthy community relations and requires the discharge of an educational task. It is worth noting that, from the early 1990s onward, the WCC tended to focus on interfaith and allied intercommunal relations, especially with respect to situations of conflict.

Belief in the one universal Creator responsible for the whole of creation in all its fullness and rich diversity is another key element in any theology for dialogue. This is the heart of the *theocentric element* of a Christian rationale for dialogue. We are all creatures of the one Creator for whom diversity and differentiation are an embedded delight of creation and who yet desires the redemption and wholeness of the fractured fallenness that is the existential hallmark of this otherwise richly diverse creation. Thus the ecumenical rationale for interreligious dialogue has been stated in terms of the concern of God for all of creation and the concomitant universal application of the divine love expressed in and through "the universality of the Christ who died for all and the eschatological expectation of the rule and reign of the Kingdom of God as fully encompassing of human diversity, including religion and culture."[6] The related idea of the encompassing love of God has also often been advocated as a theological rationale for dialogue. An ecumenical theology for dialogue would clearly have the motifs of God as Creator and Sustainer to the fore. The affirmation of the unity of the human race as the creation of God is an allied rationale for dialogue: all of humanity shares a common divine origin and a divinely desired salvific eschaton. The impetus for interreligious dialogue is very much an expression of the divine concern for all: "the divine love and salvific purpose is universal."[7] This love is of universal scope; all are included. It comprises the greatest challenge to Christian praxis, for even those who are deemed "enemy" are exhorted to "love neighbour." This universality is also an expression of the idea encapsulated in the notion of the seeds of the Word (*Logos*) of God that are germinating across creation. God is before and ahead of those who go out proclaiming the good news.

A further item of the theocentric element is belief in God as Trinity. It is faith in the Triune God, who calls Christians to human relationship with their many neighbours, which adds weight to the rationale for dialogue. Indeed, it has been said that the principal reason to engage in interreligious dialogue is because of Trinitarian relationality: the universality and encompassing pervasiveness of the love of God the Father, the enlightening Word and Wisdom given in and through God the Son, and the regenerative life-giving Spirit that "acts in the depth of people's consciences and accompanies them on the secret path of hearts toward the truth."[8] Dialogue is then regarded as a genuine give-and-take of insight and understanding which is premised on a Trinitarian relationality.

The 1992 *Catechism of the Catholic Church* is one example of an endorsement of interreligious dialogue on the basis of an innate human hunger for relationship with the Divine, the idea that religion is the product of a virtually universal response to intimations of the divine within human existence.[9] This gives a clue to understanding *the responsive element* in the rationale for interreligious dialogue. There is, arguably, a universal inherent human quest for the Transcendent—or God—for which the wide variety of religions throughout history gives evidence. This quest speaks of an inherent human capacity to respond to the divine lure. Theologically, this relates to the "Seed of the Word" motif understood as that which is present within human cultures and religions. It also allows for a measure of both validity and veracity to be attributed to religions other than Christian, so providing a further basis on which to pursue dialogue. An allied pneumatological aspect is given in that the ubiquitous efficacy of the Holy Spirit is understood to be operative at the very heart of being human, stimulating and informing the human response to the divine relational outreach. Thus, being open to the other in dialogue can be construed as a modality of being open to the God who is present in, with and through the other. The pneumatological then gives way to theological anthropology: each person "grows by encountering and sharing with others" whereby seeking after truth "is better attained, understood, and lived through encounter, and by it even one's own faith can be purified and deepened."[10] Hence the allied motif of "anonymous Christianity" or "anonymous Christian" has been fleshed out to provide a rationale for dialogue, and anthropological foundations of interreligious dialogue can be found also in respect to the deepening and enriching of faith and in the humanizing and improving elements of social interaction.[11]

Finally, the purpose of dialogue is not just a matter of coexistence. A deeper theological relationality between Christians and people of other faiths is being sought: a Christian concern for a theology of religions that would embrace the question of *God's salvific intention for all*— including those of other faiths—in contrast to engaging in dialogue with the missionary aim, in the end, of incorporating the "other" into the Christian fold of faith as the *sole* efficacious means of obtaining salvation. A Christian universalist construction of salvation is necessarily all-encompassing. The assertion that "God as creator of all is present and active in the plurality of religions" is understood to lead inexorably to the inconceivability "that God's saving activity could be confined to any one continent, cultural type, or groups of peoples."[12] Redemption is understood to be inherently universal. The singularity of creation and the universality of redemption are drawn upon, implicitly at least, as part of the supporting rationale for interreligious dialogue. Most typically it is accompanied by the specifically christocentric and exclusive affirmation that it is only in and through Christ that the fullness of the religious life can be found. Yet there is also an inclusive dimension: all of humanity shares a common divine origin and eschatological orientation.[13] But christocentric affirmation does not necessarily have to result in theological exclusivism. Either way, however, it is the implication of belief in the universality of the redeeming Creator that can be said to constitute a distinctive theological rationale for dialogue. Arguably, commitment to dialogue may be understood as a practice and a perspective which is "not merely anthropological but primarily theological" in the sense that it is irreducibly soteriological.[14] Dialogue is not just juxtaposed with proclamation; it serves, in the end, the greater cause of Christian witness. Interreligious dialogue accompanies mission on account of the soteriological imperative of the gospel.

Stanley Samartha was the first and, for a long time, the leading, theologian of dialogue within the WCC. His voice lent weight to the choice for dialogue; he expressed the rationale for dialogue in terms of "the living relationship between people of different faiths" with respect to their shared life in the wider community. The motif of community was a major component of his thinking: the idea of community as found in the gospels "inevitably leads to dialogue. . . . [A]ll may become fellow citizens in the household of God."[15] This was supported by an understanding of biblical truth as relational, not propositional: truth emerges in the interactive relational engagement such as genuine dialogue; thus "dialogue becomes one of the means of the quest for truth."[16] Interfaith dialogue is an inherent component of Christian discipleship. It is an implication of faith in Christ, an outcome of the incarnation—indeed, a function of the action of the Spirit.[17] John V. Taylor, another ecumenical voice, regards dialogue as a

> sustained conversation between parties who are not saying the same thing and who recognize and respect the differences, the contradictions, and the mutual exclusions, between their various ways of thinking. The objective of this dialogue is understanding and appreciation, leading to further reflection upon the implication for one's own position of the convictions and sensitivities of the other traditions.[18]

Religions naturally incline to what Taylor calls a "natural exclusivism" by virtue of their own particularities and the inherent assumption of religion to be dealing with a universal reality. The problem then becomes one of contending with the plurality of particularities and the challenge of dialogical engagement which requires people from the different faiths "to expose to one another the ways in which, within our separate house-holds of faith, we wrestle with the questions that other religions put to us."[19]

In general terms, a combination of theological shifts in favour of an inclusive orientation, together with a stress on theological universalisms and the quest for human community, may be said to encapsulate the lead reasons for the ecumenical embrace of interreligious relations and dialogue. Supporting corollary theological factors encompass, in particular, the paradigmatic shift from an exclusivist to an inclusive soteriology and ecclesiology, along with the application of an expanded Trinitarian theology wherein bases for dialogical relationship may also be discerned. We turn now to the matter of theology in dialogue.

Ecumenical Theology *in* Dialogue: Recurring Issues

Wesley Ariarajah has identified five phases of the work of the WCC suggestive of an underlying or implicit theology *in* dialogue. These phases view the goal of dialogue in terms of the building up of community; opening up questions of mission, relationship, and religious plurality; evolving new institutional relations in terms of religions and interfaith organizations; identifying and responding to pastoral issues (for example, prayer, worship, marriage); and the mutual exploration of the impact of globalization on religious life.[20] Early concerns about syncretism and questions about the missionary vocation of the church, together with anxieties over the suggestion that dialogue results in the compromising of faith, were among the chief issues to emerge from within the ecclesial constituency of the WCC. Similarly, from its outset, the Vatican's Secretariat for Non-Christians (SNC) was charged with forestalling "all danger of irenicism and syncretism" together with guarding against the "false idea of the equal value of the different religions."[21] Diversity might be acknowledged, but the implication of pluralism was to be kept well at bay: dialogical détente was to be no carte blanche for doctrinal innovation or signal of change to ecclesial dogma. The fear that interreligious dialogue amounts to a betrayal of mission and the opening of the flood-gates of relativism and syncretism was certainly dismissed as groundless within both the WCC and the Vatican. As we noted above, Stanley Samartha, for instance, spoke for both in asserting that any elimination of the "fundamental differences between religions in the interests of a shallow friendliness would be foolish."[22] Syncretism, as an outcome, was never, and could never be, on the dialogical agenda. Likewise, Samartha wrote, concerns that dialogue leads inevitably and irrevocably into relativism and a loss of mission are quite misplaced.[23]

In the thinking of both the WCC and the Vatican, the dual functions of the proclamation of the Good News and engagement in interreligious dialogue are deemed to be interrelated, but not interchangeable: each has its own proper sphere and application within the wider mission of the church. A related issue concerns the paradigm shift signalled by the juxtaposition of the evangelical assertion of Jesus Christ as the normative way of salvation with an admission that no limits can be set to the saving power of God. A further fundamental component of the Christian *Weltanschauung* (world-view) is a particular theological tension: on the one hand, God is at work in and through the Christ-event; on the other, God is present and at work in people of other faiths. This tension has ever been appreciated, even addressed, but little formal attempt at a theological resolution has been made. The specific Christian question may well be how "the particularity of God's revelation in Jesus Christ [is] to be understood in the larger framework of God's universal love for all humankind."[24] The answer must not be such as to foreclose the prospect of other particularities also being uniquely expressive of a shared or same universal. It is axiomatic for Samartha that in and through other religions, the self-disclosure of God may be discerned, and that it is to be accorded theological significance. Hence, Samartha states that "the relation of the particularity of the lordship of Jesus Christ to other particularities should be considered not in terms of rejection but in terms of relationships" and he goes on to argue for two possibilities.[25] One has to do with regarding "universality as the extension of just one particularity," although this can lead to either rampant exclusivism or disinterested relativism—"a sterile co-existence or . . . an unseemly competition." The other recognizes the absoluteness of God and considers "all religions to be relative" to that: particularities of religions are not denied in this case, "but the ambiguity of religions as historical phenomena is recognized" and so the relative integrity of the different faith standpoints is honoured and the need for an exclusive defence overcome.[26] Interfaith dialogical engagement—indeed the engagement of transcendental dialogue (see chapter 5)—can thus proceed in confidence.

Socio-political elements, pertaining especially to the context of the Vatican's inter-state diplomatic relationships, include advocacy for human community and religious freedoms. However, such advocacy and engagement in dialogical relations have been conducted within the horizon of a priority on mission and with an eye on the avoidance of any semblance of syncretism, relativism or false irenicism. Arguments drawing on the universality of God the Creator and of the quest for a fuller human community may be offered to counter fear of syncretism and concern for the loss of mission. Such classic issues have been joined today by the pressing concerns of pluralism and fundamentalism, among others. Furthermore, dialogue may be viewed as substituting for mission on the one hand while, on the other, "mission instrumentalizes dialogue as a means of converting adherents of other religious communities."[27] These represent, in effect, the two extreme positions often loosely identified with a pluralist perspective, in regards to the former, and an evangelical missionary outlook, with respect to the latter. However, a third way "distinguishes the two as separate, though mutually connected, activities" and is the stance formally taken by both the WCC and the Roman Catholic Church.[28] A fourth way is further suggested, that of a dialectical relation involving mutual witness: the willing sharing of religious convictions in a context of mutual questioning and respect.[29]

For both the WCC and the Vatican, the mission of evangelism is construed in the modality of dialogue, but with the implication that interreligious dialogue is effectively subsumed within this mission. The interrelationship of dialogue, mission and the witness of proclamation comprises a perennial theological issue, and yet the "theological understanding of the relation between dialogue and mission has not always been clear."[30] Nevertheless, dialogue is understood to include both witness to, and exploration of, the respective religious convictions of dialogical interlocutors. Thus the practice of dialogue can certainly involve discerning and confirming religious value in the other. But at the same time the identification of incommensurable values and genuine contradictions is seen (by Christians) to distinguish Christianity from any other religion with which it engages: from the Catholic perspective, the idea "that all religions are essentially the same; that every religion is equally a way to salvation" is regarded as erroneous.[31] This would find echo within the WCC constituency. Furthermore, I would add that it makes phenomenological sense: religions are different. Despite some common values, there are many values that are unique and resist commensurability, hence the need for dialogue to probe the reasons for that—and, where appropriate, to provide challenge and critique. This in turn enables the necessary critical self-reflective engagement of intrareligious dialogue, and so the possibility of theology *after* dialogue.

Towards the latter part of the 20th century there was mounting evidence of a widespread quest for an appropriate spirituality apparent within many societies where a new appraisal and appropriation of religious plurality was taking place. As we observed above, lying behind the impetus to dialogue, for many Christians, is the pressing question of how to live "as religiously committed people in a multi-religious society" in today's world.[32] Religious diversity, together with secularization, did not just constitute a responsive context of, and so a rationale for, dialogue; it also emerged as a significant issue that impinges directly upon dialogue. However, the future of dialogical engagement rests not just with the revisiting of recurring issues. The critical challenge for theological reflection is the addressing of theology in a *post-dialogue* context: the probing of theological questions and issues, and so the undertaking of theology consciously consequent upon dialogical engagement.

Theology *after* Dialogue: Reflection and Rethinking

David Tracy's remark that "dialogue among the religions is no longer a luxury but a theological necessity" remains an imperative.[33] Although he gives priority to the experiential praxis of dialogue, Tracy nonetheless points to the eventual need to rethink theology as a consequence. He asks: "Is it possible to have an adequate theological response to the full implications of interreligious dialogue for Christian self-understanding?"[34] In 1990 Tracy did not think such a development was close, but he did not doubt the need to "examine critically all prior Christian theological answers in the light of the interreligious dialogue."[35] That task and development are now upon us. The indomitable Stanley Samartha once noted that "what has yet to be taken seriously—not least by the academic community— are the implications of the academic study of religions for inter-religious relationships on the one hand, and the experience of actual dialogues for academic studies on the other."[36] The correlating of practitioner and academic concerns and interests with respect to interfaith engagement is an ongoing and ever challenging task. Certainly both the WCC and the Vatican, as ecumenical stakeholders in the interreligious dialogical enterprise, have made, and continue to make, significant advances. The age of interreligious engagement, emerging with vigour and commitment during the 20th century, continues apace into the 21st. So, too, must the academic work of investigating dialogue and the allied theological task of reflecting upon it—including the articulation of theology *after* dialogue. Indeed, in the middle of the 20th century Paul Devanandan, noting the evidence of resurgence within the major religions as, in part, a response and reaction to the encounter with Christianity, remarked that this provoked a challenge to Christians "to rethink their affirmations of faith."[37]

From quite early on dialogical encounter stimulated an awareness of the need for theology *after*, or arising out of, interreligious dialogue. Although, as M. M. Thomas once remarked, the wider ecumenical movement, in the form of post-Vatican II Catholicism together with the WCC, had indeed become engaged in a rethinking of theology in relation to interreligious dialogue, in reality this task has waxed and waned.[38] It is to this dimension that I now turn. With respect to dialogue and theology, what is the overall outcome suggested by an investigation of interreligious dialogue in the life and work of the Vatican and the WCC? Issues arising out of theological considerations both *for* and *in* dialogue that impact directly upon the faith perspectives, presuppositions and fundamental beliefs of dialogical interlocutors form the basis of theology after dialogue. It is here, I would argue, that the future of the interfaith enterprise stands or falls so far as Christian engagement is concerned: the extent to which some radical rethinking, even fundamental doctrinal reconceptualizing, is able to take place with respect to major issues and questions. The notion that dialogue only occurs to and between people, and does not directly involve the religious systems to which the people belong, and that theological reflection refers only to the significance of the people and their concerns, and not of their belief systems as such, is fundamentally flawed. It amounts to a confusion of process with substance.

Whilst it is people who relationally engage, dialogical encounter must involve, at some point, the depths of worldviews and allied belief systems, for it is these worldviews and systems that undergird religious identity, behaviour and values. At the level of process different models of dialogue apply according to circumstance and need. But wherever there is any substantive worldview or ideological content involved, whether in terms of articulating spiritual perceptions, religious values or theological metaphysics, then clearly what is being engaged is not just interpersonal relations. Dialogue involves a meeting of minds as much as an intercourse of friendship and collaboration on shared concerns. Dialogue aims at understanding the other and reconfiguring our stance toward the other as no longer a competitor, but a partner.[39] It requires neither the rejection nor the acceptance of the religion of the other in any cognitive sense. It requires rather an acceptance of the other as a religious person, acknowledging the place and importance of religion as such and honouring that with sincere critical engagement. It requires affirming and endorsing where appropriate, challenging and critiquing where called for. And that means being capable of both giving and receiving in authentic dialogical engagement and interfaith engagement.

Critical theological self-reflection on the part of the wider Christian church is one important key to the future of dialogue, lest the impetus to advance dissipate in a flurry of self-preserving reactions. Can the church embrace necessary theological change so as to honour the dialogical enterprise as authentic? Or will the concern not to give ground in terms of tradition and identity effectively vitiate the dialogical quest? The issue of theology after, or arising out of, dialogue prompts further reflection. Perhaps the time has come to go beyond dialogue, as it were—not so much to rethink the modality of interreligious relations as a variation on the theme of dialogue, but to begin understanding dialogue as but one element of relational engagement. The field this opens up is potentially vast: in many ways dialogue calls into question the sum of Christian theology, at least in terms of contemporary articulation and expression, if not also in terms of fundamental issues of metaphysics and interpretation. I will touch on the issue of contending with plurality to make the point, and this means revisiting some of the discussion of chapter 2.

The question of faith-identity within the context of religious plurality is critical for interfaith engagement and for theological reflection consequent upon dialogue and, indeed, with reference to the sheer fact of many faiths. For it is religious plurality *per se* that sets the context for interfaith engagement and raises questions of relativities of religious identities and presumptions of absolute truth.[40] Stanley Samartha gave voice to the sharp challenge posed by plurality in asking, if universality means just the extension of Christian particularity, "What happens if our neighbours of other faiths also have similar notions of universality, that is, of extending *their* particularities?"[41] Situations of religious plurality effectively demand dialogical engagement in order to resist a slide into exclusivism or the encroachments of an imperial inclusivism.[42] The problem of not engaging in dialogue, and so of not being open to our religious neighbour and the prospect of valid truth and meaning in their faith, too easily promotes a closed religious identity. Religious plurality is, in effect, the necessary context for mission: mission is necessarily to an "other" and presupposes some form of dialogical engagement at least.[43]

The literature addressing pluralism is, of course, considerable.[44] From the innovative work of Alan Race, Christian discourse has focused on the paradigmatic options of exclusivism, inclusivism and pluralism.[45] Exclusivism has represented the dominant Christian position towards any other religion or ideology down through the ages—at least until around the middle of the twentieth century.[46] Although formally eclipsed, it remains a lively and vexed issue.[47] Inclusivism has become the predominant Christian paradigm with respect to religious plurality, although the paradigm of pluralism, despite much contentious debate around it, holds out the prospect of a more fruitful and apposite theology of religious diversity.[48] Furthermore, with respect to religious diversity, "it is important to recognize not only the plurality of religions but also the plurality *within* religions."[49] In contrast with much of the later 20th century perspective in regard to other religions, Cracknell has proposed an alternative theological stream which he sees leading to greater openness to other religions because it enables Christians "to see what their faith has to say about the unity of creation, the purpose of God in history and about the universality of the action of the Divine word."[50] On the other hand, Donald Swearer identifies four options with respect to the contemporary task of contending with religious plurality. *Discontinuity* holds a basic stance of hostility toward other faiths, an antagonism that leads to "the denial of validity of truth claims of other religions."[51] As a Christian response to plurality, discontinuity is the basic perspective of early ecumenical leaders such as Hendrikus Kraemer and Wilhelm

Visser t' Hooft. By contrast, the *fulfilment* option of early inclusivism, where Christianity (or more specifically Christ) is viewed as the fulfilment of all other religions, has also loomed large. A third option, that of an interreligious *cooperative interchange*, means that valid truth claims are found in other religions and that Christianity and Christians may yet gain something of positive value and insight from them. This view is indicative of an early emergent pluralist perspective. But Swearer suggests a fourth option, that of *intentional dialogue*, "an encounter of religious persons on the level of their understanding of their deepest commitments and ultimate concerns."[52] This, I suggest, encapsulates my advocacy of transcendental dialogue (in chapter 5 above) together with the need for theology *after* dialogical engagement: deeper dialogue requires theological work of commensurable depth.

From a Catholic perspective, Peter Phan addresses the challenge of religious plurality for mission and theology:

> The issue at stake is whether the plurality of religions is to be regarded as a merely historical accident or as belonging to God's intention and purpose for humankind itself. If the former, then religious pluralism may be viewed as a curse to be overcome in order to achieve religious uniformity; if the latter, such pluralism is a blessing to be joyously and gratefully accepted.[53]

On the one hand, a rationale for dialogical engagement is given. On the other it appears to contradict the Church's magisterium for, as the 2001 Vatican document *Dominus Iesus* stressed, "proclamation is endangered today by relativistic theories which seek to justify religious pluralism" whereby, it is implied, certain doctrinal truths of Christianity have been superseded, whether explicitly or implicitly. But need this be the case? Surely addressing religious pluralism requires a re-envisaged theological methodology, not just a tweaking of extant doctrine. Pluralism does not necessarily imply relativism.[54] The need to continue to work at theology after dialogue—which then enables rethinking theology both for and in dialogue—is acute. As M. M. Thomas wrote in the preface to his own book on pluralism, "The churches today face no greater challenge that the one they encounter in the situation of religious, cultural and ideological pluralism."[55] Nothing has changed really; this key challenge—one of many impinging upon the development of theology after dialogue—remains. Perhaps, today, it is more urgent than ever. It is of critical import to any theology after dialogue. Indeed, the issue of theology from, or arising after, dialogue prompts further reflection.

Conclusion

I have argued in the foregoing that a theology of dialogue can be construed in terms of three elements or conceptual moments: theology *for* dialogue, theology *in* dialogue, and theology *after* or *consequent upon* dialogue. This is not to suggest a simple linear progression, but rather a developmental spiral where these elements mutually interact with and inform each other as dialogical engagement progresses. Theology *for* dialogue embraces the rationales that are given, often in the face of contrary concerns and counter-argument, in support of dialogical engagement. I have sketched a possible way forward in arriving at a more broadly ecumenical theology *for* dialogue. I have also endeavoured to discern theological concerns, issues, priorities and perspectives which could be said to point to theology *in* dialogue—problems and challenges that have emerged within the context of dialogical engagement. Thus, having explored and assessed the broad trajectory of interreligious dialogue as a Christian ecumenical concern, and reviewed the prospects of discerning theology for and in dialogue, I have been able to address theology *after* dialogue—the issues and questions that emerge from out of the dialogical encounter. Having entered dialogue with a set of presuppositions and beliefs, in what way do we need to modify, challenge and rethink them as a consequence of the dialogical engagement? A task beckons; the response awaits a fuller engagement.

The need for deepening and strengthening interfaith, and thus intercommunal, relations through interreligious dialogue has never been greater. The opportunity for the Christian church to rise to the challenge of a dialogue capable of addressing contemporary issues of rising fundamentalism, exclusivism and collusion with varying forms of terrorism has never been so inviting or obvious.[56] Furthermore, the recent invitation issued from the Muslim world to the Christian indicates that at least one interlocutor also sees the point—and the urgency.[57] The call is to engage in theological dialogue, and in depth. The argument that a Christian ecumenical theology of dialogue embraces a necessary re-thinking of theological understanding and formulation (theology *after* dialogue) as a third moment in the theology of dialogue is also amply supported by such a dialogical call. Interreligious dialogue continues to be both challenging and of vital importance to contemporary Christian faith and life, and for relations between the Christian church and peoples of other faiths. Holding together conceptually the motif of witness and proclamation with active dialogical engagement continues to be a major focus of theological interest and controversy.

Part Three

Some Questions and Issues

7. GUIDE FOR INTERFAITH RELATIONS
DIALOGUE AND DISCIPLESHIP

CHRISTIANITY IS A MISSIONARY RELIGION. CHRISTIANS ARE CALLED TO be disciples. What does this mean when it comes to relating to people of other faiths? Clearly being disciples and engaging in Christian mission, however we might think of that, takes place in a pluralist world—culturally, ethnically, religiously, to name but a few of the many diversities with which we must necessarily contend. There are a variety of issues arising out of multi-faith contexts that impinge upon Christian life today. What do these mean for the life of faith? How might Christians respond to the ever-present reality of religious diversity? What are the theological options that govern the relationship of the Christian to peoples of other faiths? Given formal changes that have occurred in the stance of the church toward other faiths during recent decades, what might be the appropriate theological position to take today? What is the proper way of thinking theologically of the relation between mission and pluralism? For instance, is evangelism—with the goal of seeking conversions—the only proper mode of Christian relationship to other religions? A key issue confronting Christians and the church today is the unavoidable presence of the multiplicity of faiths in our society. As we observed in chapter 2 above, religious diversity is here to stay.

In this chapter I shall address three questions. First, is there a biblical basis for interfaith engagement? Second, what are we to make of the missionary imperative of Christianity derived from the Great Commission at the end of Matthew's gospel? Third, what is the understanding of mission with regard to discipleship, and how might that relate to interreligious dialogue? In other words, is there any prospect for understanding discipleship that not only allows for, but actively enables positive interreligious relations with our neighbours of other faiths? In the context of manifest religious plurality, what is the relation of witness to mission? And what is the relation of mission to discipleship? Is it the case that making disciples is the goal of mission? Is interreligious dialogue enjoined, in the end, by virtue of being subsumed to mission, whose aim is something other than the pursuit of dialogical relations? Or is engagement in authentic dialogue—in all its facets and dimensions—itself an authentic component of Christian mission and witness?

As we noted above, Stanley Samartha once gave voice to the sharp challenge posed by plurality in asking: "Does universality mean simply the extension of Christian particularity? What happens if our neighbours of other faiths also have similar notions of universality, that is of extending *their* particularities?"[1] Does plurality simply mean a state of competing exclusivism? Or can there be another way of comprehending this plurality of "universalist particulars"? The question as raised by Samartha still requires to be clearly answered, and finding the answer is no easy task, for religious competition and presumptions of exclusivism seem perennial. Where religious people choose to ignore the other and reject dialogical encounter, Samartha writes, this "can only lead to a closed particularity which feeds on itself and in the process impoverishes the community."[2] Furthermore, notes another ecumenical theologian, Wesley Ariarajah, "it is important to recognize not only the plurality of religions but also the plurality *within* religions."[3] What then are the options for Christian faith? There is a long-standing uneasy accommodation, which can sometimes break out into open hostility, between those who construe Christian mission and discipleship as inherently subordinating, if not superseding, other religions, and those who would see a *prima facie* need to view other religions—or more particularly the people of other faiths—in some form of equal, or at least balanced, relationship. The question then becomes, what sort of balance? What kind of relationship? Indeed what, theologically, might be the proper relationship between a Christian and a person of another faith such that the integrity of Christian mission and discipleship, together with the integrity of the religious identity, beliefs and experience of the religiously "other," are neither compromised nor reductively relativized? And then, one may ask of course, what about the classic text of Christian exclusivity, John 14:6?

A Biblical Basis for Interfaith Engagement

Is there a biblical basis for interfaith engagement? Indeed, how may we properly use the Bible when thinking about interfaith matters? As Andrew Wingate asks, "Do we look at particular verses or the overall picture?"[4] Wingate notes that the contexts within which the Bible is being applied and interpreted are constantly changing. Questions which were right to ask yesterday have been eclipsed by others today. The use of the Bible in this regard needs to be generous in theological outlook, especially with how we understand God. As Wingate remarks, given that "the central Christian understanding of God is of a God of love, forgiveness, generosity, freedom, faithfulness and justice," then the challenge "is whether individual texts can be considered binding, or whether we need to look overall at the general thrust of scripture seeking to discover what kind of approach to people of other faiths such a God would encourage, rather than what this or that text says about such a relationship."[5] The theologian Israel Selvanayagam notes that the Bible "is distinctively a book of dialogue and it contains many dialogues within. We can misread its passages if we miss the dialogical context."[6] With this in mind, some apposite guidance can yet be derived from the consideration of specific texts and passages. In the encounter of Jesus with the Samaritan woman (John 4:1-42), for example, the interaction "demonstrates Jesus' willingness to receive from a person of another faith" wherein new insights and truths may be forthcoming.[7] The report of the conversion of Cornelius in Acts 10 prompts Peter "to the realisation that God has no favourites"[8] and this is an important theological insight to hold in mind when considering the Christian attitude towards other religions and their peoples. Similarly, Acts 17:16-34 presents "a practical example of dialogue. Paul goes to where the Greek philosophers are. He observes and listens . . . and builds on what he can affirm."[9]

Good hermeneutics (interpretation) recognizes the importance of context, and context itself can be multi-layered. We need to keep this in mind when exploring the possibility of a biblical basis for interfaith engagement. I shall confine myself to two key texts—one from the Hebrew scriptures and one from the Christian Testament—both of which are dominical commandments. That is to say, the context of each is direct revelation: they give "the word of God" as directly as is possible to ascertain. The first is the ninth of the Ten Commandments: "You shall not bear false witness against your neighbour."[10] The second is one confidently attributed to Jesus himself, who summarized the heart of faith by citing from the *Shema* (Deut. 6:4), "You shall love the Lord your God with all your heart," to which he added, "The second is this: You shall love your neighbour as yourself. There is no other commandment greater than these."[11] Does the ninth commandment, not to bear false witness against our neighbour, together with the commandment of Jesus to love our neighbour as ourselves, juxtaposed, in effect, as co-equal with loving God, provide the basis for a biblical mandate for interfaith engagement?

The Ten Commandments, when subject to careful interpretive scrutiny, can be regarded not merely as a summary set of ethical requirements but rather the distillation, in an imperative form, of the foundational principles of relational integrity that comprise the vertical and horizontal planes of our existence: our relationship with God and our relationships with our fellow human beings. I wish to suggest that we human beings experience a fundamental psychological and spiritual need to have reliable witness made as to who and what we really are. It is a commonplace that this is not always easy to acknowledge, perhaps even to recognize; but it is there, nevertheless. Perhaps the point can be demonstrated by its obverse: there is an inherent human reaction of hostility to slander, to being misrepresented, to having selfhood questioned or denied outright. Where an individual is constantly put down, demeaned and depreciated, the chances are it will result in a diminution of personhood, with depression, negative perceptions of self-worth and concomitant mental health maladies likely to ensue. On the other hand, there is, without doubt, profound value in having those who know us and whom we trust bearing true witness to and of us: confirming our identity, affirming who we are, upholding our worthiness. Mental health and spiritual health are correlated.

However, to be confronted with false witness—to have our identity denied in any form, our identity called into question, to have doubt cast on our very being—is to contend with a situation of profound betrayal. And if this is true at the personal psychological level, it can also be true for communities, for whole societies. Tragically, this has been a mark of the historic relationship between Jews and Christians. It is also a feature of the history and contemporary reality of Christian–Muslim relations, as was evidenced rather vividly in recent times courtesy of the Prophet Muhammad cartoon affair in Denmark. Perhaps the commandment proscribing false witness against our neighbour has something to tell us about intercommunal as well as interpersonal relations. The neighbour of whom we are commanded not to bear false witness is not only the person next door, but the every-body, the every-culture, every-religion, with whom we live in ever closer proximity in the modern world.

The key question is this: Is the ninth commandment to be honoured passively only? Do we fulfil it by never actually bearing false witness as such? Or do we fulfil it actively to the extent we bear, concretely and intentionally, true witness in respect of our neighbour? I suggest that in the context of understanding the commandments as providing guidance for the priorities and integrity of relationship—between us and God, between us and our fellow human beings—this commandment is the beginning point of a theological mandate for interfaith engagement. People of other faiths are our neighbours.[12] The biblical scholar and ecumenist Krister Stendahl observes that the ninth commandment carries a clear implication in favour of interreligious engagement. The fulfilling of the command requires active dialogue in order to know and honour the other as, indeed, our neighbour. Perhaps those who would honour God would do so more by seeking to bear true witness to the religious neighbour—through proper, critical, empathetic knowledge and understanding and through active sympathetic engagement—than by basing their stance on the rather odd notion that the good news of God requires that the integrity and identity of the non-Christian religious neighbour is to be denied in favour of the neighbour joining the Christian club, of becoming "one of us." After all, this is exactly the pattern of ecclesiastical one-upmanship within the Christian orbit that the ecumenical movement has striven hard to ameliorate: replacing mutual deprecation and rivalry with mutual respect and a wider encompassing theological vision. It is a similar wide theological vision that is called for in respect to interreligious relations. In the end, I suggest, the commandment not to bear false witness against our neighbour of another faith is the other side of the second great commandment: to love our neighbour as ourselves. For true love does not bear false witness; bearing true witness is itself an act of love.

But what of the classic counter-text, John 14:6? Does this not say, unequivocally, that there is but one modality of salvation, as in the only "way to God, the Father," namely through Jesus, the Son? Selvanayagam rightly notes that this text is, most usually, "taken out of context and proclaimed as an established doctrine which is non-negotiable."[13] Wingate points out that this text is preceded in John 14:2 by the cryptic

"In my Father's house there are many dwelling-places" and that this can be linked to John 10:16 ("I have other sheep that do not belong to this fold").[14] Caution and discernment, with a deep reading of the full text in its context, are required before rash claims to theological, and specifically soteriological, exclusivity can be entertained. The John 14:6 text does not carry the same revelatory weight as do the two dominical texts, for it cannot be assumed that these words, as recorded in scripture, are the actual verbatim speech of Jesus. They bear the hallmark of theological redaction by the compiler of the gospel. But it is an important text to address, nonetheless, and a number of points need to be made. The text admits of a multiple or multi-layered context of which one dimension is its inclusion in the set of "I am" sayings attributed to Jesus. One facet of this is that, so far as attribution to significant religious figures go, an "I am" saying is by no means unique to Christian texts. Similar sorts of sayings are found in the texts of other religions in reference to their specific key or divine figures. To that extent the "I am" structure is a religious-literary trope utilised by the gospel writer. The immediate relational setting is also significant, namely that "[t]he context of John 14 is the farewell discourse of Jesus addressed to his desperate disciples with passion and intimacy. 14:6 is part of a dialogue."[15]

In other words, we need to remember that the giving of abstract utterances of a philosophical kind is not in the manner of the discourse of Jesus. That which reliably reflects his known interpersonal style is more likely to be concrete and direct, with a provocative, or perhaps poetically evocative, edge: Jesus was a teacher in the Hebrew–rabbinical, not the Greek–rhetorical, mode. This is supported by the fact that the text itself comes in response to the concrete question of Thomas, raised in the context of the farewell discourse: "How can we know the way, when we don't know where you are going?" This reflects the immediate focused or narrow context. But there is also a wider context. The community for which John wrote was made up of mainly Jewish–Christians caught up in an intra-Jewish struggle and, in particular, "facing a conflict situation created by the conservative wing of the Jewish leadership."[16] In this setting, messianic interpretations, applications, and expectations were critical. So, in summary, there is a complex contextual *Sitz im Leben* for this text which cannot be ignored. At many levels it is a text that must be understood in terms of a nuanced and multi-layered dialogical setting, which certainly goes beyond its immediate context as given by John's gospel. Selvanayagam observes:

> When we highlight the intra-Jewish context of Jesus, we need to take note of and connect this with the basic affirmation that Jesus was the embodiment of the eternal divine Word—as recorded in the prologue of John. [The Word/Logos] is internally present as light and life in all human beings, struggling to enlighten them. In a Hellenistic world such an interpretation made [a] lot of sense. But what we should not forget [is] that the particular embodiment was in the form of a Jew, called teacher and prophet and confessed as Messiah and the Son of God; and also that the eternal Word which was embodied in Jesus continued to be present as light and life in every human being. . . . It is not up to us to make judgements on other embodiments whether they are claimed to be of the cosmic Word or principle, but it need not be an arrogant act if we test every claim against the claim of Jesus within the Jewish context.[17]

We may conclude, at least provisionally, that in terms of the key dominical texts that suggest relational openness to the religious other, and of the principal counter-text which has tended toward an exclusivist interpretation, it is the dominical texts which carry greater weight. The likelihood is that a biblical mandate in favour of interreligious engagement, when pressed beyond these "test texts," can be adduced. It is certainly the case that there is no compellingly conclusive biblical warrant *against* interfaith relationships and interreligious dialogue as such. But if a biblical mandate to relate dialogically to our neighbour of another faith can be ascertained, where does that leave the received tradition that has premised the relation of Christians to others on the basis of Matthew 28:16-20, the "Great Commission"? Indeed, is there an inherent tension between these "Great Commandments" and the Great Commission?

Interreligious Engagement and the "Great Commission"

What may we make of the missionary imperative of Christianity as derived from the Great Commission (Matt. 28:16-20)? The late South African missiologist, David Bosch, in observing that the author of the gospel of Matthew was a Jew addressing a predominantly Jewish–Christian community, argues that the "entire purpose of his writing was to nudge his community toward a missionary involvement with its environment."[18] Although the Protestant missionary movements during the 19th and 20th centuries, when giving account of their individual rationale, all appropriately appealed to the Great Commission that closes Matthew's gospel, such appeal, says Bosch, "usually took no account of the fact that this pericope cannot be properly understood in isolation from the gospel of Matthew as a whole."[19] For Bosch, the entire gospel may be read as a missionary text: it is not a life of Jesus so much as a guide for the community of those who would follow Jesus by living out his teachings. Thus, says Bosch, it is "inadmissible to lift these words out of Matthew's gospel . . . [and] . . . allow them a life of their own, and understand them without any reference to the context in which they first appeared."[20] Indeed, the Great Commission is perhaps the most genuinely and uniquely Matthean contribution to the entire gospel: virtually every word or expression used in these verses is peculiar to the author of this gospel.[21]

Peter Cotterell concurs that, in Matthew, the commissioning of the disciples for mission is the intentional climax of the gospel in its entirety. In the text of the pericope "the words of Jesus fall into three parts, a statement, a command, and a promise."[22] The statement amounts to the assertion of "all authority" suggestive of a new means of empowerment; the command, to "go and make [disciples]," is an exhortation to empowered action that knows no boundaries, meaning that what heretofore was a localized and particular activity is now of universal import; and the promise is that the unalloyed divine presence will surely accompany this active empowered process. In fact, the Great Commission may itself be read as an affirmation of the universal applicability of the work and mission of Jesus—into and for the whole world, not just the Jewish world—as a distinctly post-resurrection development. Terence Donaldson remarks that the climax to the gospel narrative is not so much the resurrection of Jesus *per se* but the signalling of "a new community of salvation . . . a community drawn from all nations, bound to Jesus" wherein it is the authority of Jesus which "makes it possible for his disciples to carry out the helping role for which they were initially called."[23] Further, the disciples are no religious super-heroes: Matthew depicts them in all their human frailty. In their relation to Jesus, for example, they are portrayed as slow to understand (Matt. 15:12-20; 16:5-12) and showing fear (Matt. 14:26, 30) and lack of faith (Matt. 14:31; 16:8).[24]

Matthew interprets membership of the community of Jesus' people in terms of discipleship, and the very humanity of the first disciples serves to encourage a new generation of followers to *their* life of discipleship. Thus the first disciples have an "important function, both positively and negatively, of showing the readers of the Gospel just what is involved in being a follower of Jesus and a beneficiary of his saving activity."[25] The question this then raises is whether salvation is understood by Matthew—and so may be understood by us—as primarily an *individual benefit* gained by virtue of becoming, as individuals, disciples or followers of Jesus. Or is salvation a *mark of a particular and unique community*, the membership of which is to be understood in regard to the dynamics of discipleship, of living out salvation as the qualitative guide and measure for those who comprise the body of Christ? Arguably, where the idea of mission—in essence, the action of "going out" to "make disciples"—lies with the former, then Protestant evangelicalism dominates and, consequently, religious exclusivism and competition come more to the fore. If it lies with the latter, then "making disciples" is to be understood more in terms of the spread and diversification of the "Christ community" *within* the nations of the world, and therefore presupposes the concomitant development of appropriate relations between the Christ community and those diverse communities—including religious communities—which, together with the Christian community, make up the nations.

Undoubtedly, discipleship is a leitmotiv of Matthew's gospel. Donaldson notes: "Matthew eventually makes it clear that he wants his readers to become disciples and recipients of Jesus' teaching as well."[26] The disciples, slow on the uptake, got there in the end—and were finally commissioned. In effect, says Matthew, "The same can go for you, dear reader . . ." However, the corporate dimension of Matthew's portrayal of discipleship is really quite clear: "in the only Gospel that refers to the church [*ekklesia*] ([Matt.] 16:18; 18:17), discipleship takes place in the context of a distinct, discipled community."[27] The making of disciples is thus to be read as working to bring others into a new and widely inclusive community, understood now to be of universal import, beyond the confines of its originating (Jewish) particularity. For Matthew there is "no discontinuity between the history of Jesus and the era of the church."[28]

Also, for Matthew, as discipleship "means living out the teachings of Jesus. . . . It is unthinkable to divorce the Christian life of love and justice from being a disciple."[29] Mission is not simply the narrow activity of winning converts, even though there will always be a welcome given to the new entrant to the community. Rather it may be seen as also the never-ending and much broader task of socializing or educating people into an appreciative awareness and understanding—and so a discovering and deepening—of the Christian discipline or way of life. And this may be something other than, and alongside, the joining of a particular ecclesial community by way of taking up active membership within it. What I am suggesting is that, given the propriety of positive and mutually respectful relations which even a preliminary rethinking the interpretation of the dominical commandments has shown, the relational motifs of socializing and educating may themselves be interpreted and applied quite broadly. A relationship with an other who knows, understands and sees value in my religion, and in which I know, understand and see value in the religion of the other, may well be, in certain contexts, a sufficient discharge of the task of making disciples. Let us explore this idea a little bit further.

Christian Mission and Discipleship

What is the understanding of mission in regards to discipleship, and how might that relate to interreligious dialogue? Given that the linguistic (Latin) derivation of the term disciple is literally that of pupil or "learner"—in the sense of one who learns from and becomes a follower of a particular teacher, as was the normative pattern at Hellenistic philosophical schools of the time—does it really make sense to think of the chief goal of mission in terms of some sort of programmatic "making disciples" activity? Indeed, can someone be "made" a disciple as such? Of course, a lot depends on how we interpret and apply the verb: what is the intent of "making" in this case? Equally, a lot depends on what we mean by the content of discipleship. At the very least, it has to do with mission, inasmuch as the Christian disciple is one who participates in the mission of Christ. Thus it is worth approaching the question of discipleship from the perspective of the question "What is the meaning of 'mission' inherent to discipleship?" Mission is not a matter of applying fixed or pre-determined patterns of events and expectations. To the extent that witness, for example, is integral to the idea of mission, Martin Conway usefully notes that witnessing "is not to cajole or argue other people into accepting your point of view or joining your community: it is to do no more than point to what you believe to be significant and true, or to offer a criterion and an interpretation in which you find meaning and purpose."[30] Further, Conway says, whereas undertaking witness is the responsibility of the disciple, "the response to that witness is the affair of the other."[31] And, importantly, it is God, not the disciple, who is responsible for conversion, if there is such. The mission task of bearing witness to the good news in the context of relational engagement is sufficient, for it is God alone who works in the heart and life of those to whom witness is borne. It is never the evangelist who effects conversion; conversion is only ever an outcome that occurs in and by the spirit and grace of God. So, the interconnected elements—witness, mission, discipleship—do not necessarily denote some fixed or narrow agenda for Christian action. And although these terms remain of crucial importance in the self-understanding of the church, their content is in fact both much more open and much more opaque than we might at first think.

David Bosch, following the work of Winston Crum,[32] suggests that the church may be regarded as a community gathered, elliptically as it were, around two foci:

> In and around the first it acknowledges and enjoys the source of its life; this is where worship and prayer are emphasized. From and through the second focus the church engages and challenges the world. This is a forth-going and self-spending focus, where service, mission and evangelism are stressed.[33]

Furthermore, a contemporary leading paradigm of mission sees the task of the church, or the Christian community, as being to participate in the mission of God—the *missio Dei*—wherein, strictly speaking, "mission is not primarily an activity of the church, but an attribute of God. . . . Mission is thereby seen as a movement from God to the world; the church is viewed as an instrument for that mission. . . . To participate in mission is to participate in the movement of God's love toward people."[34] Mission, in this sense, is the fulfilling of relational injunctions: to love, to bear true and proper witness, to honour and respect, to offer hospitality to the stranger. Mission is the act of reaching out to the other in both an imitation and an enacting of the outward reaching love of God. This opens us to a wider and enriching interactive understanding of mission, one which allows for interfaith engagement as a component dimension. Bosch reminds us that the

> most we can hope for is to formulate some *approximations* of what mission is all about. . . . Our missionary practice is not performed in unbroken continuity with the biblical witness; it is an altogether ambivalent enterprise executed in the context of tension between divine providence and human confusion.[35]

Now, whereas the modern era missionary enterprise was founded on notions of the inherent superiority of Christianity, the fact that we are living now in a manifestly pluralist world has produced a new context and, says Bosch, this is an element of the contemporary "crisis" of mission.[36] But a situation of crisis—if that is what it is—does not mean mission is vitiated, only that it must, as with all things theological, be constantly re-thought. In this regard Roger Bowen acknowledges that the question of the proper Christian "attitude to people of other faiths" is the "hardest theological question which faces the whole Church."[37] Although, says Bowen,

> God is at work outside the area of the Church's witness, there have been times when the Church's witness to Christ has been so false that God cannot have been in it. The obvious example is the Crusades, which were so cruel that Christians should be ashamed to use the word at all. What response should Saladin and his Muslim armies have made to the Christ whom they saw then?[38]

Christians can claim no inherent and automatic right of superiority in terms of the historical praxis of the faith, even if, as with Bowen himself, priority is yet given to Christ as the only sure means by which, in the end, the deepest reality of God may be known. Yet the christocentrism of Bowen does not preclude him from acknowledging the place and role of interreligious dialogue within the wider mission of the church which "should not be to trade bargaining points between the religions, but to admit that we all have a journey of faith to go on . . . Perhaps people of different faiths can sometimes go on part of this journey together as they talk with one another."[39]

There is yet another dimension to the question of discipleship and mission. To whom is the mission directed? Who is the other to whom the invitation to discipleship is issued, let alone who is to be the subject of a "making disciples" initiative? In other words, who is the other, theologically speaking? And what is being proposed with respect to this other? In 1302 CE Pope Boniface proclaimed that "the Catholic Church was the only institution guaranteeing salvation" and, later, the Council of Florence in 1442 CE "assigned to the everlasting fire of hell everyone not attached to the Catholic Church."[40] The legacy that these decrees have bequeathed to the Christian church today is that, in terms of Catholic dogma, outside the *church*, or at least *without* the church, there is no salvation. By contrast, for Protestants it is more the case that without the *word* there is no salvation: hence the driving force to evangelical proclamation of the word (or Word) for the winning of converts, for it is only so that salvation may be accessed. The upshot is that, historically, for "both these models mission essentially has meant *conquest* and *displacement*. Christianity was understood to be . . . the only religion which had the divine right to exist and extend itself."[41] The goal of mission had been to displace the other faith and win over the people of that faith. In either case, of course, the central point of reference is Christ. However, the interpretation and so application of the understanding of Christ differs considerably. Although the focal interpretation as to what is essentially meant by that Christianity wherein salvation is obtained— the one is ecclesiocentric, the other christocentric—the effect, vis-à-vis the person standing outside the Christian community, is the same: they are numbered among the lost. So, to that extent, people of other faiths were counted as "lost sheep," at least until they had the chance to hear the gospel and respond with belief in, and allegiance to, Christ and his church, and so enter the salvific fold. Therefore the proper relationship that predominated, at least until the middle of the 20th century, with respect to the Christian stance towards other religions and peoples of other faiths, was that they were to be the subject of evangelical outreach and the quest for conversion, all for the sake of salvation in and through

Christ. But is this overt relation to Christ the only valid mode of relationship to God?

In the early 1960s, as the World Council of Churches was beginning to develop the ecumenical journey into interreligious dialogue, the Roman Catholic Church had embarked on its epochal Second Vatican Council, at which the influence of the theologian Karl Rahner was to be felt. Rahner, Bosch reminds us, agitated "for a shift from ecclesiocentric to a christocentric approach to the theology of religions."[42] Bosch writes:

> It is important to take cognizance of the fact that Rahner's point of departure, when discussing other religions and their possible salvific value, is Christology. He never abandons the idea of Christianity as the absolute religion and of salvation having to come only through Christ. But he recognizes supernatural elements of grace in other religions which, he posits, have been given to human beings through Christ. There is a saving grace within other religions but this grace is Christ's. This makes people of other faiths into "anonymous Christians" and accords their religions a positive place in God's salvific plan. They are "ordinary ways of salvation", independent of the special way of salvation of Israel and the church. It is in the latter that they find fulfilment.[43]

From this relatively innovative perspective the position of inclusivism, as the newly governing paradigm, supplanted exclusivism; peoples of other faiths were no longer arbitrarily and comprehensively excluded from the grace of God—until such time as they came into the Christian fold— but were accorded the respect of their own integrity and the recognition that, in some sense, they already participated in salvific grace. To the extent this might be so, in a sense that hitherto had never been conceded, they were now understood to be already theologically included within the divine scope. On the other hand, the later development of a more sophisticated and intentional pluralism, one that wishes to obviate the inherent superiority of the Christian position in regards to inclusivism, is not without its own problems. Bosch, a missionary theologian, asserts "we are in need of a theology of religions characterized by creative tension, which reaches beyond the sterile alternative between a comfortable claim to absoluteness and arbitrary pluralism."[44] Although Bosch appears to dismiss both exclusivism and pluralism, he is by no means uncritically accepting of inclusivism. The problem in regard to this paradigm applied to the interreligious arena is trenchantly put: "In the end everything— and everyone!—is accounted for. There are no loose ends, no room left for surprises and unsolved puzzles. Even before the dialogue begins, all the crucial issues have been settled."[45] Bosch asserts that, in reality, "both dialogue and mission manifest themselves in a meeting of hearts rather than of minds. We are dealing with a mystery."[46] And so we are.

Conclusion

Roger Herft, the Sri Lankan-born Anglican Archbishop of Perth, Australia, in speaking of the need for theology to engage in dialogue with other faiths, asserted that "in all our efforts in dialogue we cannot lay aside the truth that God in Christ has been present and active in all nations, cultures and religions, nor can we lay aside our call to be fishers of women and men."[47] Martin Conway once wrote of mission that it amounts to the "entire task of the church," thus: "Mission is not so much one entity as a whole way of living—of feeling, of seeing, and of searching for love and truth."[48] The third question I posed above sought to address the understanding of mission with regard to discipleship, and how that might relate to interreligious dialogue. I suggest that a number of elements have emerged from the foregoing discussion which contribute to understanding discipleship as, in fact, actively enabling proper and meaningful relations with our neighbours of other faiths. In the first instance, Christians simply living out their lives in the context of everyday interactions within a religiously plural environment are engaged in non-intentional dialogue. Such engagement occurs without any conscious design as such; it simply takes place as the dialogue of life. Beyond that a range of intentional interreligious engagements can and does occur. The dialogue of life dimension itself can take on a more intentional edge in terms of the range of social intercourse necessarily taking place in the context of communal existence: in the wider society, different communities, including religious ones, may well interact conscientiously in terms of their religious identities and perspectives in the public arena, for instance in the context of participation in community councils. Further, joint responses to societal issues and cooperative actions premised on shared, or at least compatible, values and perspectives speak of a planned and intended level of interreligious relating that may be classified as representing the dialogue of action. Occasions wherein an interfaith event of a liturgical, meditative, reflective, or otherwise worshipful nature is engaged in, represent the dialogue of religious experience. Events where scholars and other allied experts from across two or more religions get together to pursue deep discussions is often referred to as the dialogue of discourse: as I have noted in chapter 5, this discursive activity is what the term "dialogue" immediately suggests, but in fact it is the most difficult to pursue, and really requires a history of relationship being built up by way of the other modalities of dialogue before it can be confidently entered into.

In light of the discussion of the biblical basis for interreligious engagement, and the contours of mission in regards to other faiths, all four of these dialogue modalities—life, action, experience, discourse—can be seen, from the perspective of Christian faith and reflection, as representing appropriate dimensions of the way of discipleship. Furthermore, there is also the indirect element of intentional interreligious engagement by virtue of a religious community (a parish church, for example) undertaking self-reflection in respect to the fact of the religious plurality in which it is set—seeking to discern and understand its role vis-à-vis its neighbours of other faiths. In this regard, Bosch usefully summarizes the attitudes, preconditions and perspectives for interreligious engagement.[49] There must be both a clear and willing acceptance of the coexistence of different faiths and an intentional cultivation of a deeper commitment to one's own faith. Dialogical engagement then proceeds in the confidence of the God who precedes us, who is there before us—from our viewpoint—in the uncharted waters of interfaith relations. Further, both dialogue and mission are to be pursued in a context of humility: this is an exercise of being open to grace. Religions are to be understood as discrete worldview systems. Thus interactions with them, or rather their followers, will vary accordingly: the form and focus of relations between Christians and Muslims will be different from that of Christian-Buddhist encounter, for example.

Interreligious dialogue neither subverts nor substitutes for mission understood in its wider sense of living out the *missio Dei* in and to the wider world. At the same time dialogue moves us beyond any sense of business as usual: the dialogical engagement of interfaith relations will effect change, if not in fundamental beliefs and values, then certainly in the modality of their interpretation and application. To that extent, a new phase of the life of discipleship is entered into when interreligious engagement is taken up. And in all this a role may be found for more sophisticated theological investigation and reflection in seeking a rationale for, and engaging in an evaluation of, interreligious relationships and allied dialogical activities; this simultaneously takes us back into our own heritage and forward into uncharted waters of understanding and new engagements. In effect, this is where this chapter—indeed the entire book—is situated, and it leads to a final comment. Discipleship, as a response to the greater reality of God, a reality that is manifestly universal in reach and inclusive in scope, implies an openness to that which necessarily falls within the purview of the *missio Dei*, namely the *oikoumene*—the whole inhabited earth. And this means all that lies therein, including the rich diversity of human culture and religion.

Interreligious engagement is not the pursuit of dialogue by an "in-group" with respect to an "out-group" on the basis of a belief that the one is within the divine encompass and the other is not. For there is no "out." Nothing is "outside" or beyond the reach and scope of the reality of God. Those who would be disciples of the Christ participate in the mission of God which is governed by this dimension of universality and inclusiveness. Therefore, discipleship is not about the attempt to gather in those who are "outside." This very bifurcation, which derives from the pastoral imagery that played a role in the early establishment and self-reflection of the Christian community, has long been eclipsed by developments in theological understanding. Rather the life of Christian discipleship is a matter of engaging both self and world in the quest for deeper knowledge of God and in living out the life which goes with that knowledge and quest. And this is a way of life that presupposes dialogical modality: the interior dialogue as one seeks and follows one's individual path; the dialogue of belonging within the community in which the quest is situated and shared; and the dialogue with others, especially others of different faith traditions and paths, who are similarly living out their own quests.

8. INTERRELIGIOUS PRAYER
DIALOGUE IN ACTION

RELIGIOUS DIVERSITY, AS WE HAVE SEEN FROM OUR DISCUSSIONS THUS far, is not just a brute fact of the contemporary age; it is a complex reality that impinges cognitively and spiritually upon religious sensibility *per se*. And whatever the cognitive response to, or the theoretical assessment of, the fact of this diversity, the allied fact of our time, namely that this plurality is a given (albeit in some instances relatively novel) component of societies and communities who must necessarily live and work together, demands also a more practical response. For irrespective of official ideological inclination, to the extent that it can be articulated, it is people holding particular beliefs and owning particular religious identities who find themselves engaged in common cause with other people of quite different religious persuasions, when occasion arises or need demands. Thus plurality of religion is not only theoretically apprehended but also actively encountered and engaged within everyday experience. The fact that a multitude of engagements at the practical and cooperative level occur between peoples of different religions is, of course, not the point at issue. That people of different religious persuasions can cooperate on projects for the common good is neither startling nor new. But the coming together of people of diverse religions to plan or reflect upon a common action or venture and to consider, let alone engage in, an act of shared spiritual experience—such as interreligious prayer or other spiritual or liturgical act—is something that is still, for many, comparatively novel and relatively rare. Yet the impetus for acts of interfaith prayer, worship, or other similar shared events, is increasing as more and more experiences of cross-religion engagement and dialogical encounter occur, and as communities encompassing religious diversity address issues in common, or respond to crises that affect all.[1]

Opportunities for sharing in multi-religious experiential events are likely also to increase. In some corners of the globe this is already the case; for some it is a relatively infrequent experience, whilst for others it is only just emerging into view on the horizon of possibility. For example, the

2012 National Interfaith Forum in New Zealand included a multi-faith Sunday service that involved a number of different faith traditions— Jewish, Muslim, Hindu, Baha'i, Christian (Anglican, Methodist, Catholic), Mormon—all of which contributed up to five minutes of reflection, reading, meditation, music, and other elements of worship. It is the kind of event that can be too easily critiqued and dismissed; in fact it proved the most highly appreciated element of the entire weekend programme of the forum and many found the experience to be very moving. It was, without doubt, quite a highlight. But what was it, exactly? In this chapter I explore the question of interreligious prayer, although what I traverse can also apply to a wider range of liturgical, devotional or other worship activities. I will commence by commenting on a joint WCC-Vatican project which will set the scene for a discussion of some phenomenological elements of interreligious prayer. This will lead to my offering a supportive theological rationale, including a discussion of the Lord's Prayer, for Christian engagement in suitable interfaith prayer and related activities.

A Project on Interreligious Prayer

There are many examples of everyday life situations wherein Christians find themselves necessarily encountering, at some depth, people of other faiths. These range from the more personal level of, for example, interfaith marriages—with concomitant religious diversity impacting upon the extended family—to corporate cooperation in some common cause, such as protesting human rights violations, opposing the proliferation of casinos, engaging climate change and ecological concerns, or challenging the damaging effects of the free-market economy. Shared community tragedies and disasters, or occasions of communal celebration, also often provide contexts where people from across a variety of faiths seek to join together in a suitable religious response. My own interest and thinking arise primarily from personal involvement in interfaith matters, including shared events such as combined "prayers for world peace" and suchlike, together with my participation in a combined World Council of Churches and Vatican study project during the 1990s.[2] This involved the then Office for Inter-Religious Relations (OIRR) of the WCC, and the Pontifical Council for Interreligious Dialogue (PCID) of the Vatican, undertaking a cooperative project on interreligious prayer.[3] The questions which lay behind this cooperative venture remain live ones today, of course, and require continual reflection and fresh thinking. When the natural human response is to pray, and the context of that response is multi-religious, what can we do together? How can we do it? Indeed, ought we to do it? And if we do, on what basis may we proceed? What justification can we give in respect of our own faith? What are the issues to be addressed? How, if at all, may they be resolved?

Following a preliminary exploratory survey of a number of churches, study centres, and theological institutions around the world, a joint consultation on the subject of interreligious prayer was convened in Bangalore, India, in July 1996. Some two dozen participants representing different Christian traditions and coming from different parts of the globe shared their experiences and understandings and drew up a preliminary report. A subsequent and smaller consultation was convened in September 1997, drawing upon theological expertise from Catholic, Protestant and Orthodox perspectives. This Joint Theological Consultation on Interreligious Prayer, co-sponsored by PCID and OIRR, was held at the ecumenical Catholic monastery, Communità di Bose, in Magnano, Italy. The group of fifteen theologians, of whom I was one, divided into three five-person work-groups to address, respectively, biblical, pastoral and theological dimensions of interreligious prayer. The consultation was charged with formulating conclusions on the basis of the earlier research and findings together with the further reflection in which the group and its sub-groups had engaged in during the course of the four-day gathering. As the findings report of the earlier Bangalore consultation pointed out, there are often occasions when the experience of working together on a social project leads to a desire to pray together. This was no less true of the Bose consultation itself, and indeed is the crux of the issue that faces us on the interreligious front.

It is not my purpose here to rehearse or summarize the outcomes of the Bose consultation. That can be found elsewhere.[4] However, the work in which I engaged as a participant stimulated my own thinking and prompted further development of lines of inquiry and reflection. Naturally, reports and findings of such a consultation are a group product reflecting consensus and compromise, the melding of individual input with corporate concern and the wisdom of the group mind. There are always strengths and weaknesses with this process. On the one hand the tentative, suggestive, initially inchoate contributions of individuals can be expanded, honed and refined through the processes of group reflection and critical interchange to form a substantial element of the outcome; on the other hand, the inevitable need for a measure of compromise and the necessary limitations of such a corporate project can mean that some otherwise sharp and incisive, or novel and exploratory, individual contributions are muted, maybe even lost, so far as the final product is concerned. Such individual reflections may belong elsewhere. The task of theological reflection and exploration is never ending and cannot be confined. Alongside the carefully considered corporate product may stand the complementary work of the individual theologian, no less carefully weighed, but perhaps freer to extend the boundaries, to be a little more adventurous and more easily able to explore cognitive options and suggest theoretical possibilities. My own thinking on the subject certainly reflects, to some extent, some aspects of the work of the consultation. In particular, I have developed that work by way of an exploration of the phenomenological and theological elements of interreligious prayer, and it is these two dimensions that I shall now discuss.

Phenomenological Explorations

It is important to delineate at the outset just what might be meant by the term "interreligious" as applied to the context of prayer or some other such experiential event—by which is meant a multi-religious occasion that may embrace more than just elements of prayer, but where prayer and/or meditation form part of an overall act of interreligious liturgical engagement. Indeed, we need also to explore what is meant by the term "prayer" in the multi-religious context. A preliminary phenomenological reflection discerns four possible modes of meaning and usage of the term "interreligious" which yield four models, or paradigms, of interreligious action in the sense of a prayer or worship event. First, and most simply, an interreligious event can be a *shared multi-religious* act wherein there is presentation, in some sort of serial or simultaneous fashion, from a number of religious traditions or groups, without necessarily presupposing any depth of coordination, nor implying any particular level of mutual acceptance or agreement: the diverse offerings are simply allowed to be; they are passively observed rather than actively apprehended or responded to by others participating in, or at least attending, the event. There may be a common theme or occasion to which the various contributions are oriented, but no attempt made to coordinate thematically, critically, and intentionally the contributions so offered on the basis of seeing them as components cohering together to make up a recognizable, and acceptable-to-all, whole. It is a matter, simply, of spiritual or liturgical pot-luck or of a smorgasbord-like spread of differently sourced religious items contributed to the worship or prayer event or other liturgical act. This was more or less the style of event that took place at the New Zealand National Interfaith Forum referred to above. It worked well enough, attracting very appreciative responses from those who both participated in the faith presentations and the majority who simply respectfully observed.

Second, there is the possibility—amply demonstrated in the two World Days of Prayer for Peace, held in Assisi, Italy, at the invitation of Pope John Paul II in 1986 and 2002, and in the 2011 event hosted by Pope Benedict XVI—of a *contiguous multi-religious* act. Here, as at Assisi, the principal event is constructed along the lines of having different religious traditions engage in their own prayer, or liturgical act, each in their allocated space, whether a different location for each group, as in the Assisi cases, or some other form of spatio-temporal demarcation. There is no intermingling of principal acts; full integrity of religious identity and the authenticity of specific actions are maintained. But at the same time this spatio-temporal demarcation is also bounded: the diversity of actions is held together by the virtue of some manifest contiguity. As at Assisi, it might be by way of being held within a uniting time and place—the same town on the same day—and including a shared opening and closing action. The essential focus and meaning of the event is found through the sheer fact of being conjoined by virtue of temporal and geographic contiguity. The theological context is clear: coming together, in order to pray; but doing that separately such that no-one is compromised, and no reductionism or relativism can be imputed. This form of multi-religious prayer is one which is not uncommon in many pastoral situations as, for example, with hospital chaplaincy work where two or more people from different faiths may find occasion to pray with and for each other, but to do so independently, as it were, even if in the same room and at the same time. There is no suggestion of an overt corporate act of multi-religious sharing. But there is a context of multi-religious contiguity enacted: people are together, praying, but they are not engaged in praying together. With respect to the Assisi occasions, whilst each religious group did its own thing, independently of each other in accord with the contiguity model, there was also a dimension of the shared multi-religious act. Typically the day concluded with an act of coming together to share, each with the other, some suitable meditative, reflective or otherwise prayerful item, and to bear common witness to the world of a shared concern, at least, with the theme of peace. So these Assisi events, in their totality, embraced both multi-religious contiguity and a measure of shared multi-religious action.

Third, and potentially most problematic, interreligious prayer can be taken as the occasion to have an *intentional combined multi-religious* act. In this case, the aim is to create, out of the resources of a multiplicity of religions involved, an act or event that produces a blended or otherwise combined content which may be effectively "owned" in its entirety by each of the participating groups, or religious representatives. Inevitably the only way this can be achieved is by utilising the approach of discerning the lowest common denominator. The distinctive and particular is shorn in order that a baseline of harmony and acceptability may prevail. In some cases, the negotiations undertaken—in dialogue—to achieve such an outcome may itself be quite considerable, as well as beneficial to those involved, even if, from the perspective of any one participating tradition, the combined outcome seems rather banal and overly simplified. Further, if this was the only mode of interreligious prayer, such prayer and allied liturgical activity could be justly criticized as a reductionist and necessarily relativizing, even syncretistic, enterprise: all the fearful concerns mounted against the cause of interreligious dialogue would come home to roost.[5] Indeed, I suspect that this is often the assumption, and the limitation, as to what the term "interreligious prayer" means for many people, and so a reason used for avoiding it.

Fourth, and seemingly reflecting the best of the reported experiences of interreligious prayer, is the occasion of prayer that has been carefully planned, but not as a syncretistic blending. This we might call *coherent-integrated interreligious* prayer wherein, from the contributing religions, there comes a thematic and critical interlinking of prayers and/or a co-ordinating of allied liturgical items. These items or components are selected and rendered mutually congruent around a particular event, need or appropriate common communal point of reference. The intention is to attain a sense of underlying unity, or internal coherence, to the outcome, yet one where the real differences, unique dimensions and contexts, as well as the different content of the contributions and the religions from which they are drawn, are mutually respected and upheld. There is no intention, through the event, of presupposing, or enacting, some form of uniting the participating being religions, nor of subsuming them under some inclusive umbrella of any one of them. There is no attempt to blend the rich diversity of contributions into a kind of spiritual porridge; nor is the outcome marked by the happy randomness of a smorgasbord. No religious tradition is compromised, no reduction of essence or denial of the religious self-identity of the participating traditions occurs. Yet, some sense of greater wholeness may emerge nonetheless: an intuition of a larger context, a wider or deeper sphere wherein a unifying spirit is at work, may be discerned. Again, this is without prejudice to the particular sensibilities of any of the contributing religions. Yet it can allow an acknowledgment and affirmation of the result by all as authentic to the occasion. The Assisi events I have referred to above did not pursue this model, of course. Nevertheless something of it was implied, even if only by virtue of an inchoate sense of the Spirit being at work in and through the shared valuation, across the different religions, given to the witness to and for peace.

To summarize, the four models or paradigms that have been identified include *shared* multi-religious; *contiguous* multi-religious; *intentional-combined* multi-religious; and *coherent-integrated* interreligious modalities. The first three are clearly activities whereby the multiplicity of religions involved are brought together, in varying degrees, in a more or less loose or serendipitous way. But with the fourth paradigm the level of cooperation, and with it a depth of dialogical consultation that is necessarily implied, means that a two-fold shift occurs. The act is planned and executed as coherent and integrated, on the one hand; on the other, the coming together of participants suggests a depth of interaction beyond what is possible to experience in terms of the other paradigms. Thus a genuinely interreligious outcome is the result and it is *inter*-religious as opposed to *multi*-religious. Something takes place between (*inter*) the participants, and between their religious systems, in the event. Yet this involves no synthesising of identities or beliefs. I do not claim that the four paradigms and my discussion of them exhaust all possibilities. However, I suggest that it is only as we can identify and refine such paradigmatic options that progress can be made.

I turn now to explore what might be meant by the term "prayer." If "interreligious" may be interpreted in terms of the four modes, what may we say about prayer itself? Keeping in mind the context of interreligious engagement, how may we understand the phenomenon of prayer? What might the term mean for us with respect to recognition of the plurality of religions? Prayer, as a category of religious phenomena, is universal. That is to say, prayer *per se* is a phenomenological category of religion: all religions may be said to include some kind of activity that would be classified as prayer. There would be no religion which, arguably, does not have some act and utterance that can be reasonably identified in this way. It may be seen as basic to all religions insofar that it manifests a variety of elements, not necessarily all together, but certainly encompassed within the broad range of the prayers of a given tradition. These elements might include vibrant expression of particular religious experience and perspective on the one hand, and on the other hand the implicit and explicit intention toward harmony and at-one-ness, both within community and with respect to the Centre of Being or Transcendental Other, however that is articulated. The elements of prayer, broadly speaking, include also various modalities of encounter with that Other or spiritual centre-point and a measure of reflectively critical self-encounter with respect to the realization of human contingency or dependency upon that Other.

There may also be found a reflective response to the encounter or experience of the world as it really is, some form of communication with, to, and from, the "Other," and that which may be called the "oikoumenal" intent as such, namely wholeness and well-being for all the earth, for all life. All these comprise elements of prayer that may be found across religions. However, although the phenomenon of prayer is universal, all actual prayers are particular and unique to the religious tradition in which they are located. Prayers found in any one religious tradition cannot be regarded as variants of a species that holds across all religions, in the sense of a common spiritual datum, either in terms of content or with respect to form. Yet the occasion of unique and particular prayer is nonetheless an instance of a universal phenomenon. At the very least it is the concrete particular act that may be classified in terms of a more general dynamic typology of prayer—thanksgiving, supplication, intercession, and so on. Furthermore, prayer may be viewed as having two modalities: personal and communal. In any given event of prayer, both modalities may be operative. In some situations one or other may predominate, or one may be the only operative mode.

In the *communal* mode, prayer gives evidence of religious identity: prayer is always the prayer of a particular religion, and indeed it may be a form of prayer belonging to an identifiable tradition from within a particular community, or sub-set, of a religion. Communal prayer is a means both by which the adherent of the religion engages in public spiritual participation, and whereby the religion itself perpetuates and sustains its unique identity. However, not all communal prayer carries the same spiritual value so far as religion is concerned. Communal prayer can have a multiplicity of levels, from the relatively general and superficial to that of expressing treasured depths of spirituality or mystic encounter. This range alludes to the sense in which communal prayer may be a vehicle for plumbing the resources of a religion for the enhancement of the religious life appropriate to it.

In the *personal* mode, prayer is a private and intimate phenomenon. Personal religious identity and allegiance are expressed; the act of prayer gives evidence of personal commitment and choice. Therefore the person at prayer is vulnerable; the act of prayer in this mode is the spiritual corollary of intimate interpersonal relation. The one at prayer may be likened to the attentive lover; the object or focus of prayer the beloved. Hence the context of prayer as sacral intimacy needs always and everywhere to be respected. Yet, as with communal prayer, there is a great variation in spiritual depth and range of religious value, from the relatively pedestrian or lightweight to the deeply personal, meditative and self-dispossessing reflection or engagement in which the soul best makes its journey alone. Some forms of personal prayer are such that they can only be engaged in solitude; others can easily occur in the public domain, in company with fellow spiritual travellers, or even in a non-religious setting, in the midst of life's daily demands and pressures.

A Theological Case for Interreligious Prayer

For theistic revelatory religion, God has already spoken: prayer is an answer. Christian prayer, for instance, is responsive to the word (or Word) which precedes prayer. Christian prayer may be said to have its source and goal in the One God, of which Christ is the fullness of revelation. At the same time Christ, the Word of God, is also the effective referent of prayer for the Christian. Prayer is often made "in and through the name of" Jesus, the Christ. Furthermore, prayer may be viewed as encompassing a variety of modalities and dimensions such as personal and relational engagement; times of meditative waiting upon the Divine; moments of resting in the aloneness of abandonment and the sense of forsakenness; occasions of expressions of joyful praise; and periods of heartfelt lamentation. Arguably dynamic parallelisms for these dimensions of a Christian perspective on prayer could be ascertained within the prayers of other religious traditions.

A Christian theological perspective on prayer may discern other undergirding dimensions which provide further criteria for the guiding of interreligious practice. Prayer is the language of love. It is the communion of heart and mind in the context of spirit. In prayer there may be discerned the affirmation of diversity in unity, the promotion of acceptance through active forgiveness and reconciliation. From a Christian point of view, prayer can be a means to a deeper communion with, if not also understanding of, the mystery of the Divine Other. It can also be a moment in which there is a deepening of self-understanding. Thus prayer serves both the cause of interreligious relations as well as self-reflective spiritual growth: in both, prayer embraces a dimension of self-encounter and the transcending of self in order to go beyond self. If prayer can be thought of as a moment of "dwelling-in" (or indwelling) one's faith, then interreligious prayer may be viewed as an occasion of "dwelling-*with*" the religiously other in that other's own indwelling of faith. Thus interreligious prayer can constitute a relational bridge, as it were, interconnecting peoples and faith communities. Interreligious prayer furthermore gives opportunity to acknowledge the sacredness that is presented in and by the other; it affirms and honours that sacredness; it may even evoke and manifest—that is, bring-into-present-being—an overarching sense of sacredness in which the particular moment of interreligious prayer is situated, and which is not inappropriate to the participating traditions.

I suggest that it is possible to identify four modalities of encounter and engagement wherein interreligious prayer may occur with theological legitimacy. These include two modes of *responsiveness type* and two modes of *hospitality type* of interactions. These types could be thought of as models for interreligious prayer, the one based on situations that evoke response, the other based on a parallelism with acts of hospitality. These basic models, or types, in their various modes, feature as common human experiences. Yet through the mundane and the familiar can be conveyed spiritual insight and novel understanding. The *responsive type* of interreligious prayer has to do with the outward facing situation of humanly reacting to an external situation or event. On the one hand there is clearly an anthropological ground for this stance. It is in the nature of human being to respond, to react as appropriate to the nature of the event: to provide succour and aid, to respond with sympathetic grieving or whatever the occasion evokes. On the other hand, the responsive mode may provide the occasion for discerning a pneumatological impulse: the Spirit at work in and through the human reaction, the response itself giving evidence of more than the merely anthropological at work. Broadly speaking, the two modes of this type are, first, occasions of communal crisis or other such significant events calling for a specifically religious response and, second, appropriate occasions of civic celebration offering opportunity for a religious contribution, dimension and witness. Christians participate in the religious response—as in an act of interreligious prayer—by virtue of the gospel imperative to love neighbour and the call to serve others with empathy. Compassion is being or standing with the other in his or her time of need; it constitutes the legitimate context for the expression of Christian values of cooperative praxis and sympathetic spirituality.

By contrast, the *hospitality* type of interreligious prayer signifies events that are inner-facing in the sense of hospitable communal ingathering of persons of different religions on occasions wherein the reciprocal roles of host and guest set the parameters for interaction. This sets the context for mutual respect. It is the respective roles that provide the two modes of this type. As host, a Christian community, for example, invites members of another community to join with it in a specific event wherein the model and intent is that of offering hospitality, whether materially, spiritually, or both. The structure of the act of hosting a guest *per se* is the practical guide to the event: invitation, reception, welcome, attending to need, offering reassurance and comfort; sharing and interacting; closure. The motif of God being found in the Christ who both goes before us among our neighbours and comes to us in the guise of the stranger in our midst provides, in part, a theological rationale for this model. And there are many biblical examples of the exercise of hospitality to stranger and neighbour, with the clear message that in so doing we are enacting an appropriate response and relationship to the Divine. In the life of the church there may be moments of eucharistic hospitality, for instance, when the Christian companion of another tradition is admitted to the intimate and tradition-specific enactment of the ritual because, in the prevailing context, for whatever reason, they have no other avenue of accessing this means of grace. The discharge of hospitality is not just a duty; it is also itself a moment of grace infused with deeper spiritual significance.

As guest, the Christian individual or community, in humility, receives and experiences that which the host offers, and in return shares the gift of the *euangelion*, the "good news," which, most simply put, states "God loves you." The life of discipleship, the witness of Christian grace, may be seen as a contribution to be added to that which the host presents. Here a biblical reference provides a scriptural example to place alongside the examples of hosting: disciples are sent to seek and respond to the invitation to enter the house of the other (see Mark 6:7-10), to offer good news and receive hospitality (or not) and so the mutuality of receiving in gratitude and with thanksgiving that which is offered. As with the host model, there is risk and vulnerability here; the prospect of insight gained on the one hand, or the possibility of indigestion resulting on the other, are equally potential outcomes for which there are spiritual equivalents to the physical. Furthermore, as a modality of interreligious engagement, the hospitality model provides an inherently asymmetrical pattern of interaction, a correlation of role and responsibility. Hospitality, given and received, offers an opportunity to learn something of, to get to understand better, to sample the cuisine of, another. And just as with cuisine, where the act of appreciation of the other implies no necessary or profound change to one's own culinary customs, so with other aspects of hospitable engagement: the interchange and sampling are for the purposes of mutual enrichment, not conversion.

Of course, culinary openness may well—indeed often does—lead to an expansion of cuisine: modifications of eating patterns, perhaps, or the acquiring of new tastes. Generally, however, this is in the context of retaining one's fundamental eating pattern: remaining with the foods that are known to nourish, which are palatable in consumption—but, adding to that, an increased range of options, an expansion of flavours, a wider appreciation of a diversity of nourishment and enrichment. We are broadly familiar with this culinary experience as cultural phenomenon; the realm of the spiritual or religious may be viewed as analogous. Interreligious prayer provides an opportunity, on the hospitality model, to enhance our spiritual being through exposure to a wider diversity of enrichment. There is no need to treat persons of other faiths as proffering an inherently threatening cuisine. The notion of a host forcing the guest to eat that which is clearly unpalatable vitiates the principles of good hospitality, as does the idea that when someone brings their contribution to a shared meal they would expect the table to be cleared of all other offerings. Such exclusivisms would be unacceptable in the culinary realm; they are no less so in the realm of interreligious engagement.

A Christian theological perspective on prayer may adduce commonality of contextual aim as a criterion for theological legitimacy and a guide to pastoral practice. Prayer, broadly speaking, is situated in the context of redemptive transformation of the *oikoumene*. Wholeness for all is affirmed and sought for in prayer as, for example, in the paradigmatic Lord's Prayer.[6] Here I find it helpful to engage in a phenomenological-theological analysis of the Lord's Prayer. That is to say, I discover meaning and significance as I attend to the theological dynamics within the phenomenon, in this case the discourse of a prayer text that conveys meaning. Theology is revealed within the dynamics of the textual datum. Let's see how this plays out.

"Our Father in heaven . . ."

The Lord's Prayer, which in the tradition of the Christian church is arguably the paradigm of all prayer, begins in an attitude of relational attunement: the opening bidding names the focus of prayer, the intentional object to whom prayer is directed, as personal being. The sacred Other ("in heaven") is personally knowable and known, and so may be intimately addressed. *Father* is really *Abba*: God, the *mysterium tremendum et fascinans* (terrifying and fascinating mystery) may be addressed legitimately with the familiar "Dad." The term evokes an image of warm trustworthiness, of sure affection and steadfast acceptance, of reliable being-there for support and nurture. This interpretation finds its analogy in the human experience of positive relationship between children and parent, specifically in the mode of the offspring-father relationship. That the image today may be tarnished by starker experiences of fatherhood—negative images of fathers as varyingly and oppressively paternalistic, abusive, and domineering, or fathers as totally absent—does not detract from the positive evocation of theological verity contained in the prayer. The Divine is that to which address may quite properly be made in a deeply personal mode; the Divine is of itself personal and knowable in relational form.

"Holy is your name . . ."

Personal address is set within the motif of sacredness and otherness inherent in the Ultimate. Having established the intimacy and familiarity of address and relationship, the prayer then invokes boundaries and limit; that which is familiarly addressed is also that which is transcendent: "*Holy* is your name." Intimacy and familiarity do not sanction diminution of sacred integrity. The dimension of the personal does not diminish the sacral value of the Divine; God is not rendered the equivalent of human Dads. The name of God is not diminished in the modality of familial interaction and familiar spiritual relationship: the immanent association is balanced by the transcendent reference.

"Your kingdom come . . ."

This petition, which follows the opening form of address in the structure of the prayer, directs attention towards purpose and intent in the divine-human relationship. There is something of the realm of the Transcendent Other that is needful for the human realm, something that is requisite for the fullness of life itself. It is not the image utilized within the words of the prayer that is here important; "kingdom" no longer bears the socio-political signification it once did. Rather, what is perennially significant is the theological dynamic: the Ultimate, the Divine, the Absolute Other who is personally addressable and knowable, has purpose and intention for the benefit of the human realm ("kingdom") which the utterance of the prayer names as divine intent ("*Your* kingdom") and for which the prayer makes petition ("Your kingdom *come*").

"*Your will be done, on earth, as in heaven . . .*"
The invocation of the sacred *telos* (goal, end) in the invocation of the divine kingdom is then immediately strengthened. The theological dynamic borne by this phrase contains three references to the sacred Other as, first, all-important for the well-being of creation ("Your will . . . *on earth*") yet, second, not imposed or predeterminedly exercised, but rather chosen, invoked, called upon and requested ("Your will *be done* on earth") in the context such that, third, the divine will is itself something perceived to be dynamic, responsive, personal, and in essential sympathy with human being. It is good and perfect and needful for us humans, even as it is acknowledged to be not yet fully operative within the realm of human existence; and it is symbolized as belonging to, or guaranteed by virtue of already being of, the realm of the Other ("Your will be done on earth, *as in heaven*").

"*Give us this day our daily bread . . .*"
The nature of the divine reference established, the prayer then addresses human need—the motif of ultimate dependency. Human sustenance requires regular attention. Human being is not self-sufficient, physically or spiritually. But dependency is neither passive nor limited to relationship with the Divine. The ensuing petition interconnects relationship with the Divine Realm to relationship between and among human beings.

"*Forgive us our sins, as we forgive those who sin against us . . .*"
The re-establishment of sundered relationship is the ground-motif: the theme of forgiveness is the life-blood, the healing balm, which effects the desired reconciliation. And this flows from the established recognition of the personal nature of the Divine and the evocation of the will of the Divine Being as the operative guide for human existence.

"*Save us from the time of trial . . .*"
The three variants on the next line of text—"And lead us not into temptation" / "Do not bring us to the test" / "Save us from the time of trial"—all speak of an underlying anxiety to human existence, that of

going beyond the boundaries of security, sanity and personal capacity. To lose control of the sense of self, to cross into an abyss from which there is no return, evokes a fear deeper than that associated with any concern for the finality of death. For it is the prospect of a living death, of a life severed from that sustenance found in deep relationships, particularly in the relationship to the ultimate ground of existence, that constitutes the greatest time of trial from which to be saved, whether thought of in temporal or eternal terms. Such is the core relationship of Christian faith, perhaps of religion *per se*, namely that of personal spiritual relationship to the Divine Other knowable as personal Divine Being.

"But deliver us from evil . . ."

The general anxiety is then given more specific focus. Evil is that which ensnares the human spirit, dehumanizing and distorting the course of relationships, deflecting the path of authentic human being. It is antithetical to all that is good and of positive benefit and value for human life. Evil is to be avoided, but avoidance requires the assistance of the Other. The pervasiveness and subtle seduction of evil is widely attested in and by all humanity. It requires more than merely human effort to counter; it requires the aid of the Divine, the gracious intervention of God, an empowerment from beyond to bring about the desired outcome within the here and now. So this most universal and widely repeated prayer, arising from the very inception of Christian religion, gives proper and realistic acknowledgment of the lot of human existence and provides for a coping dynamic: the proper relationship with the Divine.

"For yours is the Kingdom . . ."

The prayer returns to the opening theme, but now in the context of affirmation rather than petition and supplication. The language is still that of personal familiarity ("For yours") and the image associating a connection between the realm of the Divine and the domain of the human ("is the kingdom") remains unchanged. However, lest familiarity breed contempt, the majesty of the Divine Other is asserted—*the power and the glory*—and all is couched in the context of temporal transcendence—*for ever and ever*.

What, by way of summary and conclusion, can we draw from this analysis? How might the Lord's Prayer both theologically and phenomenologically inform our understanding of prayer, and so of interreligious prayer? The theological dynamic of the Lord's Prayer clearly indicates that God, the Holy One, desires to be known personally even in the context of majestic Otherness or Holiness. Prayer begins in the acknowledgment and re-establishment, or re-iteration, of this relational dimension. God has resource, intention and desire for the well-being and proper life of humanity, and it is right for human beings to seek this in prayer. There is a Way to be human that is inherently divine: prayerful attunement aids in its attainment. God is the source of all, the point of reference for daily sustenance both materially and spiritually. This is prayerfully acknowledged, and in prayer is expressed the desire for, and the affirmation of, the transformative redeeming and preserving activity of God. Phenomenologically speaking, this prayer provides a paradigm and concomitant ontological inference whereby addressing the Divine, or the Transcendent Other, is situated in personal mode: the being of this Other is relational, both immanently personal whilst yet transcendentally other-wise or Holy. The realm of the transcendental Other and that of the human intersect, with the human requiring this Other as determinative guide and as sustaining and transforming agency. The Holy Other is that which preserves and protects; the human strives to imitate and perfect itself on the example and guidance provided from the realm of the Holy Other. Thus we may say there is a dynamic here that, when explicated in phenomenological-theological terms, may be seen to provide a point of reference for an understanding of prayer that is potentially wider than a limitedly Christian perspective, yet which neither diminishes nor compromises the Christian understanding. It adds another dimension to the Christian theological rationale for engaging in acts of interreligious prayer.

Conclusion

The challenge of prayer is to listen in depth to that which is within, around and beyond, to empty oneself of self and then be open to receive and be filled with the Other. Prayer can provide a meeting point, an opportunity for significant religious interconnection. Thus it can be a sign of hope: in many contexts a sense of redeeming hopefulness may be found for a particular disquieting situation in the sheer possibility of interreligious prayer and in what that might portend for improved communal relationships. The very act of coming together, in the full knowledge of religious difference—of holding mutually exclusive identities—yet, in humility, subjecting these differences to the embrace of an inclusive action, may of itself be a vital sign of hope in an otherwise hopelessly fraught situation. Further, thus subjecting pride in specific particularities to the intuition of a unifying transcendent mystery—the *mysterium tremendum et fascinans*, which signifies the divine Other—can provide an additional fundamental motivation for pursuing interreligious action: the act is as much a moment of faithful expression of a spiritual value found within one's own tradition as it is suggestive of some level of spiritual interconnection across religions. In interreligious prayer, participants, together, come before a universal and greater spiritual "otherness" which somehow encapsulates human alterities and difference: in the end, human beings in their religious diversity sense and experience together (though not exactly in the same way) transcendental grounding oneness. This may provide both adequate justification for the hope implied in the action and confirming motivation for the action itself. On the other hand, the absence or denial of such possibility is an occasion of real despair: if the prospect of appropriate combined prayer is precluded, there is little chance that meaningful reconciliation and relational healing will occur.

This chapter has noted paradigmatic structures and perspectives as a point of reference for a particular type of interreligious contact. It is based on the notion of discerning dynamic parallels across the variety and difference inherent in the prayers and allied devotional activities of religions, rather than seeking for a close, let alone exact, measure of equivalence by way of discerning common denominators, whether in terms of form or of content. In the context of seeking a dynamic parallelism as a starting point for approaching a prospective event of interreligious prayer, the criterion of a shared sense of ultimate coherent, congruent, and constant source and reference may be met even where the conceptual articulation and the specific beliefs about this are highly variable. Despite pronounced and profound differences, all religions that espouse a belief in God ought to readily discern a dynamic commonality of perspective around which coherent interreligious prayer may be approached. Even a non-theistic religion such as Buddhism, which eschews a belief in God such as is foundational to Christianity, may be amenable to the suggestion that dynamic parallelisms of spiritual intuition and conceptual association may be discerned; hence, the notion of an appropriate interreligious prayer event is not vitiated a priori.

Among other modalities, interreligious relations may embrace cognitive engagement found in dialogical conversation on the one hand and spiritual engagement as in a shared event of prayer on the other. The cognitive and the spiritual are together required where dialogue seeks deeper understanding each of the other and in the pursuit of any deeper being-together in community. Prayer, universally speaking, is suggestive of an ultimate coherence and congruence in the sense that, whatever the perspective of the religious foreground, the background or underlying conceptuality is invariably that of a perception of an ultimate coherence to the universe, a fundamental congruence between the experience of life as lived and the spiritual context in which life is set. Interreligious prayer, especially in the *coherent-integrated* mode, offers opportunity for an appropriate and mutually respectful spiritual event of sharing, an engagement that is itself both cognitive and experiential.

9. FAITHFUL OPENNESS
IDENTITY AND INTERRELIGIOUS DIALOGUE

A FEW YEARS AGO ONE OF BRITAIN'S LEADING CHRISTIAN INTERFAITH specialists produced a book on living as a Christian in a religiously plural world.[1] As with my own approach, the book's author, Andrew Wingate, wrote in "the conviction that the question of Christian response to people of other faiths is relevant everywhere, theologically, spiritually, pastorally and practically, as well as locally, nationally and internationally."[2] The purpose of my book is to explore aspects of Christian involvement in interreligious relations as well as issues of Christian response to, and thinking about, interfaith engagement. Irrespective of our denominational church affiliation and theological inclinations that together contribute to our religious identity, Christian identity, generally speaking, involves seeing ourselves as part of a community of faith which is on a mission— God's mission (*missio Dei*) which upholds certain truths and values as God-given; which is responding to God's call to discipleship and service in and to the world. We express all this, and more besides, in many and varied ways. But a core dimension to all is the centrality of Christ, without which we could not call ourselves Christian, and an understanding that in the person of Jesus there was made manifest, historically, the redemptive action of God significant and meaningful for all humankind. This action, we Christians believe, is relevant and applicable everywhere and at all times, which is also of vital significance "theologically, spiritually, pastorally and practically, as well as locally, nationally and internationally," to repeat Wingate's sentiments. Today it is both God's action in Christ and our Christian engagement with peoples of other faiths which are of co-relative significance. Evidence for this comes from the fact that the church, in recent times, has endeavoured to hold together the motifs of both interreligious dialogue and evangelical proclamation with respect to relating to peoples of other faiths.[3]

Evidence also comes out in the often vexed issue of how we live out our identity as faithful followers of Christ without closing ourselves off to what God may be doing, revealing, and accomplishing in and through our neighbours of other faiths.[4] Often we assume that in order to be true to our Christian identity, we need to resist the encroachment of another religion: we think we need to exclude, rather than be open to, the religious other. Many Christians around the world take this position in one form or another. It is my suggestion, reinforced by exploring what has gone on with the Christian church more widely with respect to interreligious dialogue and interfaith engagement (Part II above) and by examining a range of issues (Parts I and III), that holding to our identity as Christian and being open to appropriate relationship to a person of another faith—and indeed being open to the truths, values and insights of another religion—are not mutually exclusive. Interreligious dialogue does not diminish our faith-identity; it requires us to think even more deeply about it and to strengthen and refine it. Faithful openness is not only possible; it is a valid and vibrant option that enhances Christian identity. Let us explore this idea further. How might we live out our Christian identity in a spirit of faithful openness?

Christians are monotheists. And for the most part Christians hold a Trinitarian understanding of God. Here Jesus is not another divine being alongside God (that would be bi-theism) but rather understood to manifest and present the reality of the one God in, with, and to human existence (the historical Jesus was not God *per se*; rather God was working in and through the person of Jesus: monotheism is upheld). However, Jesus' being denoted Son of God establishes first and foremost a unique relationship and role as historical figure (Jesus of Nazareth) and, post-resurrection, as the risen Christ signifying that the God present in Jesus manifests the values and dynamics of love, forgiveness, acceptance, self-giving and transcendent inspiration that are not in themselves historically or contextually bounded. It is this that invites us to go beyond the boundaries of our thinking, our assumptions, whatever we regard as the religious norm. It invites us to be open to a new future, a new way of being, one which accords with and reflects the divine purpose for human creation even more authentically than we may have imagined previously. This is all of God and is given expression in human understanding by the dynamic Christian Trinitarian concept of God: God the Father, God the Son and God the Holy Spirit—not three divine beings, but the three dynamic and relational dimensions of the one living God. Much more can be said about the Trinity, of course, but for our purposes what is essential is the sense in which we are engaged with a relationally dynamic divine reality; whilst apprehended through the legacy of tradition, this reality is nonetheless not bound or delimited in any final way by the traditions of our thinking and conceptualizations.

The task of theology involves the dynamic tension between the teachings of and about our faith, which comes to us from our respective ecclesial traditions, and the sense that, in the end, God and God's purposes are more than what our traditions encompass. If this is so, then the issue of Christian relation to and theological appreciation of other faiths is located in the midst of that tension. So it is that one of the critical issues of our time is discovering what it means to be both true to our own faith and authentically open to relationship with a person of another faith—to know and hold the truths that comprise the substantial beliefs of our religion, yet recognize, and where appropriate, acknowledge and respect, the beliefs and perspectives that comprise the truth proclaimed by another religion. However, it is not uncommon, I have found, for Christians in many parts of the world, when asked about the place of other religions, or what should be the Christian attitude to persons of other faiths, to respond with variations on the theme of exclusivism: salvation is only through faith in Christ; he is the one true way to God. People of other faiths may be well-meaning, they might say, and we need to be friendly toward them, but in essence they have got it wrong. In the end, the task of Christian mission is to bring Christ to all people and all people to Christ. I hope that if you have read through this book, you will have begun to sense the sheer limitation of this position. It is a naïve and unreflective identification of and with the Christian story of Jesus; it falls short of *God's* story. A fuller theological appreciation and understanding of God and God's story needs to take place.

Paul Hedges frames the issue, for Christians, as one of a contrast between closed, or exclusivist, and open perspectives. Although the issue of "whether those outside Christianity can be saved at all, or even whether they can be approached with any degree of openness" has been a central and dominant debate within Christian circles since the late 19th century, in reality it is now a pseudo-issue, primarily because of the generally inclusivist position that is the formal stance of all the main churches such that the portrayal of other religions as "demonic or utterly false . . . has become a fringe belief."[5] Hedges also acknowledges that even though "many ordinary Christians are exclusivist, this is due, partly, to a misunderstanding or lack of awareness as to what their church teaches, combined with the fact that, for many, they have never really considered the issue."[6] Hedges also notes the impact of ecumenism in providing a paradigm for cross-faith relationships: "Once it is accepted that there are various versions of Christian truth, and so not just one correct way of believing or being Christian (and therefore of being saved), a theological door is opened to other religions."[7] I think Hedges is on the right track. The simple rehearsal of the Jesus story, in isolation from deep reflection upon the "God story," yields a wholly inadequate response and appreciation of other religions and *their* story of God—where that applies: not all religions are equal in this regard, since not all religions believe in a God, but certainly it applies to all religions that express belief in God in some sense; who are we to declare otherwise? And this is the rub; whatever the religion, it also has a story. It may be different from ours, but it cannot be written off automatically as a non-story so far as *our* understanding of the fullness of God's story is concerned. It was what the missionary movement of the 19th century came up against and which, in part, led to the famous Edinburgh World Missionary Conference of 1910. That in turn was a spur both to the birth of the Christian ecumenical movement and to the nascent interfaith movement begun, effectively, by the 1893 Parliament of World Religions that met in Chicago.

For well over a century, Christians have been wrestling with the profound and provocative question of identity in the context of religious plurality: how to be true to our faith in Christ and at the same time how to be open to others not of our faith. Put this way, we see the question being worked out in two modes: the interchurch and the interfaith. The first is the province of ecumenism—the move to break down barriers of divisions between Christians, even working to reverse the fissiparous tendencies of the past in order to bring about full organic institutional union (or reunion) of churches. The field of interfaith relations, interreligious dialogue and interfaith cooperation presents striking dynamic similarities to ecumenism with respect to key questions and issues, but significant differences of goal and aim. Interestingly, the 1988 Lambeth Conference of the Anglican Communion spoke "of the need to correct our particular expression of Christian faith in the light of other Christian experience" on the one hand, and admitted, on the other, the prospect that Christians "may also have to correct it in the light of the commitment of non-Christians."[8] It also spoke of "daring to believe that we will see there something of the presence of the God who called them, no less than us, into being who and what they are . . . [and so] . . . it does not surprise us to find echoes of the Gospel in the deep convictions of our non-Christian brothers and sisters."[9] A potentially wider fruitful comparison of interchurch and interreligious dialogue could well be made, both for the purposes of investigating methodological and relational issues and to probe theological rationales and implications. This investigation could also be helpful, importantly, in investigating the problems and prospects of holding and maintaining discrete religious identity within a religiously pluralist milieu so as to be able to affirm both. Simple encounters are the foundational stuff of interfaith engagement—interactions where acceptance of the other in his or her otherness and respect shown in word or gesture demonstrate that acceptance is more than mere tolerance.

Without doubt there has been an upsurge of new interest in interreligious dialogue in this 21st century of the Common Era, and much of it, ironically, has been spurred on by the tragic events of 9/11 and their aftermath. To this extent, dialogue and interfaith engagement involving Islam and Muslims has tended to predominate, although there are many multifaith as well as bilateral dialogical engagements that have taken place, and continue to be undertaken, between Christians and people of other faiths. One of the effects of 9/11 has been the emergence, on the part of many political leaders, of the need to address religious issues and harness religious leadership and sensibilities for the sake of communal harmony and global security. Interfaith concerns and activities have become a priority in many quarters.[10] With respect to Christian-Muslim relations, there are two Anglican initiatives that are worth noting and reflecting on. First, there is the Al-Azhar Agreement from the "Joint Commission of Anglican Christians and Sunni Muslims" with al-Azhar University in Cairo. Second, there is the "Building Bridges" seminar series. Both of these Christian-Muslim dialogical events were set in motion in 2002 by the then Archbishop of Canterbury, George Carey. Both have resulted in a pattern of scholarly meetings, virtually on an annual basis, hosted alternately by Christian and Muslim organizers. Carey is on record as having stated: "our responsibilities as religious leaders and scholars [is] to help our communities live together in ways which do not suppress our own identities but open us up to the riches which the other offers." He has also noted that this invites Christian participants in interfaith activities to dare "to believe that God has drawn us together. In neither of our faiths is God a subject of idle curiosity. We are concerned with the living, loving God who brought all things into being and who seeks to bring his creation to its proper fulfilment, with the human family living together in justice and peace."[11] In both cases Muslim participation, full engagement, and support have been readily forthcoming. In the case of the Building Bridges seminar series, Christian involvement has not been limited to Anglicans; rather the Anglican initiative has been fulfilled on the Christian side by being also an exemplary ecumenical venture.

In his introduction to the book from the first Building Bridges meeting, Michael Ipgrave remarked that the aim of the series is "to explore how these two monotheistic religions can contribute to finding solutions rather than perpetuating problems, and—as as a first step toward that—to create an environment in which some of the obstacles to mutual understanding could be overcome."[12] On the one hand, there is the desire to see substantial outcomes; on the other the recognition that in order to achieve such outcomes, something else must first happen (and continue to happen), namely, the facilitating of relationships: engendering a climate of mutual respect, hospitality and trust. Ipgrave reflects this in his comment that "the mapping out of common ground, the respectful acknowledgement of difference, and the firm commitment to future collegiality" would not only mark out the *modus operandi* of the seminars, but would also "give some hope and encouragement to Christians and Muslims who are engaged in the issues in practical ways" wherever they may be: "the God to whom we witness is calling us to engage more deeply and trustfully with one another for the sake of his world."[13] Building relationship, as much as discerning substantive cognitive issues and outcomes, set the scene for the second of the seminar events, where the intent was "to make better sense of how we relate to the other."[14] Relationships marked by mutual trust and acceptance require the honest addressing of difficulties and stumbling blocks, and this seemed to be directly the case with the third meeting in the Building Bridges series, where relationship developed in the process of "finding the appropriate language in which difference can be talked about rather than used as an excuse for violent separation."[15] The effect of this relationship building process was seen to significant degree with the 2005 seminar co-hosted by Muslims, Serbian Orthodox and Roman Catholics of Sarajevo, following some ten years of bitter internal strife. It was the developing climate of deep relational and scholarly trust that enabled the addressing of more problematic concerns of justice and rights at the 2006 seminar. "What is remarkable about the material presented," Ipgrave writes, "is the extent to which it shows that Muslims and Christians are facing similar issues, even if the answers they give can differ quite radically."[16] This was carried over and further developed the following year when the seminar focused on "a shared sense of common purpose in addressing issues that affect us equally and inseparably."[17] Furthermore, at this 2007 event, for the first time "some Qur'anic texts were introduced by Christian scholars, and some biblical texts were introduced by Muslim scholars" and it was noted that such a cross-reading may "be seen as a sign of the collegiality that is possible when faithful believers who have grown to trust and respect one another meet in openness in the presence of their respective scriptures."[18] The relational aspirations evinced in the first would seem to have borne distinctive fruit in this, the sixth gathering.

The Building Bridges seminar series completed its first decade with the 10th meeting held in May, 2011. It may have been an Anglican initiative and commitment in the first instance; it is by no means an Anglican affair alone. *Intra*religious as well as *inter*religious relations have been drawn upon, developed and strengthened in and through this series. David Marshall notes that

> Building Bridges has developed its own distinctive approach to Muslim-Christian dialogue, stressing theological dialogue based on the study of scriptural texts. The aim has not been to achieve immediately demonstrable results but rather to nurture a long-term conversation on key issues at the heart of both faiths. . . . A number of participants have returned year after year, thus creating a committed core group which brings a valuable sense of community and continuity.[19]

Clearly this has been, and promises to continue as, a ground-breaking series. Though undertaken at a rather high scholarly level, it will nonetheless continue to witness to the propriety and possibility of such Christian-Muslim theological engagement and serve to encourage Christians and Muslims elsewhere in the world to take seriously the capacity to talk theologically together—neither to ameliorate real difference nor to act as a cover for a missionizing agenda, but to enable a better level of spiritual sharing and mutual understanding than might otherwise be the case. And, indeed, the series of books now published that contain the core material of the meetings of this series will be a significant resource which many more "grassroots" dialogical groups will find useful. Even as these Anglican initiatives were getting underway in 2002, in Germany an ecumenical group of younger scholars, based in Stuttgart, set in motion an initiative that by 2005 was to emerge as the Christian-Muslim Theological Forum (*Theologisches Forum Christentum-Islam*). This has resulted in a series of annual conferences and the production of books of valuable scholarly insight and exchange arising therefrom.[20] Without a doubt, the first decade of the 21st century has seen many activities and a plethora of institutes and centres pursuing various aspects of relationship and dialogue with the world of Islam. And where there has been an intentional Christian-Muslim theological engagement, as in the examples noted above, issues of identity and openness one to the other have been very much to the fore.

Within a few years of the establishment of these dialogical events there was a response, in 2007, emanating from the Muslim side. Admittedly it was provoked by the ill-fated "Regensburg Address" given by Pope Benedict XVI in 2006 and also by the Danish "Cartoon Affair" of 2005-06. The response was prompted by a real concern on the part of Muslim leadership for the future of both Islam and Christianity in a context of rising polarization, persecutions and extremism, mostly emanating from the Muslim side. So it was that the letter known as *A Common Word*, was sent to the Pope, the Archbishop of Canterbury and many other named Christian leaders around the globe, a letter intended, indeed, for all Christian leaders everywhere.[21] It was initially signed by well over a hundred Muslim leaders and scholars from around the world. Many hundreds more have since endorsed it. Significantly, the letter invites Christians to enter a new phase of dialogue with Muslims based on the common theological heritage that interlinks Judaism, Christianity and Islam, including the core affirmation to love God and to love neighbour. There has been a raft of responses from Christian leaders, councils and institutions, both denominational and ecumenical; as well as a number of conferences and consultations have been convened to consider the letter and reflect on its invitation. Among the more substantial responses was that of Rowan Williams, Archbishop of Canterbury. After an initial positive message in a press release in which Williams "welcomed the letter as a clear reaffirmation of the potential for further development of existing dialogue and common action between Christians and Muslims and other faith communities,"[22] he undertook a wide-ranging ecumenical consultation before composing his formal reply. The archbishop's document, *A Common Word for the Common Good,* is addressed to "the Muslim Religious Leaders and Scholars who have signed *A Common Word Between Us and You* and to Muslim brothers and sisters everywhere."[23] It has been well received. Williams notes the Muslim letter's spirit of "a helpful generosity of intention" and interprets the Muslim invitation to Christians as not seeking a facile quick accord but the more modest quest to "find a way of recognising that on some matters we are speaking enough of a common language for us to be able to pursue both exploratory dialogue and peaceful co-operation with integrity . . . without compromising fundamental beliefs." Indeed, the Muslim invitation is "a powerful call to dialogue and collaboration between Christians and Muslims" for which the "very wide geographical (43 countries) and theological diversity represented among the signatories . . . provides a unique impetus to deepen and extend the encounters." The archbishop goes on to assert: "What we need as a vision for our dialogue is to break the current cycles of violence, to show the world that faith and faith alone can truly ground a commitment to peace which definitively abandons the tempting but lethal cycle of retaliation in which we simply imitate each other's violence."[24] Williams ends his letter with by affirming mutual education, the continued engagement in living practical issues and the commitment to a long-haul process as the essence of the practical response to the Muslim letter: "to your invitation to enter more deeply into dialogue and collaboration as a part of our faithful response to the revelation of God's purposes for humankind, we say: Yes! Amen."[25] The outworking of the Christian response to the Muslim initiative is an ongoing story.

Another Anglican initiative, this time addressing more directly the ongoing issue of Christian engagement in interreligious dialogue *per se,* is found in the 2008 document arising out of work undertaken by the London-based Network of Inter Faith Concerns (NIFCON) which is a worldwide activity of the Anglican Communion. The statement addresses issues of Christian identity with respect to interfaith relations. Entitled *Generous Love*, the report of the network offers a clue in its foreword: "Many Christians are torn between wanting to affirm the importance of dialogue and not wanting to compromise their allegiance to the one Lord and Saviour whom they proclaim as the desire of all nations." It goes on to note that the document

> is offered for study to the Anglican Communion—and more widely—in the hope that it will stimulate further theological thinking . . . [concerning the] . . . double conviction that we must regard dialogue as an imperative from Our Lord, yet must also witness consistently to the unique gift we have been given in Christ.[26]

Rather than being in any sense a last word, this is a document that endeavours, in a fairly succinct manner, to articulate the contours of a broadly Anglican perspective so as to open up the question of theological reflection upon interfaith engagement for wider consideration. Grounded in the affirmation of the Trinity, reflecting on contemporary context and Anglican heritage, the document asserts the place of scripture, tradition and reason in theological method and focuses on the twin themes of the "embassy" and "hospitality" of God with respect to the *modus vivendi* of Christian engagement in interfaith relations. The concerns this Anglican document addresses, and the theological emphases it seeks to elucidate, have wider resonance in the Christian world.

So, where is all this taking us? If the above are all good examples of positive dialogical engagement and reflection in which the Christian participants are very happy to engage—participants who certainly are very clear and committed in their Christian identity—where does that leave the vast majority of Christians who are not engaged in interfaith relations in any great dialogical depth, if at all, and who might have a range of theological queries and spiritual concerns yet to be satisfactorily addressed? How might we proceed? For myself, as an Anglican who has come from a Methodist background and upbringing, I have found the so-called Wesleyan Quadrilateral of scripture, tradition, reason and experience to provide a useful methodological approach as well as a framework for engaging the question of Christian identity. John Wesley was an Anglican priest his whole life, even though his evangelical and theological work led to the rise of Methodism as, in the end, a new denomination alongside the Church of England rather than remaining a vivifying movement within it. But that is another story. What is of interest here is that this 18th century Christian thinker and priestly minister articulated these four dimensions of Christian life and authority in a way that remains pertinent and useful. As Christians, we take it as given that our faith is founded on *scripture* that bears witness to the revelation of God in history and through Christ. Further, we recognize that the church, through history, has evolved a raft of teachings, reflections and positions that are judged to appropriately extend Christian understanding, and so belief, beyond even the pages of the Bible: and so we add to the scripture the reality of *tradition*, which incorporates the historic creeds, for example, as well as much more. In essence this tells us that, although we may read the Bible as individuals and we may find God's word therein speaking to us, our individual reading and understanding sits alongside the collective wisdom of interpretation, exegesis and theological reflection that comes down to us through the history of the church, including recent history.

This brings us to the third dimension: *reason*. God has given us minds to use. The principles of rational and appropriately critical thinking have ever been applied: theology is as much "God logic" as it is "God word or talk," for the very notion of *logos* refers to both rationality (logic) and speech (word). God's word is rational; God does not speak, or act, confusedly, meaninglessly or capriciously. Together with attending to the scriptural text and the tradition of the church that accompanies it, we are called to use the best thinking we can in understanding, extending and applying our faith today. And to do that properly, we need also to take account of *experience*— that is, the contemporary insights and empirical findings of our time. This is what enables us to be rooted in the real world and not the world of some spiritual fancy or long lost past. The faith of the ages is to be—indeed must become—the faith of today. Just as the best thinkers of the past engaged in making Christian faith present and meaningful to their contemporaries, relating theological insight to current concerns and interests, so too must we engage in thinking and applying our faith afresh, not simply enacting a regurgitation of stale formulae and rancid interpretation. Daily bread is freshly baked; the bread of heaven is renewed every morning. Our lived experience—the reality of the world as we find and inhabit it, and the insights and understanding of life as we live and encounter it—is vastly different in many respects, whilst also admittedly unchanged in others, from that of our forefathers and mothers who have bequeathed us the Tradition, and traditions, in which we stand, together with the scriptures we reverently read. So, by applying this methodological quadrilateral we may and do discover that there is no necessary incompatibility in holding identity as a Christian and being open to the presence and value of other faiths.

Experience shows us that there is both good and bad in all religions, Christianity included. It has been said we ought not to compare the best of our own with the worst of another's; rather we should compare saints with saints and, if we must, sinners with sinners. And in so doing, as did missionaries early on in the modern period, we find the assumptions arising out of an uncritical acceptance of tradition being challenged. We have to think again, use our minds to look again at scripture, to reconsider tradition—and to be open, above all, to the new thing that God is perhaps showing us, endeavouring to open our eyes and our hearts. For example, the *Generous Love* document I noted above affirms not only scripture as a necessary component within interfaith dialogue, but also "that Scripture is to be interpreted in the light of tradition and reason . . . shaped by . . . lived experiences."[27] Furthermore, this document suggests,

> our human relationships at their best are marked by a dynamism and interactivity capable of changing all involved through genuine encounters which lead us into new life. Those we called "other" are no longer over against us, but present to us and us to them, human beings whose energy connects with ours and ours with theirs, those who are fellow guests in God's house with us. . . . We will listen to and receive from our neighbours even while we speak and give to them, and in this mutuality of encounter we can experience God's gracious presence in a new way.[28]

Another Anglican document notes that it is nonsensical to affirm on the one hand that God is love and yet to say, on the other hand, that "God brings millions into the world to damn them. The God of Love also longs for all to come into relationship with him, and this is his purpose in creation."[29] To be sure, religions differ on points of fact and matters of interpretation. Nevertheless, as Christians, we "assert that God can and does work in people of other religions, and indeed within other religions, and that this is by his Spirit," and it is this that provides the "essential basis for genuine dialogue."[30] Furthermore,

> by living and working with people of other faiths, and by recognising their integrity and faithfulness as well as, in many cases, their goodness and love, questions of salvation arise. Can the God of love, revealed in Christ, reject such people whom we admire? They follow a way of life based upon religious discipline, prayer and reading of Scriptures. Can the quality of their lives be separated from their religious belief? If not, how can we find an adequate way of speaking of salvation, one that both affirms the significance of the biblical witness to Christ and at the same time can take account of what we see before us?[31]

A helpful summary of a theological rationale for interreligious relations and engagement in dialogue is offered by Andrew Wingate. In many respects it echoes what we have discussed in previous chapters. In the context of reflecting on the question of Christian identity vis-à-vis interreligious dialogue, it is worth repeating and discussing here. Christian faith affirms that God is the creator of all, and that creation is good.[32] It is worth pausing a moment to reflect on the chief image of God's good creation, the Garden of Eden, and to ask: Of what did the garden consist? How might we think of this archetypal handiwork of the Creator? What would seem a just and right image of it? Would it be a minimalist garden, perhaps a single rose, together with that apple tree, in an expanse of grass? Or do we envisage more a glorious profusion of diverse plant life, a rich kaleidoscope of flora and fauna that befits our sense of the absolute majesty of the God who creates? And if we sense this is the more appropriate, why then presume that the creation of humanity, represented by the primal couple in the Garden, would have been divinely envisaged as a singularity of "look" such that the rich diversity of race, language and ethnicity that has ever comprised humanity can only ever be comprehended as a consequence of the so-called Fall? Might it not be more theologically appropriate to recognize that the diversity of God's good creation extends also to human being such that the diversity of humanity, including the religious life of human beings, is within, not outside, the divine will of the Creator? The Christian perception of the human need for redemption transcends human diversity; redemption does not vitiate this diversity but rather embraces it.

As Wingate expresses it, "Christ died for all, not just for Christians, and therefore the person I meet from another faith is someone for whom Christ died, in the same way that he died for me."[33] So we affirm God's love is for all and we respond to this love in showing love to our neighbour—who could be anyone and who, theologically, is everyone. Furthermore, in our world today, where there is a sense of an increasing polarity around religion, to engage in interfaith relations is to show "that division is not inevitable" and this, indeed, is one way of enacting love of neighbour: "Can we show that religions and cultures can co-exist in peace and harmony? . . . Are we to work together or are we to work separately, even against each other?"[34] In the context of pressing practical needs and issues, many have discovered that their faith is strengthened, not weakened or diluted, in the context of interreligious engagement and dialogical sharing. Openness to our neighbour of another faith does not vitiate our own faith; it can rather be the fulcrum around which we deepen and extend our very Christian identity as we discover what the living out of God's commandment to love entails, and as we discern the deeper meaning to our affirmation of God as Creator and Redeemer of all. Interreligious engagement can, and does, "lead to a journey of discovery." Engaging in interreligious activities and dialogue "can be an outward and visible sign that religious people can grow together and not apart," which gives rise the the challenging question: "Are we to work together or are we to work separately, even against each other?"[35] And part of that journey of discovery is that there are many shared values across a wide range of religions. Often it is this that gives a sense, sometimes overstated but nevertheless of considerable significance, that religions are but variations of the same "thing." To be sure, a common point of moral reference such as that expressed by the Golden Rule does impress with its universal import across widely differing religious contexts. To acknowledge this does not imply any amelioration of real difference. Phenomenologically speaking, there is great diversity within and between religions, hence the ongoing discussions and debates concerning the meaning of, and response to, this very plurality.

Christian identity has sometimes been expressed in reference to the Vincentian Canon, namely "that which has been believed everywhere, always, and by all people" (*quod ubique, quod semper, quod ab omnibus creditum est*).[36] There is perhaps a long-standing notion that Christian identity is, or ought to be, singular, unchanged and unchanging. The reality of Christian diversity is thus seen to be a "scandal" because it detracts from a supposed ideal of singularity. But remember the idea of the Garden of Eden: is singularity the proper mark of the Creator? I suggest not. Hedges remarks that "Christian theology is not simply about accepting a unitary and undisputed tradition . . . Rather Christianity and Christian theology is about the creation and recreation of identity."[37] Our very Christian identity, both as individuals and as communities of faith is itself something that is in process. Indeed, from the outset, "Christianity does not just appear as a 'given' and ready-made system, but is produced in interaction with the cultures and religions that surround it."[38] The history of the Christian church, including theological thinking and church teaching, is a story of change, development, contestation and variety. Our God-given identity as a people of faith is not a singularity of sameness but a rich diversity of differentiation. So it was in the Creator's garden. So it is with the Creator's creation. So it is with humanity. So it is with faith. Variety of perception, understanding and expression is part and parcel of the Christian experience and, as Hedges usefully notes,

> Christianity has always been created in interaction with other creeds, systems of belief and religious identities, and so we must allow ourselves to retell the Christian story again, and in the act to recreate it as we engage the contemporary globalized world situation and forge a sense of what Christian identity may be in this context.[39]

What holds the great diversity of Christian identities together in a family of faith is the common focus on Jesus, the Christ. In the gospel accounts of the activities and teachings of Jesus we can certainly see an example of radical openness to and acceptance of others who are otherwise shunned, despised and cast out. It is this leitmotif of the way of Jesus, understood as manifesting the divine will for the way of being human, which for me and many others of Christian faith prompts the extension of this openness to the followers of other faiths and to a consideration of the nature and reality of the religions of the world as somehow legitimately within the purview of God's diverse creation. It is this which calls us today "to adopt a radical openness in our dealing with the religious Others we encounter."[40] Such openness suggests growth in learning and in relationship across religions, as when we see the work of God in the faith of others or meet Christ in our neighbour. This has been expressed by the German theologian Reinhold Bernhardt as "an inclusivism of mutuality" wherein each commences from his or her own side, yet each is open "to the challenging otherness of other religions."[41] Openness to our neighbour of another faith may allow a mutuality of spiritual growth and fulfilment such that the integrity of the religious identity of each is enhanced by interfaith engagement and dialogue. This is the hope; for many, including myself, it is the reality.

NOTES

Preface
1. I will use "interfaith" and "interreligious" interchangeably throughout this book.

Introduction
1. Andrew Wingate, *Celebrating Difference, Staying Faithful: How to Live in a Multi-Faith World* (London: Darton, Longman and Todd, 2005), 67.

2. Ibid.

3. Ibid.

4. Mark Woods, "Talking about Religions, Doing Faith," 22 February 2006, http://www.oikoumene.org/en/news/news-management/eng/a/browse/16/article/1634/talking-about-religions-1.html.

5. For a full discussion see Douglas Pratt, *The Church and Other Faiths: The World Council of Churches, the Vatican, and Interreligious Dialogue* (Bern: Peter Lang, 2010).

6. Initially, this was, within the WCC, a programme Sub-unit on Dialogue with People of Other Faiths and Ideologies (DFI), then the Office on Inter-Religious Relations (OIRR). Later the Office for Inter-Religious Relations and Dialogue (IRRD), it is now the Programme for Interreligious Dialogue and Cooperation (IRDC). At the Vatican, this was initially the Secretariat for Non-Christians (SNC), which later became the Pontifical Council for Interreligious Dialogue (PCID).

7. Wingate, *Celebrating Difference*, 11.

8. Ibid., 5.

9. Ibid., 6.

10. Ibid., 8.

11. Ibid.

12. Ibid., 9.

13. Stanley Samartha, "Dialogue as a Continuing Christian Concern," in *Christianity and Other Religions*, ed. John Hick and Brian Hebblethwaite (London: Collins, 1980), 151.

14. Raimundo Panikkar, Preface, in *Hindu-Christian Dialogue: Perspectives and Encounters*, ed. Harold Coward (Maryknoll, NY: Orbis, 1989), xiii.

15. See Douglas Pratt, "The Dance of Dialogue," *Ecumenical Review* 51, no. 3 (July 1999): 274–87.

16. Stuart Brown, *Meeting in Faith* (Geneva: WCC Publications, 1989), 3.

17. Ibid., 4.

18. Wingate, *Celebrating Difference*, 2.

1. Preliminary Considerations
1. Andrew Wingate, *Celebrating Difference, Staying Faithful* (London: Darton, Longman and Todd, 2005), 11.

2. Ibid., 69.

3. Ibid.

4. Theodore Ludwig, *The Sacred Paths* (New York: Macmillan, 1989), 512.

5. Ibid., 514.

6. David Lochhead, *The Dialogical Imperative: A Christian Reflection on Interfaith Encounter* (London: SCM Press, 1988).

7. Ibid., 41.

8. Ibid.

9. Ibid.

10. Ibid.

11. Ibid., 12.

12. Ibid.

13. Ibid.

14. Ibid., 26.

15. Ibid.

16. Ibid., 66.

17. Ibid., 69.

18. See Norman Solomon, "The Third Presence: Reflections on the Dialogue" in *Dialogue with a Difference*, ed. Tony Bayfield and Marcus Braybrooke (London: SCM Press, 1992), 147–62.

19. See Douglas Pratt, *Religion: A First Encounter* (Auckland: Longman Paul, 1993), 5.

20. Ibid.

21. There is nothing new in this summary; it echoes many such that are found elsewhere.

22. Wesley Ariarajah, Introduction to Kuala Lumpur "Implications of Interfaith Dialogue for Theological Education Today" Consultation by WCC Sub-unit on Dialogue and WCC Programme for Theological Education (Geneva: WCC, June 1985), 3.

23. Ibid., 2.

24. Ibid.

25. Ibid., 3.

26. I will attend below in chapter 2 to the distinction between plurality and pluralism.

27. Paul Hedges, *Controversies in Interreligious Dialogue and the Theology of Religions* (London: SCM Press, 2010), 10.

28. The Lambeth Conference, *The Report of the Lambeth Conference 1978* (London: CIO Publishing, 1978), 52.

29. Ibid., 89.

30. Ibid., 92.

31. Chester Gillis, *Pluralism: A New Paradigm for Theology* (Louvain: Peeters Press; Grand Rapids: Eerdmans, 1993), 40.

32. Jonathan Sacks, *The Dignity of Difference* (London and New York: Continuum, 2007), 4.

33. Ibid., 4–5.

2. Contending with Diversity

1. Gary Bouma, *Australian Soul: Religion and Spirituality in the Twenty-first Century* (Melbourne: Cambridge University Press, 2006), 1.

2. Kenneth Cracknell, *Considering Dialogue: Theological Themes in Interfaith Relations, 1970–1980* (London: British Council of Churches, 1981).

3. See J. Mark Hensman, "Beyond Talk: The Dialogue of Life" (Unpublished DTheol thesis, Melbourne College of Divinity, 1999), 39.

4. Peter Byrne, *Prolegomena to Religious Pluralism: Reference and Realism in Religion* (London: Macmillan, 1995), vii.

5. For a wider ranging discussion, see also Paul Hedges, *Controversies in Interreligious Dialogue and the Theology of Religions* (London: SCM Press, 2010).

6. Diana L. Eck, *Encountering God: A Spiritual Journey from Bozeman to Banares* (Boston: Beacon Press, 1993), 174.

7. It was at the Council of Florence that the definitive formulation of "no salvation outside the church" took place in 1442.

8. John Hick, *God and the Universe of Faiths*, rev. ed. (London: Collins, 1977), 121.

9. W. A. Visser t' Hooft, *No Other Name: The Choice between Syncretism and Christian Universalism* (London: SCM Press, 1963), 88.

10. See Hendrik Kraemer, *The Christian Message in a Non-Christian World* (London: Edinburgh House Press, 1938).

11. Ibid., 95.

12. For a discussion of the attempt by the Exclusive Brethren Church to impose its ideology onto the political arena in New Zealand, Australia and Canada, see Nicky Hager, *The Hollow Men* (Nelson: Craig Cotton Publishing, 2006).

13. The term "anonymous Christian" was first used by the Roman Catholic theologian Karl Rahner. in the early 1960s, immediately before the Second Vatican Council.

14. Diogenes Allen, *Christian Belief in a Postmodern World* (Louisville: Westminster John Knox, 1989), 187.

15. See Raimundo Panikkar, *The Unknown Christ of Hinduism*, rev. ed. (Maryknoll, NY: Orbis, 1981).

16. Byrne, *Prolegomena to Religious Pluralism*, vii.

17. Ibid.

18. John Hick, *The Rainbow of Faiths* (London: SCM Press, 1995), 15.

19. John Hick, *God and the Universe of Faiths*, rev. ed. (London: Collins, 1977), 131.

20. Hick, *God and the Universe of Faiths*, 139.

21. Ibid., 137.

22. John Hick, *The Metaphor of God Incarnate* (London: SCM Press, 1993), 140.

23. John Hick, *The Myth of God Incarnate* (London: SCM Press, 1977), 181.

24. Hick, *The Metaphor of God Incarnate,* 140.

25. See for example, John Cobb, *Beyond Dialogue: Toward a Mutual Transformation of Christianity and Buddhism* (Philadelphia: Fortress, 1982); see also Leonard Swidler et al., *Death or Dialogue?* (London: SCM Press, 1990).

26. See S. Wesley Ariarajah, *Hindus and Christians: A Century of Protestant Ecumenical Thought* (Amsterdam: Rodopi; Grand Rapids: Eerdmans, 1991), 178.

27. Ibid.

28. See Paul Hedges, *Controversies in Interreligious Dialogue*, especially 146ff.; see also Paul Hedges, "Particularities: Tradition-Specific Post-modern Perspectives," in *Christian Approaches to Other Faiths*, ed. Alan Race and Paul M. Hedges (London: SCM Press, 2008), 112–35.

29. Mark Heim, *Salvations: Truth and Difference in Religion* (Maryknoll, NY: Orbis, 1995) and idem, *The Depth of the Riches: A Trinitarian Theology of Religious Ends* (Grand Rapids: Eerdmans, 2001).

30. See Paul F. Knitter, *No Other Name? A Critical Survey of Christian Attitudes Toward the World Religions* (Maryknoll, NY: Orbis, 1985) and idem, *One Earth Many Religions: Multifaith Dialogue & Global Responsibility* (Maryknoll, NY: Orbis, 1995).

31. Cited in Ariarajah, *Hindus and Christians*, 177.

32. Ninian Smart, *The World's Religions* (Cambridge: Cambridge University Press, 1989). See also Theodore Ludwig, *The Sacred Paths* (New York: McGraw-Hill, 1991) and Douglas Pratt, *Religion: A First Encounter* (Auckland: Longman Paul, 1993).

33. Hans Küng, *Global Responsibility: In Search of a New World Ethic* (London: SCM Press, 1991).

34. See Knitter, *One Earth Many Religions*.

35. See: Stanley J. Samartha, *Courage for Dialogue: Ecumenical Issues in Inter-religious Relationships* (Geneva: WCC Publications, 1981) and idem, *One Christ, Many Religions: Toward a Revised Christology* (Maryknoll, NY: Orbis, 1991).

36. Israel Selvananagam, "Theological Positions in Christian Approach to Religous Pluralism—The Fourth Way" (Unpublished paper, n.d.), 10.

3. From Conversion to Conversation

1. Mark Woods, "Talking about Religions, Doing Faith," 22 February 2006. http://www.oikoumene.org/en/news/news-management/eng/a/browse/16/article/1634/talking-about-religions-1.html.

2. Ibid.

3. Marcus Braybrooke, *Faith and Interfaith in a Global Age* (Grand Rapids: CoNexus Press, 1998), 9.

4. See ibid., 17ff.

5. This meeting brought together official representatives from many missionary societies: 46 British societies represented by over 500 delegates; 60 American societies represented by over 500 delegates; 41 European continental societies represented by 170 delegates; 12 South African and Australian societies represented by 26 delegates.

6. Jan Hendrik Pranger, *Dialogue in Discussion: The World Council of Churches and the Challenge of Religious Plurality between 1967 and 1979*, IIMO Research Publication 38 (Utrecht-Leiden: IMO, 1994), 1.

7. S. Wesley Ariarajah, *Hindus and Christians: A Century of Protestant Ecumenical Thought* (Amsterdam: Rodopi; Grand Rapids: Eerdmans, 1991), 45.

8. Ibid., 51.

9. Pranger, *Dialogue in Discussion*, 46.

10. Ibid., 55.

11. See Hendrik Kraemer, *The Christian Message in a Non-Christian World* (London: Edinburgh House Press, 1938).

12. Ariarajah, *Hindus and Christians*, 85.

13. Ibid., 91.

14. Ibid., 94.

15. Ibid., 95.

16. Ibid., 46.

17. Ibid., 131.

18. Ataullah Siddiqui, *Christian–Muslim Dialogue in the Twentieth Century* (London: Macmillan; New York: St Martin's Press, 1997), 35.

19. The pertinent documents of Vatican II are: *Nostra Aetate* (Declaration on the Relationship of the Church to Non-Christian Religions), *Lumen Gentium* (Dogmatic Constitution on the Church), *Dei Verbum* (Dogmatic Constitution on Divine Revelation), *Apostolicam Actuositatem,*(Decree on the Apostolate of the Laity), *Dignitatis Humanae* (Declaration on Religious Freedom), *Ad Gentes* (Decree on the Church's Missionary Activity) and *Gaudium et Spes* (Pastoral Constitution on the Church in the Modern World). See Francesco Gioia, ed., *Interreligious Dialogue: The Official Teaching of the Catholic Church from the Second Vatican Council to John Paul II (1963–1995)* (Boston: Pauline Books and Media / Pontifical Council for Interreligious Dialogue, 1997).

20. Papal and other formal Vatican statements, including the documents of Vatican II, are known by the first two words of their Latin text.

21. Ariarajah, *Hindus and Christians*, 129.

22. *Nostra Aetate* 2. See Gioia, *Interreligious Dialogue*, 38.

23. *Lumen Gentium* 16; see Gioia, *Interreligious Dialogue*, 42.

24. Pranger, *Dialogue in Discussion*, 123.

25. "Christians in Dialogue with Men of Other Faiths."

26. Pranger, *Dialogue in Discussion*, 60.

27. Ibid.

28. Ibid., 63,

29. Ibid., 67.

30. Ariarajah, *Hindus and Christians*, 138.

31. Ibid., 18.

32. Pranger, *Dialogue in Discussion*, 69.

33. Ibid.

34. Ibid.

35. See ibid., 76ff.

36. Principal examples are found in Gioia, *Interreligious Dialogue*, 117–217.

37. Siddiqui, *Christian–Muslim Dialogue*, 44; see Pietro Rossano, "The Secretariat for Non-Christian Religions from the Beginnings to the Present Day: History, Ideas, Problems," *Bulletin [of the Secretariat for Non-Christians* 41-2 (XIV/2-3) (1979): 90.

38. Michael Fitzgerald, "The Secretariat for non Christians and Muslim-Christian Dialogue." *Bulletin [of the Secretariat for Non-Christians* 37 (XIII/1) (1978): 9.

39. See the full report in Stanley J. Samartha, ed., *Dialogue Between Men of Living Faiths* (Geneva: WCC, 1971).

40. An *aide-mémoire* (or aide-memoire) is a memory aid or memorandum, but it is also a term used in diplomacy and international relations for an unofficial agreement or discussion paper.

41. See *International Review of Mission* 59, no. 236 (Oct 1970); see also Stanley J. Samartha, ed., *Living Faiths and the Ecumenical Movement* (Geneva: WCC, 1971), 33–43.

42. Pranger, *Dialogue in Discussion*, 75.

43. Ibid., 89.

44. See *The Ecumenical Review* 24, no. 3 (July 1971); see also Samartha, *Living Faiths*, 47–54.

45. Pranger, *Dialogue in Discussion*, 98.

46. See ibid., 99.

47. Ibid., 117.

48. Ibid., 124.

49. Ibid.

50. Siddiqui, *Christian–Muslim Dialogue*, xvi.

51. Ibid., 5.

52. Pranger, *Dialogue in Discussion*, 43.

53. Ibid., 126.

54. Ibid., 127.

55. Ibid.

4. Ecumenical Interreligious Engagement

1. Stanley J. Samartha, "The Progress and Promise of Inter-Religious Dialogue," *Bulletin [of the Secretariat for Non-Christians* 26 (IX/2) (1974): 110–21.

2. Ibid., 110.

3. Ibid., 115.

4. Ibid., 119.

5. See ibid., 116.

6. Ibid., 110.

7. Ibid.

8. S. Wesley Ariarajah, *Hindus and Christians: A Century of Protestant Ecumenical Thought* (Amsterdam: Rodopi; Grand Rapids: Eerdmans, 1991), 141.

9. Jan Hendrik Pranger, *Dialogue in Discussion: The World Council of Churches and the Challenge of Religious Plurality between 1967 and 1979*, IIMO Research Publication 38 (Utrecht and Leiden: IMO, 1994), 133.

10. See David Paton, *Breaking Barriers: Nairobi 1975; The Official Report of the Fifth Assembly of the World Council of Churches* (Geneva: WCC Publications, 1975), 72.

11. Pranger, *Dialogue in Discussion*, 140.

12. Ibid., 143ff.

13. That is, the Sub-unit on Dialogue with People of Living Faiths and Ideologies.

14. Ariarajah, *Hindus and Christians*, 149.

15. World Council of Churches, *Guidelines on Dialogue with People of Living Faiths and Ideologies* (Geneva: WCC Publications, 1979).

16. Pranger, *Dialogue in Discussion*, 150.

17. World Council of Churches, *Guidelines on Dialogue*, 16.

18. Ibid., 22.

19. Jutta Sperber, *Christians and Muslims: The Dialogue Activities of the World Council of Churches and Their Theological Foundation* (Berlin and New York: de Gruyter, 2000), 27.

20. Pranger, *Dialogue in Discussion*, 98.

21. See ibid., 99.

22. Ans Joachim van der Bent, *Sixteen Ecumenical Concerns* (Geneva: WCC Publications, 1986), 60.

23. World Council of Churches, *My Neighbour's Faith—and Mine: Theological Discoveries through Interfaith Dialogue; A Study Guide*, 2nd ed. (Geneva: WCC Publications, 1987).

24. See Pranger, *Dialogue in Discussion*, 164.

25. Siddiqui, *Christian-Muslim Dialogue*, 32.

26. Pranger, *Dialogue in Discussion*, 164.

27. Marlin VanElderen, *From Canberra to Harare: An Illustrated Account of the Life of the World Council of Churches 1991–1998* (Geneva: WCC Publications, 1998), 47.

28. Ibid, 48.

29. World Council of Churches, *Assembly Workbook* (Harare: WCC Publications, 1998),10ff.

30. *Jubilee*, daily newspaper of the 8th assembly, no. 4 (8 Dec. 1998): 1.

31. Diane Kessler, ed., *Together on the Way: Official Report of the Eighth Assembly of the World Council of Churches* (Geneva: WCC Publications, 1999), 83.

32. Kessler, *Together on the Way*, 48.

33. Ibid, 50.

34. See ibid., 66.

35. See documents of the conference in Hans Ucko, ed., *Changing the Present, Dreaming the Future: A Critical Moment in Interreligious Dialogue* (Geneva: WCC Publications, 2006).

36. Hans Ucko, "Editorial," *Current Dialogue*, no. 45.

37. Catholicos Aram I, "Our common calling," in Ucko, ed., *Changing the Present*, 10–11.

38. John Paul II, Encyclical *Redemptor Hominis*, March 4, 1979. See Francesco Gioia, ed., *Interreligious Dialogue: The Official Teaching of the Catholic Church (1963-1995)* (Boston: Pauline Books and Media / Pontifical Council for Interreligious Dialogue, 1997), 87–89.

39. Pontifical Council for Interreligious Dialogue, *Recognize the Spiritual Bonds which Unite Us: 16 years of Christian-Muslim Dialogue* (Rome: Pontifical Council for Interreligious Dialogue, 1994), 13.

40. Gioia, *Interreligious Dialogue*, 87.

41. Ibid.

42. As listed in Gioa, *Interreligious Dialogue*. The Solemn Magisterium is the formally (and relatively rarely) issued teaching of popes and councils of the Roman Catholic Church, as opposed to the Ordinary Magisterium, which refers to the ongoing teaching of the Roman Catholic Church.

43. Pietro Rossano, "The Secretariat for Non-Christian Religions from the beginnings to the present day: history, ideas, problems," *Bulletin [of the Secretariat for Non-Christians]* 41 (1979): 88.

44. Ibid., 90.

45. See Marcus Braybrooke, *Pilgrimage of Hope: 100 Years of Global Interfaith Dialogue* (London: SCM Press, 1992), 248ff.

46. Braybrooke, *Pilgrimage of Hope*, 250. See also Pierre Humbertclaude, "The Secretariat for Non-Christians: Its Place and Specific Role in the Church," *Bulletin [of the Secretariat for Non-Christians* 4 (II/1) (March 1967): 29–40.

47. Braybrooke, *Pilgrimage of Hope*, 249.

48. Siddiqui, *Christian-Muslim Dialogue*, 45. See Michael L. Fitzgerald, "The Secretariat for Non-Christians Is Ten Years Old," *Encounter* 9 (Nov. 1974): 2.

49. Pietro Rossano, "Dialogue in the World: Notes on Method," *Bulletin [of the Secretariat for Non-Christians* 26 (IX/2) (1974): 142.

50. Ibid., 143.

51. Ibid.

52. Ibid.

53. Ibid.

54. See address of John Paul II to Representatives of Various Religions on the World Day of Prayer for Peace: John Paul II, *Insegnamenti* (1986) IX/2, 1249–52; Gioia, *Interreligious Dialogue*, 343–45.

55. See address of John Paul II to Representatives of the Christian Communities on the World Day of Prayer for Peace: John Paul II, *Insegnamenti* (1986) IX/2, 1244–56; Gioia, *Interreligious Dialogue*, 345–47.

56. Ibid.

57. See Gioia, *Interreligious Dialogue*, 658–59.

58. See Cardinal Francis Arinze, *Bulletin [of the Pontifical Council for Interreligious Dialogue* 69 (1988):185.

59. See Gioia, *Interreligious Dialogue*, 658.

60. Pontifical Council for Interreligious Dialogue, *Recognize the Spiritual Bonds which Unite Us: 16 Years of Christian-Muslim Dialogue* (Rome: Pontifical Council for Interreligious Dialogue, 1994), 69.

61. See also Vatican website: http://www.vatican.va/roman_curia/pontifical_councils/interelg/documents/rc_pc_interelg_doc_19051991_dialogue-and-proclamatio_en.html. Also published in *Bulletin [of the Pontifical Council for Interreligious Dialogue* 77 (XXVI/2) (1991).

62. See Gioia, *Interreligious Dialogue*, 100–104.

63. *Redemptoris Missio* 29; see Gioia, *Interreligious Dialogue*, 101.

64. *Redemptoris Missio* 57; see Gioia, *Interreligious Dialogue*, 103–104.

65. *Dialogue and Proclamation*: see Gioia, *Interreligious Dialogue*, 608–42.

66. Catholic ecumenist Michael Fitzgerald himself cites from an editorial of the ecumenical journal *Areopagus* (Easter 1992), 4–6: "The document, while officially a statement of a particular Christian tradition, goes far in expressing the essential nature of the task of dialogue for Christians across the spectrum of denominations and confessions." *Bulletin [of the Pontifical Council for Interreligious Dialogue* 82 (XXVIII/1) (1993): 26.

67. *Dialogue and Proclamation* 79; see Gioia, *Interreligious Dialogue*, 638.

68. *Dialogue and Proclamation* 80; cf. *Lumen Gentium* (Dogmatic Constitution on the Church) 1.

69. Ariarajah, *Hindus and Christians*, 148.

5. Dialogue Praxis

1. See Douglas Pratt, "Religious Fundamentalism: A Paradigm for Terrorism?" *Australian Religion Studies Review* 20, no. 2 (2007): 195–215.

2. J. Mark Hensman, "Beyond Talk: The Dialogue of Life" (Unpublished DTheol thesis, Melbourne College of Divinity, 1999), 4.

3. Raimundo Panikkar, *The Intra-Religious Dialogue*, rev. ed. (New York: Paulist, 1999), 73.

4. Chester Gillis, *Pluralism: A New Paradigm for Theology* (Louvain: Peeters Press; Grand Rapids: Eerdmans, 1993), 28.

5. Notto R. Thelle, "Interreligious Dialogue: Theory and Experience" in *Theology and the Religions: A Dialogue*, ed. Viggo Mortensen (Grand Rapids: Eerdmans, 2003), 132.

6. See, for example, Part I of *The Concept of God in Global Dialogue*, ed. Werner G. Jeanrond and Aasulv Lande (Maryknoll, NY: Orbis, 2005); cf. Bob Robinson, *Christians Meeting Hindus: An Analysis and Theological Critique of the Hindu-Christian Encounter in India* (Oxford: Regnum Books, 2004), 60ff.

7. Hans Ucko, ed., *Changing the Present, Dreaming the Future: A Critical Moment in Interreligious Dialogue* (Geneva: WCC Publications, 2006), 94.

8. Report from Inter-Religious Consultation on "Conversion—Assessing the Reality," Lariano, Italy, 12–16 May 2006, 1.

9. Ibid., 3.

10. Francis Arinze, "Meeting Other Believers: Introduction to the Plenary Assembly 1992," *Bulletin [of the Pontifical Council for Interreligious Dialogue]* 82 (XXVIII/1) (1993): 17.

11. Francis Arinze, *Meeting Other Believers* (Herefordshire, UK: Gracewing, 1997), 29.

12. Ibid., 41.

13. Ibid.

14. See, for example, Michael Ipgrave and David Marshall, eds., *Humanity: Texts and Contexts. Christian and Muslim Perspectives* (Washington, DC: Georgetown University Press, 2011) for the most recent publication from this series.

15. See, for example, Hansjörg Schmid, Ayse Basol-Gürdal, Anja Middlebeck-Varwick, and Bülent Ucar, eds., *Zeugnis, Einladung, Bekehrung: Mission in Christentum und Islam* (Regensburg: Verlag Friedrich Pustet, 2011).

16. See Leonard Swidler, *After the Absolute: The Dialogical Future of Religious Reflection* (Minneapolis: Fortress, 1990), 26.

17. Paul J. Griffiths, *An Apology for Apologetics: A Study in the Logic of Interreligious Dialogue* (Maryknoll, NY: Orbis, 1991), xi.

18. S. Mark Heim, ed., *Grounds for Understanding: Ecumenical Resources for Responses to Religious Pluralism* (Grand Rapids: Eerdmans, 1998), 9.

19. See Swidler, *After the Absolute*, 194.

20. See Douglas Pratt, "Trinity: The Christian Identity of God," *Colloquium* 20, no. 2 (1988): 34–43.

21. See Douglas Pratt, "Christian-Muslim Theological Encounter: The Priority of *Tawhid*," *Islam and Christian-Muslim Relations* 7, no. 3 (1996): 271–84.

22. See Douglas Pratt, *Relational Deity: Hartshorne and Macquarrie on God* (Lanham, MD: University Press of America, 2002).

23. *"A Common Word Between Us and You": An Open Letter and Call from Muslim Religious Leaders* (Jordan: The Royal Aal al-Bayt Institute for Islamic Thought, 2007CE / 1428AH; http://acommonword.com/ index.php?lang=en&page=option1).

24. Editorial, *Pro Dialogo*, 2007/2, 105.

25. See, for example, Douglas Pratt, "Pluralism, Postmodernism and Interreligious Dialogue," *Sophia* 46, no. 3 (Dec 2007): 243–59.

26. Hensman notes an early tension between the "WCC's Commission on World Mission and Evangelism (CWME) which in 1970 recognised 'interreligious dialogue as a Christian activity in its own right' and the evangelical opposition's Committee on World Evangelism (CWE) whose 1971 Frankfurt Declaration 'upheld the primacy of preaching and rejected other religions as loci for the saving presence of Christ.'" Hensman, "Beyond Talk," 39.

27. S. Wesley Ariarajah, "A Future that May be Greater than its Past" in *A Great Commission: Christian Hope and Religious Diversity*, ed. Martin Forward, Stephen Plant, and Susan White (Bern: Peter Lang, 2000), 185.

28. Ibid.

29. Chester Gillis, *Pluralism: A New Paradigm for Theology* (Louvain: Peeters Press; Grand Rapids: Eerdmans, 1993), 40.

6. Toward a Theology of Dialogue

1. Maurice Wiles, *Christian Theology and Inter-religious Dialogue* (London: SCM Press, 1992), 3.

2. Ibid, 4.

3. J. Mark Hensman, "Beyond Talk: The Dialogue of Life" (unpublished DTheol thesis, Melbourne College of Divinity, 1999), 45.

4. Martin Conway, *The Undivided Vision* (London: SCM Press, 1966), 71.

5. "Life setting," especially the sociological or socio-cultural setting.

6. Ans Joachim van der Bent, *Sixteen Ecumenical Concerns* (Geneva: WCC Publications, 1986), 46.

7. Ibid.

8. Secretariat for Non-Christians [later Pontifical Council for Interreligious Dialogue], "The Attitude of the Church Towards the Followers of Other Religious Traditions: Reflections and Orientations on Dialogue and Mission" (also known as "The Attitude of the Church towards the Followers of Other Religions" or ACTFOR), *Bulletin [of the Secretariat for Non-Christians]* 56 (XIX/2) (1984): 24. See Francesco Gioia, ed. *Interreligious Dialogue: The Official Teaching of the Catholic Church (1963–1995)* (Boston: Pauline Books and Media / Pontifical Council for Interreligious Dialogue, 1997), 574. See also Bradford Hinze, *Practices of Dialogue in the Roman Catholic Church* (New York and London: Continuum, 2006), 6ff.

9. *Catechism of the Catholic Church* (Vatican City: Libreria Editrice Vaticana, 1993; http://www.vatican.va/archive/ENG0015/_INDEX.HTM).

10. Marcello Zago, "Dialogue in the Mission of the Church" *Bulletin [of the Secretariat for Non-Christians]* 57 (XIX/3) (1984): 267.

11. Risto Jukko, *The Trinity in Unity in Christian-Muslim Relations: The Work of the Pontifical Council for Interreligious Dialogue* (Leiden: Brill, 2007), 243–46.

12. See anonymous unpublished document "Religious Plurality—Theological Perspectives and Affirmations" (WCC Archive File Box 4612.064/5).

13. See Francis Arinze, "Interreligious Dialogue: Problems, Prospects and Possibilities," *Bulletin [of the Secretariat for Non-Christians]* 66 (XXII/3) (1987): 254.

14. See *DP* 38; see also Gioia, *Interreligious Dialogue*, 621.

15. Stanley Samartha, "Dialogue as a Continuing Christian Concern," in *Christianity and Other Religions*, ed. John Hick and Brian Hebblethwaite (London: Collins, 1980), 164.

16. Ibid.

17. See ibid., 166–68.

18. John V. Taylor, "The Theological Basis of Interfaith Dialogue," in *Christianity and Other Religions*, ed. Hick and Hebblethwaite, 212.

19. Ibid., 229.

20. Wesley Ariarajah, *Not Without My Neighbour: Issues in Interfaith Relations*, Risk Book Series 85 (Geneva: WCC Publications, 1999), 7–9.

21. Paul VI, "To the Secretariat for Non-Christians" 3, Rome, 25 September 1968, clause 3; see Gioia, *Interreligious Dialogue*, 159.

22. Stanley J. Samartha, "The Progress and Promise of Inter-Religious Dialogue," *Bulletin [of the Secretariat for Non-Christians]* 26 (IX/2) (1974): 119.

23. See Samartha, "The Progress and Promise," 116.

24. Stanley J. Samartha, *Courage for Dialogue: Ecumenical Issues in Inter-religious Relationships* (Geneva: WCC Publications, 1981), 96.

25. Ibid., 97.

26. Ibid.

27. Volker Küster, "Toward an Intercultural Theology: Paradigm Shifts in Missiology, Ecumenics, and Comparative Religion" in *Theology and the Religions: A Dialogue*, ed. Viggo Mortensen (Grand Rapids: Eerdmans, 2003), 179.

28. Ibid.

29. Ibid.

30. Zago, "Dialogue in the Mission of the Church," 268.

31. Ibid., 264.

32. See Diana Eck, Report of the Moderator to the WCC Dialogue Working Group Meeting, 1988, 19 (WCC Archive File Box 4612.062/1).

33. David Tracy, *Dialogue with the Other: The Inter-religious Dialogue* (Louvain: Peeters Press, 1990), 95.

34. Ibid.

35. Ibid., 97.

36. Stanley J. Samartha, *Courage for Dialogue*, ix.

37. P. D. Devanandan, *Christian Issues in Southern Asia* (New York: Friendship Press: 1963), 90.

38. M. M. Thomas, *Risking Christ for Christ's Sake: Towards an Ecumenical Theology of Pluralism* (Geneva: WCC Publications, 1987), 15.

39. See Ariarajah, *Not Without My Neighbour*, 15.

40. See, for example, Michael Barnes, *Religions in Conversation: Christian Identity and Religious Pluralism* (London: SPCK, 1989) and Israel Selvanayagam, *Relating to People of Other Faiths* (Tiruvalla, Kerala, India: CSS-BTTBPSA Joint Publication, 2004), among others.

41. Samartha, *Courage for Dialogue*, 88.

42. See Douglas Pratt, "Pluralism and Interreligious Engagement: The Contexts of Dialogue," in *A Faithful Presence: Essays for Kenneth Cragg*, ed. David Thomas with Clare Amos (London: Melisende Press, 2003), 402–18; and Douglas Pratt, "Contextual Paradigms for Interfaith Relations," *Current Dialogue* 42 (Dec. 2003): 3–9.

43. See Theo Sundermeier, "*Missio Dei* Today: On the Identity of Christian Mission," *International Review of Mission* 92, no. 367 (Oct 2003): 560–78.

44. See, for example, Gavin D'Costa, *Theology and Religious Pluralism* (Oxford: Basil Blackwell, 1986); Barnes, *Religions in Conversation* (1986); Harold Netland, *Dissonant Voices: Religious Pluralism and the Question of Truth* (Grand Rapids: Eerdmans; Leicester, UK: Apollos, 1991); Peter Byrne, *Prolegomena to Religious Pluralism: Reference and Realism in Religion* (London: Macmillan, 1995); Jacques Dupuis, *Toward a Christian Theology of Religious Pluralism* (Maryknoll, NY: Orbis, 1997); and Kenneth Cracknell, *In Good and Generous Faith: Christian Responses to Religious Pluralism* (Peterborough, UK: Epworth, 2005).

45. See Alan Race, *Christians and Religious Pluralism*, 2nd ed. (London: SCM Press, 1993).

46. See Douglas Pratt, "The Dance of Dialogue: Ecumenical Interreligious Engagement," *Ecumenical Review* 51, no. 3 (July 1999): 274–87.

47. See Douglas Pratt, "Exclusivism and Exclusivity: A Contemporary Theological Challenge," *Pacifica* 20, no. 3 (Oct. 2007): 291–306.

48. Cf. Douglas Pratt, "Contextual Paradigms for Interfaith Relations," *Current Dialogue* 42 (Dec. 2003): 3–9 and idem, "Pluralism, Postmodernism and Interreligious Dialogue," *Sophia* 46, no. 3 (Dec. 2007): 243–59.

49. Ariarajah, *Not Without My Neighbour*, 22.

50. Cracknell, *In Good and Generous Faith*, 5.

51. Donald K. Swearer, *Dialogue: The Key to Understanding Other Religions* (Philadelphia: Westminster Press, 1977), 28.

52. Ibid., 35.

53. Peter C. Phan, *In our Own Tongues: Perspectives from Asia on Mission and Inculturation* (Maryknoll, NY: Orbis, 2003), 175.

54. Ibid., 184.

55. M. M. Thomas, *Risking Christ for Christ's Sake: Towards an Ecumenical Theology of Pluralism* (Geneva: WCC Publications, 1987).

56. See Douglas Pratt, "Ideological Containment: Islamic Extremism and Option of Theological Dialogue" in *Proceedings of the 2008 GTReC International Conference*, ed. Sayad Khatab, Muhammad Bakashmar, and Ela Ogru (Melbourne: Global Terrorism Research Centre, Monash University, 2009), 217–32.

57. See *"A Common Word Between Us and You": An Open Letter and Call from Muslim Religious Leaders* (Jordan: The Royal Aal al-Bayt Institute for Islamic Thought, 2007CE / 1428AH; http://acommonword.com/index.php?lang=en&page=option1); and Douglas Pratt, "An Uncommon Call: Prospect for a New Dialogue with Muslims?" *Asian Christian Review* 2, nos. 2-3 (Summer/Winter 2008): 36–53.

7. Guide for Interfaith Relations

1. Stanley J. Samartha, *Courage for Dialogue* (Geneva: WCC Publications, 1981), 88.

2. Ibid., 100.

3. S. Wesley Ariarajah, *Not Without My Neighbour: Issues in Interfaith Relations*, Risk Book Series 85 (Geneva: WCC Publications, 1999), 22.

4. Andrew Wingate, *Celebrating Difference, Staying Faithful: How to Live in a Multi-Faith World* (London: Darton, Longman and Todd, 2005), 70.

5. Ibid., 71.

6. Israel Selvanayagam, *Relating to People of Other Faiths: Insights from the Bible* (Tiruvalla & Bangalore: CSS Books / BTTBPSA, 2004), 32.

7. Ibid., 73.

8. Ibid., 74.

9. Ibid.

10. Exodus 20:16.

11. Mark 12:31; cf. Matthew 22:39; Luke 10:27.

12. See, for example, S. Wesley Ariarajah, *Not Without My Neighbour*.

13. Selvanayagam, *Relating to People of Other Faiths*, 229.

14. Wingate, *Celebrating Difference, Staying Faithful*, 75.

15. Selvanayagam, *Relating to People of Other Faiths*, 230.

16. Ibid.

17. Ibid., 232.

18. David J. Bosch, *Transforming Mission: Paradigm Shifts in Theology of Mission* (Maryknoll, NY: Orbis, 1992), 55.

19. Ibid.

20. Ibid., 57.

21. Ibid.

22. Peter Cotterell, *Mission and Meaninglessness: The Good News in a World of Suffering and Disorder* (London: SPCK, 1990), 96.

23. Terence L. Donaldson, "Guiding Readers—Making Disciples: Discipleship in Matthew's Narrative Strategy," in *Patterns of Discipleship in the New Testament*, ed. Richard Longenecker (Grand Rapids: Eerdmans, 1996), 40.

24. Ibid., 36; see also ibid., 42.

25. Ibid., 41.

26. Ibid., 43.

27. Ibid., 46.

28. Bosch, *Transforming Mission*, 74.

29. Ibid., 81.

30. Martin Conway, *The Undivided Vision* (London: SCM Press, 1966), 78.

31. Ibid., 79.

32. See Winston F. Crum, "The *Missio Dei* and the Church," *St Vladimir's Theological Quarterly* 17 (1973): 285–89.

33. Bosch, *Transforming Mission*, 385.

34. Ibid., 390.

35. Ibid., 9.

36. See ibid., 3.

37. Roger Bowen, *So I Send You: A Study Guide to Mission* (London: SPCK, 1996), 210.

38. Ibid., 212.

39. Ibid., 220.

40. Bosch, *Transforming Mission*, 474.

41. Ibid., 475.

42. Ibid., 481.

43. Ibid.

44. Ibid., 483.

45. Ibid.

46. Ibid.

47. Roger Herft, "The Gospel and Communication," in *Mission in a Broken World: Report of ACC-8, Wales 1990* (London: Anglican Consultative Council, 1990), 78.

48. Conway, *The Undivided Mission*, 65.

49. Bosch, *Transforming Mission*, 483ff.

8. Interreligious Prayer

1. Cf. Andrew Wingate, *Celebrating Difference, Staying Faithful: How to Live in a Multi-Faith World* (London: Darton, Longman and Todd, 2005), 82–114, for a discussion on interfaith prayer and worship. Wingate's chapter complements my own.

2. See Douglas Pratt, "Parameters for Interreligious Prayer: Some Considerations," *Current Dialogue* 31 (Dec. 1997): 21–27.

3. See Hans Ucko, "Inter-religious Worship and Prayer," *Current Dialogue* 24 (June 1993): 35–39; and idem, "Report on Inquiry on Interreligious Prayer and Worship," *Current Dialogue* 28 (June 1995): 57–64.

4. See the joint issue of *Pro Dialogo* and *Current Dialogue* in which are contained a selection of preliminary papers and the formal reports and findings of the study. Pontifical Council for Interreligious Dialogue and Office for Inter-Religious Relations of the World Council of Churches, "Interreligious Prayer," Special Issue of *Pro Dialogo* and *Current Dialogue, Pro Dialogo* 98 (XXXIII/2) (1998).

5. See, e.g., Joseph Ratzinger, *Truth and Tolerance: Christian Belief and World Religions*, trans. Henry Taylor (San Francisco: Ignatius Press, 2004), 108–109.

6. See Douglas Pratt, "Dominical Paradigm for Interreligious Prayer: Theological Reflections," *Colloquium* 30, no. 1 (1998): 45–59.

9. Faithful Openness

1. Andrew Wingate, *Celebrating Difference, Staying Faithful: How to Live in a Multi-Faith World* (London: Darton, Longman and Todd, 2005).

2. Ibid., 4.

3. See Pontifical Council for Interreligious Dialogue and Congregation for the Evangelization of Peoples, *Dialogue and Proclamation: Reflections and Orientations on Interreligious Dialogue and the Proclamation of the Gospel of Jesus Christ* (Rome: Pontifical Council for Interreligious Dialogue, 19 May 1991).

4. See World Council of Churches, Pontifical Council for Interreligious Dialogue, and World Evangelical Alliance, *Christian Witness in a Multi-Religious World: Recommendations for Conduct* (28 June 2011), http://www.oikoumene.org/resources/documents/wcc-programmes/interreligious-dialogue-and-cooperation/christian-identity-in-pluralistic-societies/christian-witness-in-a-multi-religious-world.html). See also World Council of Churches, *Ecumenical Considerations for Dialogue with People of Other Religions* (Geneva: WCC Publications, 2003 and http://www.oikoumene.org/en/resources/documents/wcc-programmes/interreligious-dialogue-and-cooperation/interreligious-trust-and-respect/ecumenical-considerations-for-dialogue-and-relations-with-people-of-other-religions.html).

5. Paul Hedges, *Controversies in Interreligious Dialogue and the Theology of Religions* (London: SCM Press, 2010), 11.

6. Ibid.

7. Ibid., 12.

8. The Lambeth Conference, *The Truth Shall Make You Free: The Lambeth Conference 1988; The Reports, Resolutions & Pastoral Letters from the Bishops* (London: Church House Publishing for the Anglican Consultative Council, 1988), 94.

9. Ibid.

10. See Douglas Pratt, "Secular Government and Interfaith Dialogue: A Regional Asia-Pacific Initiative," *Studies in Interreligious Dialogue* 20, no. 1 (2010): 42–57.

11. George Carey, "Introduction," in *The Road Ahead: a Christian-Muslim Dialogue*, ed. Michael Ipgrave (London: Church House Publishing, 2002), x.

12. Ipgrave, *The Road Ahead*, 1.

13. Ibid., 3.

14. Michael Ipgrave, ed., *Scriptures in Dialogue: Christians and Muslims Studying the Bible and Qur'an Together* (London: Church House Publishing, 2004), xii.

15. Michael Ipgrave, ed., *Bearing the Word: Prophecy in Biblical and Qur'anic Perspective* (London: Church House Publishing, 2005), 12.

16. Michael Ipgrave, ed., *Justice and Rights: Christian and Muslim Perspectives* (Washington, DC: Georgetown University Press, 2009), x.

17. Michael Ipgrave and David Marshall, eds., *Humanity: Texts and Context: Christian and Muslim Perspectives* (Washington, DC: Georgetown University Press, 2011), xvi.

18. Ibid.

19. Ibid., 1.

20. See Hansjörg Schmid, Ayse Basol-Gürdal, Anja Middlebeck-Varwick, and Bülent Ucar, eds., *Zeugnis, Einladung, Bekehrung: Mission in Christentum und Islam* (Regensburg: Verlag Friedrich Pustet, 2011).

21. *"A Common Word Between Us and You": An Open Letter and Call from Muslim Religious Leaders* (Jordan: The Royal Aal al-Bayt Institute for Islamic Thought, 2007 CE / 1428AH; http://acommonword.com/index.php?lang=en&page=option1).

22. "Archbishop's Response to 'A Common Word.'" Press Release (London: Lambeth Palace, 11 October 2007; http://www.archbishopofcanterbury.org/articles.php/1148/archbishops-response-to-a-common-word).

23. Rowan Williams, *A Common Word for the Common Good* (London: Lambeth Palace, 4 July 2008; http://www.acommonword.com/lib/downloads/Common-Good-Canterbury-FINAL-as-sent-14-7-08-1.pdf).

24. Williams, "A Common Word for the Common Good."

25. Ibid.

26. Anglican Communion Network for Inter Faith Concerns, *Generous Love: The Truth of the Gospel and the Call to Dialogue: An Anglican Theology of Inter Faith Relations* (London: The Anglican Consultative Council, 2008).

27. Anglican Communion Network for Inter Faith Concerns, *Generous Love*, 7.

28. Ibid., 15.

29. Doctrine Commission of the Church of England, *Contemporary Doctrine Classics from the Church of England* (London: Church Publishing House, 2005), 419.

30. Ibid.

31. Ibid., 298.

32. Wingate, *Celebrating Difference*, 13.

33. Ibid., 13–14.

34. Ibid., 14.

35. Ibid.

36. Hedges, *Controversies in Interreligious Dialogue*, 32.

37. Ibid.

38. Ibid., 34.

39. Ibid., 43.

40. Ibid., 145.

41. Cited in Hedges, *Controversies in Interreligious Dialogue*, 246.

BIBLIOGRAPHY

"A Common Word Between Us and You": An Open Letter and Call from Muslim Religious Leaders. Jordan: The Royal Aal al-Bayt Institute for Islamic Thought, 2007 CE / 1428AH. http://acommonword.com/index.php?lang=en&page=option1.

Ali, Tariq. *The Clash of Fundamentalisms: Crusades, Jihads and Modernity.* London: Verso, 2002.

Allen, Diogenes. *Christian Belief in a Postmodern World,* Louisville: Westminster/ John Knox, 1989.

Anderson, Gerald H., and Thomas F. Stransky, eds. *Christ's Lordship and Religious Pluralism.* Maryknoll, NY: Orbis, 1981.

Anglican Communion Network for Inter Faith Concerns. *Generous Love: The Truth of the Gospel and the Call to Dialogue: An Anglican Theology of Inter Faith Relations.* London: The Anglican Consultative Council, 2008.

Anglican Consultative Council. *Towards a Theology for Inter-Faith Dialogue.* London: Anglican Consultative Council, 1986.

Antes, Peter, Armin W. Geertz, and Randi R. Warne, eds. *New Approaches to the Study of Religion, Volume I: Regional, Critical and Historical Approaches.* Religion and Reason 42. Berlin and New York: de Gruyter, 2004.

Arai, Tosh, and S. Wesley Ariarajah. *Spirituality in Interfaith Dialogue.* Maryknoll, NY: Orbis, 1989.

Ariarajah, S. Wesley. *Not Without My Neighbour: Issues in Interfaith Relations.* Risk Book Series 85. Geneva: WCC Publications, 1999.

Ariarajah, S. Wesley. *Hindus and Christians: A Century of Protestant Ecumenical Thought.* Amsterdam: Rodopi; Grand Rapids: Eerdmans, 1991.

Ariarajah, S. Wesley. *The Bible and People of Other Faiths.* Risk Book Series 26. Geneva: WCC Publications, 1985.

Arinze, Francis. *Meeting Other Believers.* Herefordshire, UK: Gracewing, 1997.

Arinze, Francis. *Church in Dialogue: Walking with Other Believers.* San Francisco: Ignatius Press, 1990.

Barnes, Michael. *Theology and the Dialogue of Religions.* Cambridge: Cambridge University Press, 2002.

Barnes, Michael. *Religions in Conversation: Christian Identity and Religious Pluralism.* London: SPCK, 1989.

Bayfield, Tony, and Marcus Braybrooke, eds. *Dialogue with a Difference.* London: SCM Press, 1992.

Bennett, Clinton. *Understanding Christian–Muslim Relations.* London: Continuum, 2008.

Bernhardt, Reinhold. *Ende des Dialogs? Die Begegnung der Religionen und ihre theologische Reflexion.* Zürich: Theologischer Verlag Zürich, 2005.

Bosch, David J. *Transforming Mission: Paradigm Shifts in Theology of Mission.* Maryknoll, NY: Orbis, 1992.

Bouma, Gary. *Australian Soul: Religion and Spirituality in the Twenty-first Century.* Melbourne: Cambridge University Press, 2006.

Bowen, Roger. *So I Send You: A Study Guide to Mission.* London: SPCK, 1996.

Braybrooke, Marcus. *Faith and Interfaith in a Global Age.* Grand Rapids: CoNexus Press, 1998.

Braybrooke, Marcus. *Pilgrimage of Hope: 100 Years of Global Interfaith Dialogue.* London: SCM Press, 1992.

Brown, Stuart. *Meeting in Faith.* Geneva: WCC Publications, 1989.

Brown, Stuart. *The Nearest in Affection: Towards a Christian Understanding of Islam.* Geneva: WCC Publications, 1984.

Bulliet, Richard W. *The Case for Islamo-Christian Civilization.* New York: Columbia University Press, 2004.

Byrne, Peter. *Prolegomena to Religious Pluralism: Reference and Realism in Religion.* London: Macmillan, 1995.

Cobb, John. *Beyond Dialogue: Toward a Mutual Transformation of Christianity and Buddhism.* Philadelphia: Fortress, 1982.

Conway, Martin. *The Undivided Vision.* London: SCM Press, 1966.

Cornille, Catherine, ed. *Many Mansions? Christian Identity and Multiple Religious Belonging.* Maryknoll, NY: Orbis, 2002.

Cotterell, Peter. *Mission and Meaninglessness: The Good News in a World of Suffering and Disorder.* London: SPCK, 1990.

Coward, Harold. *Pluralism in the World Religions: A Short Introduction.* Oxford: Oneworld, 2000.

Coward, Harold, ed. *Hindu-Christian Dialogue: Perspectives and Encounters.* Maryknoll, NY: Orbis, 1989.

Cragg, Kenneth. *Muhammad and the Christian: A Question of Response.* Oxford: Oneworld, 1999.

Cracknell, Kenneth. *In Good and Generous Faith: Christian Responses to Religious Pluralism.* Peterborough: Epworth Press, 2005.

Cracknell, Kenneth. *Considering Dialogue: Theological Themes in Interfaith Relations, 1970-1980.* London: British Council of Churches, 1981.

Crum, Winston F. "The *Missio Dei* and the Church." *St Vladimir's Theological Quarterly* 17 (1973): 285–89.

D'Costa, Gavin. *The Meeting of Religions and the Trinity.* London: Continuum, 2000.

D'Costa, Gavin, ed. *Christian Uniqueness Reconsidered: The Myth of a Pluralistic Theology of Religions.* Maryknoll, NY: Orbis, 1990.

D'Costa, Gavin. *Theology and Religious Pluralism.* Oxford: Basil Blackwell, 1986.

DiNoia, J.A. [Joseph Augustine]. *The Diversity of Religions: A Christian Perspective.* Washington, DC: Catholic University of America Press, 1992.

Doctrine Commission of the Church of England. *Contemporary Doctrine Classics from the Church of England.* London: Church Publishing House, 2005.

Dupuis, Jacques. *Christianity and the Religions: From Confrontation to Dialogue.* Maryknoll, NY: Orbis; London: Darton, Longman and Todd, 2002.

Dupuis, Jacques. *Toward a Christian Theology of Religious Pluralism.* Maryknoll, NY: Orbis, 1997.

Eck, Diana L. *Encountering God: A Spiritual Journey from Bozeman to Banares.* Boston: Beacon Press, 1993.

Esposito, John. *The Islamic Threat: Myth or Reality?* 2nd ed. London: Oxford University Press, 1995.

Esposito, John. *Islam: The Straight Path.* Oxford: Oxford University Press, 1994.

Fisher, Eugene J. *Visions of the Other: Jewish and Christian Theologians Assess the Dialogue.* Mahwah, NJ: Paulist, 1994.

Fitzgerald, Michael L. "The Secretariat for Non Christians and Muslim-Christian Dialogue." *Bulletin [of the Secretariat for Non-Christians],* no. 37 (XIII/1) (1978).

Fitzgerald, Michael L. "The Secretariat for Non-Christians is Ten Years Old." *Encounter,* no. 9 (1974).

Fitzgerald, Michael L., and John Borelli. *Interfaith Dialogue: A Catholic View.* Maryknoll, NY: Orbis, 2006.

Forward, Martin. *Inter-religious Dialogue: A Short Introduction.* Oxford: Oneworld, 2001.

Forward, Martin, Stephen Plant, and Susan White, eds. *A Great Commission: Christian Hope and Religious Diversity.* Bern: Peter Lang, 2000.

Gillis, Chester. *Pluralism: A New Paradigm for Theology.* Louvain: Peeters Press; Grand Rapids: Eerdmans, 1993.

Gioia, Francesco, ed. *Interreligious Dialogue: The Official Teaching of the Catholic Church (1963-1995).* Boston: Pauline Books and Media / Pontifical Council for Interreligious Dialogue, 1997.

Griffiths, Paul J. *Problems of Religious Diversity.* Oxford: Blackwell, 2001.

Griffiths, Paul J. *An Apology for Apologetics: A Study in the Logic of Interreligious Dialogue.* Maryknoll, NY: Orbis, 1991.

Hager, Nicky. *The Hollow Men.* Nelson: Craig Cotton Publishing, 2006.

Hallencreutz, Carl F. *Dialogue and Community: Ecumenical Issues in Inter-religious Relationships.* Geneva: WCC Publications; Uppsala: Swedish Institute of Missionary Research, 1977.

Heck, Paul L. *Common Ground: Islam, Christianity and Religious Pluralism.* Washington, DC: Georgetown University Press, 2009.

Hedges, Paul. *Controversies in Interreligious Dialogue and the Theology of Religions.* London: SCM Press, 2010.

Heim, S. Mark. *The Depth of the Riches: A Trinitarian Theology of Religious Ends.* Grand Rapids: Eerdmans, 2001.

Heim, S. Mark, ed. *Grounds for Understanding: Ecumenical Resources for Responses to Religious Pluralism.* Grand Rapids: Eerdmans, 1998.

Heim, S. Mark. *Salvations: Truth and Difference in Religion.* Maryknoll, NY: Orbis, 1995.

Hensman, J. Mark. "Beyond Talk: The Dialogue of Life." Unpublished DTheol thesis, Melbourne College of Divinity, Australia, 1999.

Herft, Roger. "The Gospel and Communication" in *Mission in a Broken World: Report of ACC-8, Wales 1990.* London: Anglican Consultative Council, 1990.

Hick, John. *The Rainbow of Faiths.* London: SCM Press, 1995.

Hick, John. *The Metaphor of God Incarnate.* London: SCM Press, 1993.

Hick, John. *An Interpretation of Religion: Human Responses to the Transcendent.* Basingstoke: Macmillan, 1989.

Hick, John. *God and the Universe of Faiths.* Rev. ed. London: Collins, 1977.

Hick, John. *The Myth of God Incarnate.* London: SCM Press, 1977.

Hick, John, ed. *Truth and Dialogue in World Religions.* Philadelphia: Westminster, 1974.

Hick, John, and Brian Hebblethwaite, eds. *Christianity and Other Religions.* London: Collins, 1980.

Hick, John, and Paul F. Knitter, eds. *The Myth of Christian Uniqueness: Toward a Pluralistic Theology of Religions.* Maryknoll, NY: Orbis, 1987.

Hinze, Bradford E. *Practices of Dialogue in the Roman Catholic Church.* New York and London: Continuum, 2006.

Hinze, Bradford E., and Irfan A. Omar, eds. *Heirs of Abraham: The Future of Muslim, Jewish, and Christian Relations.* Maryknoll, NY: Orbis, 2005.

Humbertclaude, Pierre. "The Secretariat for Non-Christians: Its Place and Specific Role in the Church." *Bulletin [of the Secretariat for Non-Christians]* 4 (II/1) (1967).

Ipgrave, Michael, ed. *Justice and Rights: Christian and Muslim Perspectives.* Washington, DC: Georgetown University Press, 2009.

Ipgrave, Michael, ed. *Bearing the Word: Prophecy in Biblical and Qur'anic Perspective.* London: Church House Publishing, 2005.

Ipgrave, Michael, ed. *Scriptures in Dialogue: Christians and Muslims Studying the Bible and Qur'an Together.* London: Church House Publishing, 2004.

Ipgrave, Michael, ed. *The Road Ahead: A Christian-Muslim Dialogue.* London: Church House Publishing, 2002.

Ipgrave, Michael, and David Marshall, eds. *Humanity: Texts and Contexts; Christian and Muslim Perspectives.* Washington, DC: Georgetown University Press, 2011.

Isizoh, Chidi Denis, ed. *Milestones in Interreligious Dialogue.* Rome: Ceedee Publications, 2002.

John Paul II. Encyclical *Redemptor Hominis,* 4 March 1979.

Jukko, Risto. *Trinity in Unity in Christian-Muslim Relations: The Work of the Pontifical Council for Interreligious Dialogue.* Leiden and Boston: Brill, 2007.

Kärkkäinen, Veli-Matti. *Trinity and Religious Pluralism: The Doctrine of the Trinity in Christian Theology of Religions.* Aldershot: Ashgate, 2004.

Kepel, Gilles. *The Revenge of God: The Resurgence of Islam, Christianity and Judaism in the Modern World.* Cambridge, UK: Polity Press, 1994.

Kessler, Diane, ed. *Together on the Way: Official Report of the Eighth Assembly of the World Council of Churches.* Geneva: WCC Publications, 1999.

Kessler, Gary E. *Studying Religion: An Introduction Through Cases.* Boston: McGraw Hill, 2003.

Kimball, Charles. *Striving Together: A Way Forward in Christian-Muslim Relations.* Maryknoll, NY: Orbis, 1991.

Knitter, Paul F. ed. *The Myth of Religious Superiority: A Multifaith Exploration.* Maryknoll, NY: Orbis, 2005.

Knitter, Paul F. *One Earth Many Religions: Multifaith Dialogue and Global Responsibility.* Maryknoll, NY: Orbis, 1995.

Knitter, Paul F. *No Other Name? A Critical Survey of Christian Attitudes Toward the World Religions.* Maryknoll, NY: Orbis, 1985.

Kraemer, Hendrik. *The Christian Message in a Non-Christian World.* London: Edinburgh House Press, 1938.

Küng, Hans. *Tracing the Way: Spiritual Dimensions of the World Religions*. London and New York: Continuum, 2002.

Küng, Hans. *Global Responsibility: In Search of a New World Ethic*. London: SCM Press, 1991.

Küng, Hans. *Christianity and the World Religions: Paths of Dialogue with Islam, Hinduism, and Buddhism*. London: Collins, 1987.

Küng, Hans, and Karl-Josef Kuschel, eds. *A Global Ethic: the Declaration of the Parliament of the World's Religions*. London: SCM Press, 1993.

The Lambeth Conference. *The Report of the Lambeth Conference 1978*. London: CIO Publishing, 1978.

The Lambeth Conference. *The Truth Shall Make You Free: The Lambeth Conference 1988; The Reports, Resolutions and Pastoral Letters from the Bishops*. London: Church House Publishing for the Anglican Consultative Council, 1988.

Lochhead, David. *The Dialogical Imperative: A Christian Reflection on Interfaith Encounter*. London: SCM Press, 1988.

Longenecker, Richard N., ed. *Patterns of Discipleship in the New Testament*. Grand Rapids: Eerdmans, 1996.

Ludwig, Theodore. *The Sacred Paths*. New York: Macmillan, 1989.

Molloy, Michael. *Experiencing the World's Religions: Tradition, Challenge, and Change*. Mountain View, CA: Mayfield, 1999.

Mortensen, Viggo, ed. *Theology and the Religions: A Dialogue*. Grand Rapids: Eerdmans, 2003.

Nazir-Ali, Michael. *Frontiers in Muslim-Christian Encounter*. Oxford: Regnum Books, 1991.

Neill, Stephen. *Christian Faith and Other Faiths: The Christian Dialogue with Other Religions*. London: Oxford University Press, 1961.

Netland, Harold A. *Encountering World Religions: The Challenge to Christian Faith and Mission*. Leicester, UK: Apollos, 2001.

Netland, Harold A. *Dissonant Voices: Religious Pluralism and the Question of Truth*. Grand Rapids: Eerdmans; Leicester, UK: Apollos, 1991.

Newbigin, Lesslie. *The Gospel in a Pluralist Society*. London: SPCK; Grand Rapids: Eerdmans, 1989.

Nigosian, Solomon A. *World Religions: A Historical Approach*. 3rd ed. Boston: Bedford/St Martin's, 2000.

Second Vatican Council. *Nostra Aetate: Declaration on the Relationship of the Church to Non-Christian Religions*. Rome: 1965.

Ogden, Schubert M. *Is There Only One True Religion or Are There Many?* Dallas: Southern Methodist University Press, 1992.

Panikkar, Raimundo. *The Unknown Christ of Hinduism*. Rev. ed. Maryknoll, NY: Orbis, 1981.

Panikkar, Raimundo. *The Intrareligious Dialogue*. New York: Paulist, 1978.

Paton, David, ed. *Breaking Barriers: Nairobi 1975; The Official Report of the Fifth Assembly of the World Council of Churches*. Geneva: WCC Publications, 1975.

Phan, Peter. *Being Religious Interreligiously: Asian Perspectives on Interfaith Dialogue*. Maryknoll, NY: Orbis, 2004.

Plantinga, Richard J., ed. *Christianity and Plurality: Classic and Contemporary Readings*. Oxford: Blackwell, 1999.

Plaw, Avery, ed. *Frontiers of Diversity: Explorations in Contemporary Pluralism.* Amsterdam and New York: Rodopi, 2005.

Pontifical Council for Interreligious Dialogue. *Recognize the Spiritual Bonds which Unite Us: 16 Years of Christian-Muslim Dialogue.* Rome: Pontifical Council for Interreligious Dialogue, 1994.

Pontifical Council for Interreligious Dialogue and Congregation for the Evangelization of Peoples. *Dialogue and Proclamation: Reflections and Orientations on Interreligious Dialogue and the Proclamation of the Gospel of Jesus Christ.* Rome: Pontifical Council for Interreligious Dialogue, 19 May 1991.

Pontifical Council for Interreligious Dialogue. *Guidelines for Dialogue between Christians and Muslims.* Rev. ed. by Maurice Borrmans. New York and Mahwah, NJ: Paulist, 1981.

Pontifical Council for Interreligious Dialogue and Office for Inter-Religious Relations, World Council of Churches. "Interreligious Prayer." Special Issue of *Pro Dialogo* and *Current Dialogue. Pro Dialogo* 98 (XXXIII/2) (1998).

Pranger, Jan Hendrik. *Dialogue in Discussion: The World Council of Churches and the Challenge of Religious Plurality between 1967 and 1979.* IIMO Research Publication 38. Utrecht and Leiden: IMO, 1994.

Pratt, Douglas. "Religious Identity and the Denial of Alterity: Plurality and the Problem of Exclusivism." In *The Relationship of Philosophy to Religion Today,* ed. Paolo Diego Bubbio and Philip Andrew Quadrio. Newcastle upon Tyne: Cambridge Scholars Publishing, 2011.

Pratt, Douglas. *The Church and Other Faiths: The World Council of Churches, the Vatican, and Interreligious Dialogue.* Bern: Peter Lang, 2010.

Pratt, Douglas. "Secular Government and Interfaith Dialogue: A Regional Asia-Pacific Initiative." *Studies in Interreligious Dialogue* 20, no. 1 (2010): 42–57.

Pratt, Douglas. "Christian Discipleship and Interfaith Engagement." *Pacifica* 22 (Oct. 2009): 317–33.

Pratt, Douglas. "An Uncommon Call: Prospect for a New Dialogue with Muslims?" *Asian Christian Review* 2, nos. 2-3 (2008): 36–53.

Pratt, Douglas. "Pluralism, Postmodernism and Interreligious Dialogue." *Sophia* 46, no. 3 (Dec. 2007): 243–59.

Pratt, Douglas. "Exclusivism and Exclusivity: A Contemporary Theological Challenge." *Pacifica* 20 (Oct. 2007): 291–306.

Pratt, Douglas. "Religious Fundamentalism: A Paradigm for Terrorism?" *Australian Religion Studies Review* 20, no. 2 (2007): 195–215.

Pratt, Douglas. *The Challenge of Islam: Encounters in Interfaith Dialogue.* Aldershot: Ashgate, 2005.

Pratt, Douglas. *Rethinking Religion: Exploratory Investigations.* Adelaide: ATF Press, 2003.

Pratt, Douglas. "Contextual Paradigms for Interfaith Relations." *Current Dialogue,* no. 42 (Dec. 2003): 3–9.

Pratt, Douglas. "The Dance of Dialogue." *Ecumenical Review* 51, no. 3 (1999): 274–87.

Pratt, Douglas. "Dominical Paradigm for Interreligious Prayer: Theological Reflections." *Colloquium* 30, no. 1 (1998): 45–49.

Pratt, Douglas. "Parameters for Interreligious Prayer: Some Considerations." *Current Dialogue*, no. 31 (Dec. 1997): 21–27.

Pratt, Douglas. *Religion: A First Encounter.* Auckland: Longman-Paul, 1993.

Race, Alan. *Interfaith Encounter: The Twin Tracks of Theology and Dialogue.* London: SCM Press, 2001.

Race, Alan. *Christians and Religious Pluralism.* 2nd ed. London: SCM Press, 1993.

Race, Alan, and Paul M. Hedges, eds. *Christian Approaches to Other Faiths: A Reader.* London: SCM Press, 2009.

Race, Alan, and Paul M. Hedges, eds. *Christian Approaches to Other Faiths.* London: SCM Press, 2008.

Ratzinger, Joseph. *Truth and Tolerance: Christian Belief and World Religions.* Translated by Henry Taylor. San Francisco: Ignatius Press, 2004.

Rossano, Pietro. "The Secretariat for Non-Christian Religions from the Beginnings to the Present Day: History, Ideas, Problems." *Bulletin [of the Secretariat for Non-Christians]* 41-42 (XIV/2-3) (1979).

Sacks, Jonathan. *The Dignity of Difference.* London and New York: Continuum, 2007.

Samartha, Stanley J. *One Christ, Many Religions: Toward a Revised Christology.* Maryknoll, NY: Orbis, 1991.

Samartha, Stanley J. *Courage for Dialogue: Ecumenical Issues in Inter-religious Relationships.* Geneva: WCC Publications, 1981.

Samartha, Stanley J. "The Progress and Promise of Inter-Religious Dialogue." *Bulletin [of the Secretariat for Non-Christians]* 26 (IX/2) (1974).

Samartha, Stanley J., ed. *Dialogue between Men of Living Faiths.* Geneva: WCC Publications, 1971.

Samartha, Stanley J., ed. *Living Faiths and the Ecumenical Movement.* Geneva: WCC Publications, 1971.

Schmid, Hansjörg, Ayse Basol-Gürdal, Anja Middlebeck-Varwick, and Bülent Ucar, eds. *Zeugnis, Einladung, Bekehrung: Mission in Christentum und Islam.* Regensburg: Verlag Friedrich Pustet, 2011.

Schmidt-Leukel, Perry. *Transformation by Integration: How Inter-faith Encounter Changes Christianity.* London: SCM Press, 2009.

Schmidt-Leukel, Perry, and Lloyd Ridgeon, eds. *Islam and Inter-Faith Relations.* London: SCM Press, 2007.

Secretariat for Non-Christians [later Pontifical Council for Interreligious Dialogue]. "The Attitude of the Catholic Church Towards the Followers of Other Religious Traditions: Reflections and Orientations on Dialogue and Mission." *Bulletin [of the Secretariat for Non-Christians]* (XIX/2) (1984).

Selvanayagam, Israel. *Relating to People of Other Faiths: Insights from the Bible.* Tiruvalla and Bangalore: CSS Books / BTTBPSA, 2004.

Selvanayagam, Israel. "Interfaith Dialogues: A Clarification of Perspectives and Issues." *Current Dialogue* 23 (Dec. 1992): 20–25.

Siddiqui, Ataullah. *Christian–Muslim Dialogue in the Twentieth Century.* London: Macmillan; New York: St Martin's Press, 1997.

Smart, Ninian. *The World's Religions.* Cambridge: Cambridge University Press, 1989.

Smith, Wilfred Cantwell. *Religious Diversity.* New York: Crossroad, 1982.

Smock, David R. *Interfaith Dialogue and Peacebuilding.* Washington, DC: United States Institute of Peace, 2002.

Solomon, Norman. "The Third Presence: Reflections on the Dialogue." In *Dialogue with a Difference*, ed. Tony Bayfield and Marcus Braybrooke, 147–62. London: SCM Press, 1992.

Sperber, Jutta. *Christians and Muslims: The Dialogue Activities of the World Council of Churches and Their Theological Foundation*. Berlin and New York: de Gruyter, 2000.

Swearer, Donald K. *Dialogue: The Key to Understanding Other Religions*. Philadelphia: Westminster, 1977.

Swidler, Leonard. *After the Absolute: The Dialogical Future of Religious Reflection*. Minneapolis: Fortress, 1990.

Swidler, Leonard et al. *Death or Dialogue? From the Age of Monologue to the Age of Dialogue*. London: SCM Press, 1990.

Thomas, David, ed., with Clare Amos. *A Faithful Presence: Essays for Kenneth Cragg*. London: Melisende Press, 2003.

Timmerman, Christiane, and Barbara Segaert, eds. *How to Conquer the Barriers to Intercultural Dialogue: Christianity, Islam and Judaism*. Brussels: P.I.E.-Peter Lang, 2005.

Tracy, David. *Dialogue with the Other: The Inter-Religious Dialogue*. Grand Rapids: Eerdmans, 1990.

Ucko, Hans, ed. *Changing the Present, Dreaming the Future: A Critical Moment in Interreligious Dialogue*. Geneva: WCC Publications, 2006.

Ucko, Hans, ed. *Faces of the Other*. Geneva: WCC Publications, 2005.

Ucko, Hans. "Report on Inquiry on Interreligious Prayer and Worship." *Current Dialogue* 28 (June 1995): 57–64.

Ucko, Hans. "Inter-religious Worship and Prayer." *Current Dialogue* 24 (June 1993): 35–39.

Van der Bent, A. J. [Ans Joachim]. *Sixteen Ecumenical Concerns*. Geneva: WCC Publications, 1986.

VanElderen, Marlin. *From Canberra to Harare: An Illustrated Account of the Life of the World Council of Churches 1991–1998*. Geneva: WCC Publications, 1998.

Visser t' Hooft, W. A. [Willem A.] *No Other Name: The Choice between Syncretism and Christian Universalism*. London: SCM Press, 1963.

Volf, Miroslav, Ghazi bin Muhammad, and Melissa Yarrington, eds. *A Common Word: Muslims and Christians on Loving God and Neighbor*. Grand Rapids: Eerdmans, 2010.

Wigoder, Geoffrey. *Jewish-Christian Relations since the Second World War*. Manchester: Manchester University Press, 1990.

Wiles, Maurice. *Christian Theology and Inter-religious Dialogue*. London: SCM Press, 1992.

Williams, Rowan. "A Common Word for the Common Good." London: Lambeth Palace, 14 July 2008. http://www.acommonword.com/lib/downloads/Common-Good-Canterbury-FINAL-as-sent-14-7-08-1.pdf.

Wingate, Andrew. *Celebrating Difference, Staying Faithful: How to Live in a Multi-Faith World*. London: Darton, Longman and Todd, 2005.

Wingate, Andrew. *Encounter in the Spirit: Muslim-Christian Dialogue in Practice*. Geneva: WCC Publications, 1991.

Woods, Mark. "Talking about Religions, Doing Faith." 22 February 2006. http://www.oikoumene.org/en/news/news-management/eng/a/browse/16/article/1634/talking-about-religions-1.html.

World Council of Churches. *Ecumenical Considerations for Dialogue with People of Other Religions.* Geneva: WCC Publications, 2003. http://www.oikoumene.org/en/resources/documents/wcc-programmes/interreligious-dialogue-and-cooperation/interreligious-trust-and-respect/ecumenical-considerations-for-dialogue-and-relations-with-people-of-other-religions.html).

World Council of Churches. *Assembly Workbook.* Harare: WCC Publications, 1998.

World Council of Churches. *My Neighbour's Faith—and Mine: Theological Discoveries Through Interfaith Dialogue; A Study Guide.* 2nd ed. Geneva: WCC Publications, 1987.

World Council of Churches. *Guidelines on Dialogue with People of Living Faiths and Ideologies.* Geneva: WCC Publications, 1979.

World Council of Churches, Pontifical Council for Interreligious Dialogue, and World Evangelical Alliance. *Christian Witness in a Multi-Religious World: Recommendations for Conduct.* 28 June 2011. http://www.oikoumene.org/resources/documents/wcc-programmes/interreligious-dialogue-and-cooperation/christian-identity-in-pluralistic-societies/christian-witness-in-a-multi-religious-world.html.

Zebiri, Kate. *Muslims and Christians Face to Face.* Oxford: Oneworld, 1997.

INDEX

inclusivism, 6, 22, 26–30, 37–38, 93, 104–105, 124–25, 162

Interreligious Dialogue and Cooperation, WCC Programme for (IRDC), 68

International Missionary Council (IMC), 43–45, 47

Ipgrave, Michael, 152–53

Irenaeus, 27

Islam, ix, xi, xvii, 21, 26, 28, 34, 49–50, 66, 86, 151, 154. *See also* Muslims

Jesus, 10, 17, 23, 27, 29, 44, 63–64, 73, 85, 99, 113–20, 137, 147–50, 161. *See also* Christ

Jew(s), 8, 18, 26, 49, 68, 114, 116, 117, 118, 129

Judaism, ix, 28, 34, 87, 154

justice, 17–19, 78, 81, 86, 90, 93–94, 113, 120, 152–53. *See also* rights, human; freedom, religious; peace

Knitter, Paul, 35–36

Kraemer, Hendrik, 24, 44–45, 104

Küng, Hans, 36

Life and Work Movement, 43, 45

Lochhead, David, 6–7

Logos, the, xvi, 26–27, 85, 95, 117, 157. *See also* Word

Ludwig, Theodore, 4–5

Lumen Gentium, 50, 167n.19

Marshall, David, 153

Martyr, Justin, 27

Maurice, F. D., 27

missio Dei (God's mission), 53, 91, 121, 126–27, 147

mission, xv, 3, 21, 42, 50–53, 61, 62, 66, 73, 91, 100, 104–105, 111–12, 117–20, 126

    and dialogue, 16, 50, 53, 56, 59, 65, 69, 79–80, 90, 97–100, 111, 15, 125–26

    and discipleship, 111–12, 120–25

    and evangelism, 56, 63–64, 67, 72, 89, 100, 121

of the church, xix, 17, 21, 45–46, 50, 54, 61, 67–73, 88, 99, 111, 122, 149

morality, 10–11

Muslim(s), viii, xvii, 8, 27, 41, 49–50, 57, 68, 79, 86–87, 106, 122, 126, 129, 151–55. *See also* Islam; dialogue, Christian–Muslim

Niles, D. T., 46

Nostra Aetate, 49–50, 54, 167n.19

Office for Inter-Religious Relations (OIRR), 63, 65–66, 129–30, 163n.6

Office for Inter-Religious Relations and Dialogue (IRRD), 67, 163n.6

Orthodox
    Churches, vii, 50, 153
    theologians, 15, 51, 65, 130

Panikkar, Raimon, xv, 29, 75, 92

Parliament of World Religions, 41–42, 150

peace, vii–viii, 4, 17–19, 36, 60, 70, 74, 76, 78, 86, 90, 93, 129, 132–34, 152, 155, 160

Phan, Peter, 105

phenomenological method, 8–11, 35, 101, 129, 131–35, 140–44

plurality, religious, 4–5, 15–16, 20–38, 44, 47, 52, 55–56, 58, 60–62, 66–67, 73, 88, 93, 96–98, 101, 103–105, 111–12, 126, 128, 135, 150, 160

pluralism, 15-16, 20–22, 24, 28, 30–38, 44, 61, 65, 67, 73, 74, 93, 98, 100, 104–105, 111, 124

    common goal, 31–33
    common ground, 31–32
    complementary holistic, 35, 38
    comprehensive integrated, 36, 38
    differentiated, 33–34
    dynamic parallel, 35–36, 38
    eschatological, 34–35
    ethical, 36
    interdependent, 35–36
    paradigms of, 22, 30–38, 104
    radical, 33–35

religious, 15–16, 21, 30–38, 44, 65, 67, 73–74, 93, 105
Pontifical Council for Interreligious Dialogue (PCID), 49, 64, 66–67, 71–72, 79–81, 129–30, 163n.6
Pope
  Benedict XVI, 89, 132, 154
  Boniface, 123
  John XXIII, 48
  John Paul II, 49, 68, 70, 72, 132
  Paul VI, 48, 54, 68
Pranger, Jan Hendrik, 55
prayer
  interfaith, 68, 71, 128–29
  interreligious, xv, xix, 66, 76, 128–31, 133, 137–40, 144–46, 159
  Lord's, 129, 140–44
  multi-religious, 131–32
  phenomenon of, 131–37, 144–46
  theology of, 137–38, 140–44
proclamation, *see* witness
Protestant churches, xvii, 15, 23, 25–26, 43, 45–46, 50, 123

Race, Alan, 104
Rahner, Karl, 124
reason, theological, viii, 27, 70, 85, 95, 156–58
redemption, 44, 72, 94, 96, 159
Redemptor Hominis, 68
Redemptoris Missio, 72
reductionism, *see* relativism
relativism, xvii, 16, 31–32, 37, 46, 59, 98–100, 105, 132. *See also* syncretism
religion(s)
  meaning of, 5, 8–15, 19, 24, 35–36, 126
  theology of, 15, 88, 96, 103–104, 124
  world/major, xi, xiii, xvi, xviii, 26, 35–36, 45, 49, 73
religious diversity, xi, xix–xx, 3–4, 15–16, 20–22, 84, 93, 101, 104, 111, 128–29, 145. *See also* plurality
religious experience, 4, 31, 64, 70, 81–82, 126, 135
religious freedom, 26, 81, 89, 100

revelation, 24, 27, 44–45, 86, 99, 113, 137, 155, 157
rights, human, 81, 90, 129
Roman Catholic Church, xii, xvii–xix, 16, 26, 47–49, 68, 72, 78–79, 89, 100, 123–24
Rossano, Pietro, 70

Sacks, Jonathan, 19
salvation, 10, 14, 17, 23, 28–31, 44, 46, 50, 69, 73, 86–87, 96, 99–100, 115, 118–19, 123–24, 149, 159, 165n.7
Samartha, Stanley, xv, 37, 59–60, 62, 97–99, 101, 104, 112
Secretariat for Non-Christians (SNC), 48–49, 54, 64, 68–71, 98, 163n.6
secularism, 44, 52, 73, 93
secularization, 20, 47, 52, 93, 101
Selvanayagam, Israel, 37, 113, 115, 117
Smart, Ninian, 35
Solomon, Norman, 10
Spirit, *see* Holy Spirit
spirituality, 3–4, 14–15, 27, 53, 68, 101, 136, 138
Sub-unit on Dialogue (WCC), 55, 62, 64–65, 163n.6
Swearer, Donald, 104–105
syncretism, xvii, 7, 16, 24, 30, 46, 55–56, 59, 61–62, 65, 71, 73, 98, 100. *See also* relativism

Taylor, John V., 97
Ten Commandments, the, 113–14
terrorism, xi, 22, 26, 75, 88, 106
Thomas, M.M., 29–30, 61, 102, 105
t' Hooft, Willem Visser, 24, 105
Tracy, David, 101
transformation, *see* salvation
Trinity, the, 95, 148, 156. *See also* God—Triune
truth, the, xv, 4, 9, 17, 22–23, 28, 31, 35, 49–51, 64, 82-83, 86, 95, 96-97, 104–105, 125, 149, 150
  biblical, 97

Ucko, Hans, 67

Vatican, the, xii–xiv, xvii, xix, 18, 42–43,
48–51, 57, 64, 66, 68–70, 76–81,
83, 89–90, 98–100, 102, 105, 129,
163n.6, 165n.13, 167n.20
Vatican I, 48
Vatican II, 26, 48–50, 54, 89, 102, 124,
167nn.19, 20

Williams, Rowan, 155
Wingate, Andrew, xi–xii, xiv–xv, xix,
112–13, 115, 147, 159–60
witness, xv, xvii, 16, 27, 30, 51, 53, 55,
62–64, 67, 72, 80, 91, 97, 100, 107,
111–15, 121–22, 133–34, 138–39,
152–53, 156–57, 159
Word, the, 26–27, 46–47, 51, 85, 95, 104,
113, 117, 123, 137
of God, 68, 85, 95, 113, 117, 137, 157
World Council of Churches (WCC),
ix, xii–xiv, xvii–xix, 16, 18, 37, 41–43,
45–47, 50–51, 53, 55–59, 61–69, 74,
76–78, 81–83, 89–90, 94, 97–100,
102, 124, 129
World Missionary Conference
Edinburgh (1910), 42–43, 73, 150
Jerusalem (1928), 44
Tambaram (1938), 44–46, 52

AUTHOR NOTES

The Rev. Canon Professor Douglas Pratt, PhD, DTheol
Douglas Pratt is a New Zealand Anglican priest and Canon Theologian emeritus with longstanding interest and involvement in interreligious activities. He is Professor of Religious Studies at the University of Waikato, Hamilton, New Zealand, and Adjunct Professor in Theology and Interreligious Studies at the University of Bern, Switzerland. Professor Pratt is also an Adjunct Associate Professor (Research) of the School of Social and Political Inquiry at Monash University, Melbourne, Australia, and an Associate of the Centre for the Study of Religion and Politics (CSRP) at the University of St Andrews, Scotland. Active also in ecumenical affairs, he is the New Zealand Associate of the UNESCO Chair in Interreligious and Intercultural Relations–Asia Pacific.

Twice Chair of the National Interfaith Forum of New Zealand, Pratt has been active in the development of interfaith activities in New Zealand and and in supporting bilateral organizations such as, in the city of Auckland, the Council for Christians and Jews and the Council for Christians and Muslims. Together with the then Inter Faith Secretary to the Archbishop of Canterbury, he co-organized a Christian Presence and Interfaith Engagement conference (2006) in Oxford, England and has a long-standing involvement with the Network of Interfaith Concerns (NIFCON) of the Anglican Communion. Among his recent books are *The Church and Other Faiths: The World Council of Churches, the Vatican and Interreligious Dialogue* (Peter Lang, 2010) and *The Challenge of Islam: Encounters in Interfaith Dialogue* (Ashgate, 2005). He is a coeditor of and contributor to *Understanding Interreligious Relations* (OUP, 2013).